Challenges
to Canadian
Federalism

EDITED BY

Martin Westmacott
University of Western Ontario

Hugh Mellon
University of Western Ontario

Prentice Hall Canada Inc., Scarborough Ontario

Canadian Cataloguing in Publication Data
Main entry under title:
Challenges to Canadian federalism
ISBN 0-13-646845-4

1. Federal government - Canada. 2. Canada - Politics and government - 1993 -   . I. Westmacott,
M.W. (Martin William), 1943-   . II. Mellon, Hugh.

JL27.C424   1998   320.471   C97-931005-9

"Whose Constitution is it, anyway?" by Patrick Boyer, Q.C. copyright 1997 Patrick Boyer and
Canadian Shield Communications Corporation. Permissions granted by application to Canadian Shield
Communications Corporation, 2583 Lakeshore Boulevard West, Etobicoke, Canada M8V 1G3. Tel 416-
255-3930. Fax 416-252-8291.

"The Secession of Quebec" by Robert Young, copyright 1997 Robert Young.

Prentice-Hall, Inc., Upper Saddle River, New Jersey
Prentice-Hall International (UK) Limited, London
Prentice-Hall of Australia, Pty. Limited, Sydney
Prentice-Hall Hispanoamericana, S.A., Mexico City
Prentice-Hall of India Private Limited, New Delhi
Prentice-Hall of Japan, Inc., Tokyo
Simon & Schuster Asia Private Limited, Singapore
Editora Prentice-Hall do Brasil, Ltda., Rio de Janeiro

ISBN 0-13-646845-4

Vice President, Editorial Director: Laura Pearson
Acquisitions Editor: Cliff Newman
Developmental Editor: Carol Whynot
Production Editor: Susan James
Copy Editor: Deborah Viets
Production Coordinator: Leora Conway
Cover and Interior Design: Monica Kompter
Cover Image: Gallant/The Image Bank
Page Layout: Hermia Chung

1 2 3 4 5 RRD   01 00 99 98 97

Printed and bound in the United States of America.

Visit the Prentice Hall Canada Web site! Send us your comments, browse
our catalogues, and more. **www.phcanada.com** Or reach us through e-mail at
phabinfo_pubcanada@prenhall.com

Every reasonable effort has been made to obtain permissions for all articles and data used in this
edition. If errors or omissions have occurred, they will be corrected in future editions provided written
notification has been received by the publisher.

Contents

Contents

PREFACE

Federalism is a governing system that by its very nature is complex and multifaceted. Students and instructors have long laboured over the intricacies of the division of powers, the interrelationships of federal *and* provincial governments, and the history of disputes over the Constitution. These have become traditional staples in Canadian government courses. Yet the events and forces at work during the 1980s and 1990s have buffeted and undercut many traditional assumptions. Challenges have emerged that threaten the continued existence of the country. This book is an effort to introduce students to the depth of these challenges and the questions they raise for the conduct of politics and government. Attention has been paid to the diversity of relevant issues and to the need for making the contributions suitable for an undergraduate audience.

This collection is divided into six sections dealing with federalism and key elements of national politics. Following an introductory essay, there are sections on federalism and its relation to political culture, political institutions, constitutional controversies, public policy, and to the deep-seated challenges facing the country's future health and stability. There is a short introductory note at the commencement of each section accompanied by a list of discussion questions for classroom or seminar use.

The contributors to this volume have worked hard to convey their subjects with sensitivity to the potential background knowledge of undergraduate students. Each section draws students into a different set of debates involving the constraints and opportunities offered by our federal arrangements.

As a contribution to the literature on Canadian politics, this collection has several noteworthy features. First is the expertise of the various authors who have records of achievement in diverse fields ranging from legislative responsibilities to journalism to academe. Second is the range of issues covered (cultural, comparative, philosophical, judicial, constitutional, fiscal, democratic, etc.) amid an attentiveness to an undergraduate audience. Third is the collective intention of awakening students to the tensions and controversies being fought out over their country's future.

The text has benefitted from the attentiveness of the contributors, the able assistance of Jane Borecky and Lyn Hill, the support of King's College and of The University of Western Ontario, the research help of the Carter Library staff (King's College), and the friendship and guidance of our families. Prentice Hall's staff, including Cliff Newman and Carol Steven, have been supportive and co-operative. We thank all of them for their assistance and look forward to feedback from you the readers.

INTRODUCTION—The World of Federalism

The opening chapter explores the concept of federalism and its place in Canada's governing arrangements. Reference is made to other countries, particularly the United States, but the focus is largely Canadian. Students are encouraged to see that federalism is an important ongoing feature of national political life.

Students should reflect upon the definitions or descriptions of federalism offered by various writers. Some explanations stress the division of powers and reference to constitutional documents. Others emphasize the co-existence of provincial or territorial communities of interest sharing common cultural values, with an overarching national community. Differing interpretations yield diverse insights and offer room for discussion.

Key concepts, like the division of powers, first ministers' conferences, and executive federalism, are introduced. This is the language of federalism. To participate in Canadian political life one needs to acquire the vocabulary suitable for explaining the complexities at hand. Although terms like *constitution* have come to be viewed suspiciously by many politicians and journalists, this should not deter us. Knowledge of such subjects and their political significance prepares us for participation in public debate and alerts us to deeper meanings within slogans and popular rhetoric.

Intergovernmental discussions, and occasional confrontations, are a vital feature of federalism at work. The various channels of representation built into the system are not always capable of defusing tensions. Sources of conflict are many and the means of reconciliation are often limited. Students should gain a sense of why this is often the case.

The roles of the federal and provincial governments and the interfaces between them are thus topics for assessment.

Overall, the chapter is designed to offer a guide to the world of federalism, a sense of the uneasy co-existence of differing levels of government, an introduction to the language of federalism, and an indication of why official meetings, governmental manoeuvring, and occasional confrontation mark federal life. Subsequent chapters will build upon these insights. It is hoped that students will review the following discussion questions and return to them after completing the chapter. They provide a means of assessing how well the material has been understood and integrated.

DISCUSSION QUESTIONS

1. Can citizens be simultaneously loyal to two different levels of government? How is it possible to be both a proud Canadian and a proud member of a provincial community?

2. What is federalism meant to accomplish? Could there be other ways of meeting these objectives?

3. Why might provincial and federal governments not always get along? How might their disagreements be worked out?

4. Why is a constitution a central concern of federal states? What factors should guide the distribution of powers? How often should the division of powers be updated?

5. What values or beliefs are common among citizens of your province? How might these beliefs or values be different from those held in other provinces? How might they be similar?

A ROAD MAP TO THE
WORLD OF FEDERALISM

Hugh Mellon

The lead article in the June 21, 1996, edition of Canada's self-described "national news-paper," the *Globe and Mail*, bore the headline "Premiers Try to Avoid the C Word."[1] Canada's Constitution, the dreaded "C word," loomed once again on the political horizon. Within the newspaper, headlines declared that "Assertiveness Grows on Premiers"[2] and that a particular premier, Ontario's Mike Harris, would be keeping his "Options Open."[3] The immediate cause of the concentrated publicity was a long-awaited meeting of Canadian first ministers (prime minister and premiers) in Ottawa. Coming after the razor-thin "victory" of the No forces in the 1995 Quebec referendum and the continued federal-provincial spar-ring over budgets and fiscal arrangements, the conference atmosphere was charged. Murmurs of discussion on employment and infrastructure projects, on tax harmonization, and on the possibility of joint federal-provincial trade missions percolated among the observers at hand. While participants and their communications advisers downplayed expectations, media pundits searched for patterns of shifting alliances or angry confrontation. Outside, voices were raised about the exclusivity of the proceedings. Aboriginal complaints of iso-lation from the corridors of power were receiving media attention. Financial markets awaited clues regarding spending and taxation intentions. Advocates of increased efforts in fields as diverse as culture, child care and environmental protection searched equally diligently for indicators of federal-provincial action.

Meanwhile, Canadians waited, alert if not necessarily inspired, to emanations from the meeting. For most, these political developments were just an added example of the federation engaged in another of a long string of gatherings aimed at social and policy accommodation. This first ministers' meeting was coming on the heels of an equivalent meeting of federal and provincial finance ministers. Such gatherings are part and parcel of the conduct of public busi-ness in Canada: politicians, bureaucrats, academics and reporters congregating to ponder the workings of the country. Sensitive to the folks back home, but endeavouring to influence the national and provincial agendas, these participants in Canadian public life go about their business.

Their efforts are but one manifestation of the underlying federal character of Canadian political institutions and culture. This federal character has had a long and turbulent history and continues to shape contemporary political life. In subsequent chapters different elements of Canada's federal experience will be explained, analyzed, and reflected upon. The objective will be to provide an account of how federalism affects political developments and to offer an explanation of the challenges currently facing the federal system on a multiplicity of fronts.

A standard definition of federalism as a governing principle is that offered by K. C. Wheare, long recognized as an international authority on the issue. "By the federal principle I mean the method of dividing powers so that the general and regional governments are each, within a sphere, co-ordinate and independent."[4] He emphasized the co-existence of governing authority among two independent types of government, one ruling over the country (the general), and one ruling over smaller territorial units (regional). Both types, most often called levels or orders of government, have matters about which they may legislate independently as well as certain matters on which they share authority. They also have direct links to citizens and separate representational structures through the maintenance of distinct legislative bodies at each level or order of government.

In Canada, the general government is often referred to as the federal government, but this should not obscure the co-existence of accomplished and active provincial governments. Fostering a political community in a federal system involves the bringing together of these separate constituent elements, the national and provincial. Federalism as a project involves the effort to forge an enduring political partnership. This bonding activity was stressed by Carl Friedrich, who understood federalism as "perhaps primarily the process of federalizing a political community, that is to say, the process by which a number of separate political communities enter into arrangements for working out solutions, adopting joint policies, and making joint decisions on joint problems, and, conversely, also the process by which a unitary political community becomes differentiated into a federally organized whole."[5]

Federalism is thus rooted in the understanding that law-making authority can be divided and that differing orders or levels of government can co-exist and co-operate. These differing levels are engaged in the process of community formation amid the preservation of diversity. Citizens need to maintain awareness of their respective governments and their capabilities. The identification, loyalty, and support of individuals or groups can be simultaneously expressed towards two levels of authority and community. This reality is captured in the title of a classic work on Canadian federalism, *Divided Loyalties*.[6] Citizens are, at one and the same time, members of both national and regional political groupings.

The notion that law-making ability, or sovereignty, could be divided among differing levels of government was one of the revolutionary insights offered by the early creators of the American republic. Previously, most had assumed that sovereignty could not be divided and redivided within a country. However, the theorists of the early American political struggle developed a paradigm wherein sovereignty resided in the people, who could then delegate certain tasks to regional legislators and others to their national counterparts. Douglas Verney argues that "Like socialism and liberalism, federalism is based on a normative concept of human nature and social relations. Indeed, as developed in the United States as a set of principles, federalism was the forerunner of the assumptions underlying the post-

1789 liberal state, with its emphasis on the liberty of the individual."[7] Federalism was part of a constellation of initiatives involving limits on government and citizen rights which was consistent with the tenets of modern liberal ideology. Governments were not understood as the source or foundation of authority and were instead part of an arrangement meant to recognize individual rights and institutionally generated checks and balances on the use of power. In the words of Samuel Beer, "a single sovereign power, the people of the United States, created both the federal and state governments, delegating to each a certain limited authority."[8]

Since the American federal experiment began, a range of countries have adopted federalism. Germany, Australia, India, Switzerland, and Canada are among the world's assorted federal systems. There are wide differences in the particularities of their institutional arrangements, but the federal character is common.

While principles of limited government and liberty have often figured into discussions of federalism, pragmatism and political necessity have also been common ingredients in forging governing arrangements. Ethnic, linguistic, regional, or other sorts of political cleavages constrain the application of centralized governing systems and lead to adoption of federal alternatives. The decentralization offered by federalism yields room for the accommodation of diversity through negotiation. As former prime minister Pierre Trudeau once wrote, "Federalism is by its very essence a compromise and a pact. It is a compromise in the sense that when national consensus on *all things is not desirable or cannot readily obtain, the area of consensus is reduced in order that consensus* on *some* things be reached."[9]

Canada's confederation experience exhibited the co-existence of federal union and compromise. The environment of the mid-nineteenth century featured a set of complex challenges—British re-examination of the merits of colonial attachments, American militarism, growing economic opportunities in the west, political deadlock in the united colony of Canada, colonial particularities and loyalties, and expanding colonial aspirations. Efforts to reform political institutions to cope with these developments led to considerations of federalism. Peter Russell points out that "Here is where the British North Americans had to be creative. They were departing from Britain's unitary system and, with the United States in the throes of a civil war, the only federal system they knew, the American, seemed thoroughly flawed."[10] A federal solution was needed that was capable of preserving the linguistic and religious particularity of Quebec, as well as offering the Maritime provinces a degree of autonomy from their larger and more powerful central Canadian partners.

The creativity of the colonial architects of the 1860s fostered a highly centralized federal system coupled with limited but significant allowances for provincial autonomy. Ideologically, though, the outlook was different from that animating the creation of the United States. As Peter Smith has argued, it was a vision inspired by dreams of political growth and economic expansion to be carried out under the auspices of a powerful central government. "Only a state with strong central controlling power could bring the desired political stability. The American Revolution and Civil War had proved that."[11] Despite the founders' intentions, the visions of a centralized federation went unfulfilled. Underlying political divisions and subsequent re-interpretation of the confederation agreement emphasized decentralization rather than the centripetal forces of centralization.

Canada was not the only country to engage in the quest for a distinctive form of federalism to meet its needs. In each case the search was for institutional responses capable of reconciling the interaction of national, territorial, cultural, and other pressures. Central to most evaluations of the varying federal arrangements is the allocation of power between the respective governments (national and regional or territorial). William Riker is expressing this standard when he observes that "The numerous possible federal constitutions may be arranged in a continuum according to the degree of independence one kind of the pair of governments has from the other."[12] At one extreme lies a highly centralized model where most authority resides with the national government. If all authority resides with the national government, the system loses its federal essence. At the other end lies a confederal model where power rests basically with legally equal territorial states or provinces which may opt, on occasion or in times of crisis, to assign powers to the central government. This latter model was very influential in the earliest efforts to frame the American republic (1781–87). Given its high level of decentralization, confederal models carry with them problems of co-ordination.

Federalism assumes that territory is a salient attachment for people. It leads to the definition of issues and governmental remedies on a geographical basis. While accepting that other types of political cleavages (ethnic, gender, class) may co-exist with the territorial division, federalism reinforces consideration of territorial solutions.

Allocating powers among governments is a primary feature of any federal system. Given the existence of a division of powers and the coincidence of citizen identification with differing levels or orders of government, it is vitally important that federal systems be based upon respect for constitutional government. As Wheare and many others have pointed out, constitutions are "essential ... to a federal government."[13] Constitutions involve the foundational legislation and documents, court rulings, political practices and conventions, and deeply held values and principles aspired to by the populace. These shape the basic character and conduct of government and interaction between people and authority. Adherence to constitutional values allows for democratic life and citizenship. As Donald Smiley once observed, "What a constitution can do is to confer on the office-holders of government the legal authority to govern and to give the people a measure of protection against such powers being exercised in excessive and arbitrary ways."[14] It is true that some governing arrangements, such as those in the former Union of Soviet Socialist Republics, have had federal features without being democracies, but adherence to constitutional government fosters open and free public life.

Federal systems exhibit marked differences in the character of the actual division of authority, but each requires some common understandings and practices relating to the co-existence of territorial communities. In the case of Canada, much of the formal division of powers stems from sections 91 to 95 of the Constitution Act, 1867, formerly known as the British North America Act. Note that while the term *constitution* can apply to the range of foundational governing arrangements (documents, conventions, values, etc.), countries often label key founding documents with the title Constitution to signify their importance.

Section 91 deals with the powers of the national parliament. The preamble to this section begins "It shall be lawful for the Queen, by and with the Advice and Consent of the Senate and House of Commons, to make Laws for the Peace, Order, and good Government of Canada, in relation to all matters not coming within the Classes of Subjects by this Act assigned exclusively to the Legislatures of the Provinces...." It is then asserted that for the sake of "greater Certainty" various "Classes of Subjects" which fall under the federal parliament's legislative authority will be specified. Among these one finds headings such as

(91.2) "The Regulation of Trade and Commerce," (91.3) "The raising of Money by any mode or System of Taxation," (91.7) "Militia, Military and Naval Service, and Defence," (91.24) "Indians and Lands reserved for the Indians," and (91.27) "The Criminal Law, except the Constitution of Courts of Criminal Jurisdiction, but including the Procedure in Criminal Matters."

Section 92 includes those matters which the legislatures of each province "may exclusively make Laws in relation to...." Among this list are (92.2) "Direct Taxation within the Province in order to the raising of a Revenue for Provincial Purposes," (92.5) "The Management and Sale of the Public Lands belonging to the Province and of the Timber and Wood thereon," (92.7) "The Establishment, Maintenance, and Management of Hospitals, Asylums, Charities, and Eleemosynary Institutions in and for the Province, other than Marine Hospitals," (92.8) "Municipal Institutions in the Province," (92.13) "Property and Civil Rights in the Province," and (92.14) "The Administration of Justice in the Province, including the Constitution, Maintenance, and Organization of Provincial Courts, both of Civil and of Criminal Jurisdiction, and including Procedure in Civil Matters in those Courts." Bear in mind that the provincial level of government has authority over municipal or local governments. These local units thus derive their authority from another, more senior level of government.

Section 93 awards responsibility over education to the provincial legislatures subject to allowances for then existing denominational school systems while 94 recognizes the federal parliament's ability to work for legislative uniformity among the provinces. Section 95 recognizes that both levels of government would share authority (Concurrent Powers) over agriculture and immigration. Provincial legislation on these matters could not be contrary to acts of the federal parliament, though.

Other elements of the Constitution Act, 1867, also have potential impact on the interrelationship of the two levels of government. An example is section 58, which provides for the governor general on the advice of the Privy Council (the prime minister and the cabinet) to appoint provincial lieutenant-governors. Another example is section 121, dealing with trade in Canadian goods, "All Articles of the Growth, Produce, or Manufacture of any one of the Provinces shall, from and after the Union [Confederation], be admitted free into each of the other Provinces."

From even this brief taste it must be apparent that the term "division of power" may sound neater and easier than the reality of the underlying experience. What, for example, does the power to regulate trade and commerce imply in a conflict with provincial claims to independent authority over the management and sale of public lands, over property and civil rights, or over provincially-imposed direct taxation? How do federal and provincial taxation powers interrelate? Canada is not alone in having ambiguity and skirmishes over jurisdictional authority. In the United States, for example, jurisdictional debates over civil rights or economic regulation (labour standards, safety and pollution laws, product regulation, etc.) persist. In fact, a current thrust of the electorally resurgent congressional Republicans has been the restriction of new federal mandates for state and local governments unaccompanied by financial reimbursement.

Jurisdictional conflicts often lead to legal disputes. Governments may oppose the perceived encroachments of other governments. Individuals, groups, and/or companies may find themselves attempting to please different legislative requirements from differing levels of government. Opponents of legislative change may use jurisdictional confusion as an argument for transferring authority to a more compliant level of government. Dilemmas such as these often require an arbiter, a role played by the courts as part of their responsibility to provide judicial review of constitutionality. In the United States this role was articulated through judgments in cases such as *Marbury v. Madison* (1803), where Chief Justice John Marshall staked out the case for such review. Judicial review involves the work of the courts in adjudicating disputes and rendering judgments on what is legally acceptable under a country's constitutional setup. This review involves rendering judgments in cases involving matters like the division of powers, recognition of particular constitutional conventions, and respect for guaranteed rights and freedoms.

The Canadian experience was different from that of the U.S. The British retained final authority as the Constitution Act, 1867, was British legislation and Canadian statutes had to conform to British laws. Yet, this was to change. As Russell et al. have reminded us, "over time, with the waning of the imperial connection and the experience of so many controversies associated with the division of powers between federal and provincial legislatures, judicial review came to be seen as an imperative of federalism."[15] For many years the final authority over judicial review in Canada was the British Judicial Committee of the Privy Council. Beginning in the late 1940s, due to the federal government of Louis St. Laurent (1948–57), the right of Canadians to appeal to the British courts was curtailed and the Canadian Supreme Court became the ultimate court of appeal.

While many base their conception of federalism on a legal-constitutional vantage point stressing the division of powers and legal allocations of power, others use cultural differentiation as their starting point. Instead of beginning with the division of powers and constitutional structures, their focus is upon cultural heterogeneity. Federal systems and subnational territorial governments (provinces, states, etc.) are seen as products of underlying cultural divergence. Perhaps the foremost exponent of this theoretical approach was William Livingston who asserted that the structures of government "are only the surface manifestations of the deeper federal quality which lies beneath the surface. The essence of federalism lies not in the constitutional or institutional structure but in the society itself."[16]

In the Canadian case, territorial identity and regionalism have long been major contributors to politically significant cleavages. While Smiley is correct to note that region is a somewhat ambiguous term,[17] it does have wide popular and political usage. Provinces are the pertinent political units and provincial legislative assemblies are the existing territorial legislative institutions. There is provision for regional representation in the composition of the Canadian Senate, but even here there are provincial allocations within the regional categories. Despite all this, regional consciousness and disagreements about political and economic rewards are deeply engrained features of public life. As Janine Brodie noted in 1990, "While it is obvious that provincial governments have been very visible political actors in the past two decades, it is equally clear that the major conflicts over the past two decades reflect divisions between *groups* of provinces, especially resource-producing and -consuming provinces."[18] Alliances like the efforts of the Atlantic premiers on issues such as regional development and unemployment insurance policy testify to the notion of group pressure in support of regional interests.

National governments within federal systems often face choices that leave them vulnerable to provincial counterattack. Territorial trade-offs often provoke bitter controversy. The U.S. Civil War, for example, evolved out of differing views on matters of human rights, race, and competing socio-economic outlooks. While other countries may have been spared the brutal carnage of the U.S. in the 1860s, disputes over public policy and its territorial application are endemic to federations. A dramatic example of this can be seen in the observation by Mike Harris, the Ontario premier, concerning unemployment insurance funding, "The amount of money that is contributed by Ontario workers and employers is about $8 billion and there's about $4 billion coming back."[19] In the federal-provincial conference of June 1996, B.C. and Quebec declined to participate in the emerging federal-provincial consensus around a new national securities commission. The resulting impact, given the practical interrelationship of the country's three largest stock exchanges (Toronto, Montreal, and Vancouver), will likely take years to sort out.

The courts are not the only institutions ensuring deference toward the federal character of a political system. Representational structures such as legislatures and party systems, and schemes for fiscal redistribution all help nourish provincial communities and the voicing of territorial grievances. Again, there are differences in how these structures work within differing countries, but these variations should not obscure elements of commonality. Party systems and legislative activity provide a direct link between the workings of the subnational governments and the people. They mediate citizen requests and offer venues for sharing particular concerns. Fiscal redistribution reinforces the common national bond while permitting territorial units to retain a level of autonomy in expenditure and taxation decisions.

Recognition of the cultural dimension facilitates a deeper sense of the important roles played by provincial legislative bodies. These bodies speak to the needs of territorially defined communities and offer voters an alternative to national decision-making bodies. Early on in Canadian history it was not uncommon for a politician to be elected to both the House of Commons and a provincial assembly. Critics feared that this would promote conflicts of loyalty and a preference for national rather than local concerns. Since 1874 this practice has vanished and a sense has grown that "Federalism, like all social relations, was essentially competitive."[20] For parties and politicians this means that efforts must be made at both the provincial and nation levels to craft appeals, nominate impressive candidates, aggregate interests, and articulate visions of governance.

The possibility for integration through party networks exists, but even here there are limits born of the separate electoral venues. Canadian history is replete with examples of heated disagreements between federal and provincial governments even when headed by representatives of the same political party. Here, for example, are the reflections of former Liberal prime minister Lester Pearson (1963–68) on dealings with Quebec under Liberal premier Jean Lesage (1960–66). "There were times when we in Ottawa judged that the Quebec government had decided the best way to handle its problems, and particularly their extreme manifestations, was not so much to quarrel with Ottawa as to stand resolutely against us, to show what good provincial nationalists they were."[21] Joe Clark's (1979–80) difficulties in hammering out an energy policy with fellow Progressive Conservative, Alberta premier Peter Lougheed, illustrate that the frustration felt by Pearson and Lesage was not confined to Liberal leaders. The issues leading to federal-provincial party splits may change, but the discord persists. Present-day tensions between the federal Liberals and their Quebec counterparts speak to the continuation of this discord.

Available evidence suggests that provincial and federal politicians in Canada follow distinct career paths (federal or provincial) with limited cross-flow. Doreen Barrie and Roger Gibbins studied the political careers of numerous women and men who served in the House of Commons and/or the Senate between 1867 and 1984. They uncovered the finding "that provincial legislative experience is not common among national parliamentarians in Canada, and that it has become even less common with the passage of time."[22]

In 1992 the U.S. electorate made Bill Clinton, the governor of Arkansas, president. He followed in the footsteps of such other presidents as Ronald Reagan (California) and Jimmy Carter (Georgia). Canadian premiers seem not to have shared in this opportunity for electoral "elevation." There has not been, over the past several decades, a substantial history of provincial politicians successfully transferring to the prime ministership. Parties have recruited leaders from provincial ranks: the Conservatives opted for Nova Scotia premier Robert Stanfield in 1967 and the NDP chose Tommy Douglas in 1961. Neither were able to unseat their Liberal counterparts, although Stanfield did come within a handful of seats in 1972. A large number of federal politicians have gone on to serve as provincial premiers. Examples include New Brunswick's Hugh John Fleming in the 1950s, Quebec's Jean Lesage in the 1960s, Nova Scotia's Gerald Reagan in the 1960s and 1970s, and, in the 1990s, Newfoundland's Brian Tobin.

Various Canadian political parties focus their efforts on only one level of government to direct attention to certain sets of issues and to target their campaigning energies. Preston Manning, for example, has consistently argued that his party needs to develop a greater national following before venturing into the electoral waters provincially. Even a senior party like the Progressive Conservatives, which has held national and provincial office, has endured long periods of provincial level weakness in British Columbia and Quebec.

Just as governing institutions and representational vehicles reflect federal divisions, so too does public finance. Differing levels of government are each empowered to raise revenue for the costs of providing public services and servicing accumulated debt. Provisions are usually made for a system of transfers between the differing levels and subnational units in the hope of achieving certain types of objectives. These objectives can include redistribution in the interests of territorial equality, achievement of nationally set service standards, and/or promotion of national unity. In the case of Canada, all three goals have come into play. Equalization payments transfer funds from richer provinces, typically Ontario, Alberta and British Columbia, to less well-off provinces. Reference to national standards can be found in the national medicare scheme, whereby provincial programs must meet certain fundamental criteria to receive federal funds. National unity and the promotion of national symbols are part of the rationale for federal support of bilingual education across Canada and support for culture and sports.

For decades Canadian provinces warned of the national government's tendency to use its financial resources to shape provincial programs to meet federal objectives. The influence resulting from greater spending capability, known as the federal spending power, was a source of frustration for many provincial governments. Their complaint was that the imposition of federal plans into areas of provincial authority undermined provincial autonomy and the division of powers. Times have changed, though, and now the federal government is re-examining its transfer commitments. Deficit reduction rather than federal usurpation of authority is now the watchword. Across the board, in the areas of health, social services, regional development, urban transit, housing, etc., the federal government is retrenching and repositioning itself. As the fiscal landscape is being redefined, questions grow about the future of transfers and the ability of the national authorities to fulfill their hopes of national consistency in program delivery and services.

Given the jurisdictional and legal conflicts, the provincial and regional sensitivities, the public policy dilemmas, and the difficulties faced by possible mechanisms of national integration (parties, executive federalism, etc.), the task of updating and amending the Canadian constitutional framework has proven to be highly contentious. Amendment of a federal constitution requires provision for input and the exercise of veto rights on the part of both levels of government. In a true federation, one level may not do away with, or substantially alter, the authority of the other without joint agreement. Nonetheless, changing circumstances can necessitate updating or remodelling the federal bargain. In the Canadian situation, provinces were added, aboriginal self-government acquired momentum, citizens became attached to notions of individual rights, Quebec elected separatist governments, and deficit fighting led to talk of downloading responsibilities onto other levels of government. While these are particular to the Canadian scene, constitutional refurbishment is a challenge for all federations.

Canada has endured several rounds of what Russell has referred to as "mega constitutional" politics.[23] These rounds have involved a fundamental re-examination of complex issues—government roles, the status of citizenship, the aspirations of Quebec, aboriginal grievances, etc. Such intense soul-searching may have left Canadians dispirited and cynical, hence the already-noted reluctance to use the "C word." However, the 1995 Quebec referendum, coming on the heels of the demise of both the Meech Lake (1987–90) and Charlottetown (1992) efforts at reform, has left a dangerous vacuum.

Reform of the Canadian federal system often brings issues of national attachment up against provincial loyalties. In the case of Quebec this involves consideration of the coincidence of territorial identification with ethnic and linguistic identity. There are many francophones outside Quebec in provinces like New Brunswick (Canada's only officially bilingual province), Ontario, and Manitoba, but the government of Quebec occupies a special place as the presumed protector of francophone linguistic and cultural attributes. At a time when a sizeable portion of Canada outside Quebec is absorbed by visions of rights and equality among provinces, many within Quebec aspire to recognition of Quebec's distinctiveness and the ability of that province's government to ensure long-term cultural and linguistic preservation. This tension leads to the ongoing search for peaceful constitutional restructuring, a search made more pressing by the close results of the Quebec referendum. Some may feel that successful amendment is impossible, while others such as Jeremy Webber of McGill University's law faculty offer a more optimistic view of the present impasse. "Lying behind the often awkward or bitter terms of our present debate, Canadians (including Quebecers) hold a vision of their country that embraces the whole and draws upon our history for symbols of identity and models of justice. It is a vision that needs expression, a Canada that needs reimagining."[24]

Representatives of the federal and provincial governments continue to meet despite the ever-present possibility for discord. The practice of first ministers' conferences and gatherings of federal and provincial ministerial counterparts representing such portfolios as finance, agriculture, health, etc. has become a hallmark of Canadian intergovernmental relations. As indicated in the opening of this essay, these conferences draw together the federal and provincial heads of government (the prime minister and the premiers). Territorial and aboriginal leaders are, on occasion, invited to participate, but their role is ill-defined and vulnerable to change according to the prime minister's and premiers' agendas and/or the issue(s) at hand. First ministers' meetings have evolved into a vehicle for discussing tricky issues involving federal-provincial sensitivities. As a result, there are often private bargaining sessions in which compromise is attempted and, on occasion, achieved. The term *executive federalism* is used to characterize this type of federal-provincial interaction.

First ministers' conferences and executive federalism typify the twin influences of parliamentary government with its cabinet dominance (hence the idea of the legislative executive able to broker influences and make decisions) and constitutional elitism along the lines of consociational democracy. As Peter Russell reminds us, "This top-down form of democracy is thought to be most appropriate for a deeply divided society that can only be held together through accommodations reached by leaders who speak effectively for their respective segments of the community."[25] In the modern era, consciousness of individual rights and public questioning of political institutions challenge this conception of Canadian democracy. Many question the future of executive federalism, but the search for workable alternatives is daunting.

Given the high stakes and the complexity, judging the success of meetings like the first ministers' conference of June 1996 is difficult. Quebec premier Lucien Bouchard made a point of leaving the room when the Constitution was raised. Ontario premier Mike Harris publicly voiced reservations about the costs and benefits of current arrangements for Ontario. Glen Clark, premier of British Columbia, slammed federal fisheries policy and labelled the meeting "a complete failure."[26] Assembly of First Nations Chief Ovide Mercredi attacked the exclusion of aboriginal representatives. However, inside agreement did emerge about a first ministers' trade mission overseas, the possibility of national tax collection and food inspection agencies; eight provinces also signed on to discuss a national securities commission. In response to Clark, Prime Minister Jean Chrétien argued that constructive incrementalism was his preferred option. "And for me, I solve one problem at a time. Nobody's more flexible than I. I don't think I would have been in politics 33 years at a certain level if I had been that stupid."[27]

Judging the impact of events such as the June first ministers' conference is complicated not simply by the attendant domestic pressures already mentioned, but also by the changing international landscape. With the intensification of pressures toward globalization in economics, communications, and disarmament planning, federalism has come under new sets of pressures. International trade agreements leave provincial barriers suspect. Global bond raters assess national creditworthiness, perhaps leading to questioning of regional development initiatives. Provincial and federal governments run international trade missions. Intergovernmental deliberations contemplate agendas derived from both national and international conditions.

Students are urged to remember that federalism, like other key political concepts, is amenable to assorted conceptual and analytical understandings. The legal-constitutional approach stresses formal divisions of power and constitutional guides to institutional operation. This method of dealing with federalism has a long and proud history. It has drawn attention to the importance of political institutions while illuminating a range of possible constitutional adaptations. Critics suggest that the institutional focus obscures the diversity of modern communities while downplaying the potential for grassroots democracy. Lightning rods for this kind of attack are the first ministers' conferences and their attendant closed sessions and public posturing. Advocates urge recognition of the occasional need for private deliberations among elected decision-makers from both levels of government. Yet, since the mid-1980s there has been a steady chorus of complaints from those who deem executive federalism elitist, secretive and manipulative.[28]

Sociocultural approaches to federalism offer a sort of antidote to the dangers of rigid institutionalism. Attention is drawn to the underlying provincial communities in their cultural plurality. Likewise the relationship between regionalism and variations in the characteristics of the political cultures is laid out for in-depth examination. However, here too we find cautionary notes from critical commentary. One is the common difficulty of defining distinctive territorial cultures in an era of modern, mass culture. The generality of the reliance upon sociocultural factors is a constraint. Richard Simeon, while having great respect for this analytical approach, asserts that "overall social differences are too general to provide a satisfactory explanation by themselves of the varying patterns of adjustment found in federal systems."[29] A second conceptual difficulty is that voiced most notably in Canadian debate by Alan Cairns. He reminds us that provincial governments have powerful tools at their disposal to mould and foster provincialism and regional tensions. It may simply be in their institutional interest to rally around notions of special provincial communities. "The sociological perspective pays inadequate attention to the possibility that the support for powerful, independent provincial governments is a product of the political system itself, that it is fostered and created by provincial government elites employing the policy-making apparatus of their jurisdictions, and that such support need not take the form of a distinct culture, society, or nation as these are conventionally understood."[30] Someone like Livingston, who refers to societies having a federal character can, nonetheless, offer a valued reminder that federalism is more than simply a matter of lawyers and constitutional aficionados.

NOTES

1. Susan Delacourt, Rhéal Séguin, and Edward Greenspon, "Premiers Try to Avoid the C Word," the *Globe and Mail*, June 21, 1996, A1, A4.

2. Edward Greenspon, "Assertiveness Grows on Premiers," the *Globe and Mail*, June 21, 1996, A4.

3. "Harris Keeps Options Open," the *Globe and Mail*, June 21, 1996, A4.

4. K. C. Wheare, *Federal Government,* 4th ed. (London: Oxford University, 1963), 10.

5. Carl J. Friedrich, *Trends of Federalism in Theory and Practice* (New York: Praeger, 1968), 7.

6. Edwin R. Black, *Divided Loyalties: Canadian Concepts of Federalism* (Montreal: McGill-Queen's University Press, 1975).

7. Douglas Verney, "Federalism, Federative Systems, and Federations: The United States, Canada and India," *Publius* 25, no. 2 (Spring 1995): 82.

8. Samuel H. Beer, "Federalism, Nationalism, and Democracy in America," *American Political Science Review* 72, no. 1 (March 1978): 12.

9. Pierre Trudeau, *Federalism and the French Canadians* (Toronto: Macmillan, 1968), 191.

10. Peter Russell, *Constitutional Odyssey: Can Canadians Become a Sovereign People?* 2nd ed. (Toronto: University of Toronto Press, 1993), 23.

11. Peter J. Smith, "The Ideological Origins of Canadian Confederation," *Canadian Journal of Political Science* 20, no. 1 (March 1987): 26.

12. William H. Riker, *Federalism: Origin, Operation, Significance* (Boston: Little Brown, 1964), 5.

13. Wheare, *Federal Government*, 55.

14. D. V. Smiley, *The Federal Condition in Canada* (Toronto: McGraw-Hill Ryerson, 1987), 33.

15. Peter H. Russell, Rainer Knopff, and Ted Morton, *Federalism and the Charter: Leading Constitutional Decisions, a new edition* (Ottawa: Carleton University Press, 1989), 4.

16. William S. Livingston, *Federalism and Constitutional Change* (Oxford: Clarendon Press, 1956), 4.

17. See, for example, his comments on pp. 22–23 of *The Federal Condition* (Toronto: McGraw-Hill Ryerson, 1987).

18. Janine Brodie, *The Political Economy of Canadian Regionalism* (Toronto, Harcourt Brace Jovanovich, 1990), 16.

19. William Walker, "Harris Demands `Fair Share' of Jobs Funding," the *Toronto Star,* June 22, 1996, A20.

20. Robert C. Vipond, *Liberty and Community: Canadian Federalism and the Failure of the Constitution* (Albany: SUNY Press, 1991), 40.

21. Lester B. Pearson, *Mike: The Memoirs of the Rt. Hon. Lester B. Pearson, 1957–68, vol. 3* (Scarborough: Signet, 1976), 263.

22. Doreen Barrie and Roger Gibbins, "Parliamentary Careers in the Canadian Federal State," *Canadian Journal of Political Science* 22, no. 1 (March 1989): 144.

23. Russell, *Constitutional Odyssey*. Russell's use of the term and his periodization of events have gained wide currency.

24. Jeremy Webber, *Reimagining Canada: Language, Culture, Community, and the Canadian Constitution* (Kingston: McGill-Queen's University Press, 1994), 33.

25. Russell, *Constitutional Odyssey*, 5.

26. Tim Harper, "Ottawa Slammed for 'Inertia, Stupidity'," the *Toronto Star,* June 22, 1996, A20.

27. Edward Greenspon, "Ministers' Progress Doesn't Appease Bouchard, Clark," the *Globe and Mail*, June 22, 1996, A4.

28. On the contemporary intellectual origins of this critique, reference might be made to Donald Smiley's "An Outsider's Observations of Federal-Provincial Relations Among Consenting Adults," in Richard Simeon, ed., *Confrontation and Collaboration: Intergovernmental Relations in Canada Today* (Toronto: IPAC, 1979), 105–13.

29. Richard Simeon, *Federal-Provincial Diplomacy: The Making of Recent Policy in Canada* (Toronto: University of Toronto, 1972, reprinted in 1977), 7.

30. Alan C. Cairns, "The Governments and Societies of Canadian Federalism," *Canadian Journal of Political Science* 10, no. 4 (December 1977): 699.

II

FEDERALISM AND POLITICAL CULTURE

Federalism involves constitutional recognition of co-existing national and provincial governments and political communities. These communities are defined along geographic lines and reflect various influences such as European settlement patterns, geographical features, court rulings, and treaties with aboriginal peoples. The notion of a political community raises diverse philosophical and analytical complexities. One of these is the relationship of federally defined political boundaries with the concept of political culture. A political culture is a distinctive group of people who share values, outlooks, and patterns of transmitting community norms to youths and newcomers. There is the belief that members of communities share particular world views and relate to each other in accordance with common understandings. These understandings are the reflection of diverse factors including, but not limited to, common historical experiences, geographic isolation, religious beliefs, language, and/or a common colonizing power.

In this section various authors explore the character of Canadian political communities and the relationship between cultural values and the character of governments. They encourage readers to reflect upon the way people see their relevant political communities and how ideas about politics evolve. Comparisons with the United States are also offered.

Robert Vipond examines the evolution of federalism in Canada and the United States. He searches for insights into national variations and the differences that develop between the political intentions of national founders and the resulting systems of government. His insights remind us that there is no one model of federalism. They also encourage us to consider the evolution and adaptation over time of political systems. We should not see federalism as a "one size fits all" static concept.

Richard Vernon and Sam La Selva provide a philosophical introduction to federalism. Federalism is far from being simply an institutional model of government. It is a means of dividing sovereignty subject to differing political values and co-existing political communities. The rationales for this, and the moral principles offered in support of it, merit study.

Attention also needs to be paid to the daily challenges emanating from the co-existence of national and regional communities. Roger Gibbins focusses on the debates relating to the accommodation of regionalism within a federation. This involves consideration of constitutional models, political adaptation, and regional sensitivities.

DISCUSSION QUESTIONS

1. Is there anything unique about the politics or social outlook of people in your province? Why or why not?

2. How do you see yourself in terms of political debates—as being a citizen of a municipality? A province? A region? A country? Are these political identities mutually exclusive?

3. What lessons do you draw from Vipond's Canada-U.S. comparison? Why do you think different countries have different political systems and outlooks?

4. Would it be possible to go back to the original intentions of Canada's modern founders in the 1860s? Why or why not? Would it be wise? Why or why not?

5. What kinds of philosophical arguments have people developed about federalism?

6. Can federalism be defended theoretically? Why or why not?

7. Should federations be designed to accommodate regionalism or should we search for national efficiency? Why?

8. Can institutions of the central government (e.g., the Senate, regional ministers in the federal cabinet, etc.) adequately speak for the diverse regions of Canada? Why or why not?

9. Explain how you see the role of a provincial premier; of *your* provincial premier; of a premier like Lucien Bouchard.

10. Could regional alienation ever be dealt with completely? What are your suggested remedies?

CANADIAN AND AMERICAN FEDERALISM: A Comparative Perspective

Robert C. Vipond

The political movement to create a Canadian federation took shape in the mid-1860s—at precisely the historical moment that Americans were struggling through an intense and bloody civil war to keep their own federal union from disintegrating. The Canadian Fathers of Confederation were quick to connect the two events. From their perspective, the U.S. Civil War stemmed from a basic design flaw in the U.S. Constitution: Because the Constitution gave the states too much power, states came to believe that they were actually sovereign entities that could secede from the federation at will. The architects of the Canadian federation were determined to ensure that no similar misunderstanding would occur in Canada; consequently they stacked the constitutional deck in favour of the federal (or national) government. Yet, some 130 years later we confront an enormous irony: it is Canada that faces a serious threat of disintegration, while the United States has become one of the most centralized federations in the world. What has happened?

This chapter has two interrelated purposes. The first is to illuminate just how it is that these two federations, Canadian and American, could have developed in such different ways. The second is to introduce some of the key concepts and categories of comparative politics that you will find helpful in sorting through or explaining a puzzle of this sort.

CONSTITUTIONAL STRUCTURES

The U.S. Constitution was drafted in the summer of 1787 and immediately became the focus of an intense, rich, and frequently divisive debate as, state by state, special conventions were held to ratify or reject the new Constitution. The ratification debate was enormously wide-ranging and touched on everything from basic questions of democratic theory to quibbles about where commas should be placed. But if there was one question that stood out, if there was one question that crystallized both the support for and the opposition to the Constitution, it was federalism. Indeed, in the end it was federalism that really defined the

17

ratification debate. Supporters and opponents were not known as Democrats and Republicans, or liberals and conservatives, or hawks and doves. Rather, supporters of the Constitution were called Federalists, opponents were called Anti-Federalists, and the most famous published defence of the Constitution came to be known as *The Federalist Papers*.

One of the reasons federalism was so prominent and so controversial in 1787 was that those responsible for drafting the Constitution, men like James Madison and Alexander Hamilton, claimed to have made a theoretical breakthrough in political science that allowed them to create a new form of federalism that was previously thought impossible. In the past, constitution-makers had been governed by the basic principle that in every stable political system there could be one, and only one, sovereign or supreme authority. If there was no final authority in a political system, order would sooner or later break down; as the English philosopher Thomas Hobbes argued, the absence of a sovereign authority inevitably produced a "war of all against all."

For those who wanted to bring separate political communities together in some way, therefore, there appeared to be only two alternatives. One was to leave the individual units sovereign and have them "delegate" limited political authority for limited purposes to a common body; this was known as confederalism and was the basic inspiration for the Articles of Confederation that brought the states together for a brief period following the Revolutionary War. The other alternative was to vest sovereignty in a central political authority and have it delegate limited authority to the constituent elements or parts that composed it; this was known as the national model and was most powerfully represented at the time by Great Britain, where full legal sovereignty was vested in Parliament. From the perspective of Madison and his reforming colleagues, neither confederalism nor nationalism was terribly attractive. Under the Articles of Confederation, Congress was so weak that it was soon discredited and the presidency was so unimpressive that it became difficult to find anyone of distinction willing to take the position. But the national model was not the answer either. After all, the discontent that led to the American Revolution was deepened by British opposition to giving the colonies more freedom to legislate and govern themselves on matters that largely affected the colonies. And one of the stock arguments that was made in the 1770s against the Americans was that to give colonies full self-government could not be reconciled with the need to maintain the legal sovereignty of the British Parliament.

The Constitution that emerged over the summer of 1787 was so striking and so controversial because James Madison and the other Framers who drafted it maintained that they had found a way to combine the best aspects of both confederalism and nationalism; that they had created a system that was "neither wholly national, nor wholly federal," but a combination of both. Madison maintained that under the Constitution both national and state governments would be equally sovereign in the sense that both would be fully-equipped governments, possessing the power to legislate directly on their citizens, that the powers of government would be divided between a single national government and many state governments, and that neither would be legally subordinate to the other. Did this not contradict the idea that there can only be one sovereign in any political community? Not really, because, according to Madison, both national and state governments would be created by and would depend upon a common authority that was superior to both—the people of the United States. It was the people, Madison maintained, who were the ultimate, indivisible sovereign authority because it was they who created the Constitution. It is therefore no coincidence that the U.S. Constitution begins with the words "We the People of the United States ..."

The opponents of the Constitution, usually called the Anti-Federalists, were deeply sceptical of this novel form of federalism and profoundly worried that it would ultimately destroy the states altogether. The Anti-Federalists clung to the view that sovereignty is indivisible, and they quickly concluded that the Federalists' attempt to divide sovereignty in this novel way was actually a rather transparent ploy to centralize all decision-making in Washington and to establish a military dictatorship in the rest of the country. Once the Constitution was ratified, the friends of state power tended to argue from a completely different perspective. From that point until at least the Civil War, the argument from "states' rights" was that the position of the states after the Constitution was ratified was basically the same as it had been under the Articles of Confederation: individual states were sovereign. According to one popular theory of the time, individual states had the right to "nullify" (or not abide by) acts of Congress; and from this eventually developed the idea that states could secede from the (federal) union if they so desired. Ultimately, however, neither the Anti-Federalists nor the advocates of states' rights prevailed. If the Civil War settled anything, it settled the modern definition of federalism. From the mid-nineteenth century onwards constitution-makers and textbook writers have defined federalism the way James Madison defined it—as a division of power between co-ordinate governments, each of which is sovereign within the sphere granted to it by a constitution. And this is the crucial point: the core ideas of federalism, the ideas that inform federalism in Canada and in many other parts of the world, were really made in the U.S.

If federalism is a political system in which power is divided between two sets of government, one national, the other regional, then it becomes crucial to understand exactly how the constitution has distributed power. The U.S. Constitution bolstered the national government in three related ways. First, it assigned broad power to regulate "commerce among the states" to the national government and so effectively made Congress and the president responsible for managing the national economy. Second, the Constitution explicitly prohibited the states from acting in certain legislative areas; for instance, states could not coin their own money or impose taxes on imports or exports. Moreover, in those areas in which federal and state governments might conceivably both be active, the Constitution provided, through what is called the "supremacy clause," that valid federal laws trumped or took precedence over state laws or constitutions. In other words, if there was a conflict or collision between federal and state law, the federal law (or policy) prevailed. And third, the Constitution implicitly established the power of "judicial review." If the federal government and one or more states disagreed about which level of government had the constitutional power or right to legislate in a given area, the Supreme Court of the United States, a national court appointed by the president and confirmed by the Senate, would act as the final "umpire."

Over the years the U.S. Supreme Court has been extremely important in setting the legislative "boundaries" between national and state governments. And although there have been some spectacular exceptions, in general the Court has been extremely sympathetic to the idea of a powerful national government. In the 1810s and 1820s, Chief Justice John Marshall handed down a series of crucial decisions that early on established Congress's authority to manage the economy. In the late nineteenth century, Congress established the Interstate Commerce Commission and passed legislation outlawing monopolies. Both initiatives helped the federal government establish itself as a major player in the national economy; both were upheld by the Supreme Court. And in the 1930s, the Court finally (and only after creating a constitutional crisis) accepted most of Franklin Delano Roosevelt's New Deal—at the foundation of which lay broad federal powers to regulate the market, re-distribute income, create a modest welfare system, and manage the relationship between workers and employers.

The most dramatic court-aided expansion of the federal government's power, however, has come in the area of civil rights. Through the early decades of this century, the federal gov-ernment was notoriously slow in acting to eliminate the system of state-sanctioned racial seg-regation that created a legal apartheid in much of the South. One of the reasons (or pretexts) given to explain why Congress dragged its feet on civil rights was that it lacked the jurisdiction to act. The framers of the 1964 Civil Rights Act got around that problem by linking their goal of eliminating segregation to the commerce power. Thus the Civil Rights Act banned dis-crimination because, and to the extent that, it substantially "affected interstate commerce." Not only did the Supreme Court accept that rationale, it turned out to be willing to interpret extremely broadly what it meant to "affect interstate commerce." For example, in the late 1960s, an Arkansas man was convicted under the Civil Rights Act because he owned an amusement park that prohibited entry to blacks. He protested that his conviction was illegal because his amusement park was not located near an interstate highway, was not adver-tised as an attraction for out-of-state vacationers, and in fact served a clientele that was al-most exclusively local. Since his business was essentially "local" and not "interstate," he argued that the Civil Rights Act, an act of Congress, could not and should not apply. The Supreme Court disagreed. While it was true that there was little evidence to suggest that the amusement park served anyone but local citizens, the Court noted that the jukebox, hot dogs and other supplies came from out of state and the paddleboats were leased from a company in Oklahoma. That, in the Court's view, was enough to demonstrate that this out-of-the-way amusement park actually did have a substantial effect on interstate commerce.[1] With that the conviction was upheld, and with examples such as this, both Congress and the state legislatures learned that if Congress wanted to use the commerce power to regulate social behaviour—no matter how apparently local or insignificant the target—the courts would probably not stand in its way.

Political scientists are interested in explaining why and how certain political phenomena or patterns occur as they do. In this case the puzzle is to understand how it is that a federal system that almost disintegrated through civil war now allows the national government to act almost without restriction, including on matters that seem to be "local" in nature. We have now encountered one possible explanation, namely that American federalism has become so centralized because the courts, especially the final "umpire" of the federal system, the Supreme Court, have interpreted the Constitution in a way that has been generous to the federal government. Call this the "constitutional" explanation. It surely is a possible expla-nation for the evolving centralization of the American federal system, but is it a convincing one? Are there other persuasive ways to explain centralization that we should examine? And if so, how do we evaluate these competing explanations to determine which is the most compelling?

One way to evaluate competing explanations is to broaden the focus of inquiry so as to compare what we're trying to explain to some other relatively similar system in the hope of identifying the factors or "variables" that have the most explanatory power. In this case, we want to understand the relative centralization of the American federal system, so our next step is to consider the relative centralization of the Canadian federal system. And since we want to test the idea that judicial interpretation is crucial to understanding why the American system is as centralized as it is, it makes sense to focus on judicial interpretation in the Canadian federal system. To put the point in the language that is associated with experimental science, the degree or extent of centralization in federal systems is the dependent variable; this is what we are trying to explain. Judicial interpretation is the independent variable; this is what explains it.

The American and Canadian federal systems are such rich objects of comparison because, as we saw at the outset, their historical development seems so different. Whereas in the U.S. there has been a decided trend over the past century to give Congress greater and greater scope for action, often at the expense of the states, in Canada the provincial governments have become increasingly important players in the federal system. But terms like "more centralized" or "less powerful" are rather vague. Is there a better or more precise way to describe the phenomena of centralization and decentralization? One graphic way to compare the relative centralization of the two federal systems is to compare the amounts of money national and provincial/state governments spend in the two countries. Though not a perfect measure of political power, comparing expenditures does show the extent to which each level of government is active in making and executing policy, for without control over money it is difficult for a government to control policy-making.

Table 1 compares governmental expenditures in the United States and Canada, taken as a percentage of each country's gross domestic product (GDP) over time. As you can see from the table, provincial governments in Canada used to spend far less than the federal government did; in the 1950s, for example, the federal government spent roughly three times what the provinces did—14.9 percent of GDP as opposed to 5.1 percent. The fundamental reason for this difference is that the federal government was far more active in policy-making and program implementation than were the provinces. Since then there has been a dramatic increase in provincial expenditures, so that by the 1980s the federal and provin-

Table 1	**Government Expenditures as a Percent of Gross Domestic Product**			
	Federal		**Provincial/State**	
	Canada	U.S.	Canada	U.S.
1926	5.7%	n/a	3.1%	n/a
1943	37.8	n/a	3.4	n/a
1955	14.9	17.5	5.1	3.5
1960	14.6	17.8	7.1	4.3
1965	12.4	17.3	8.5	4.5
1970	13.3	18.8	12.5	5.7
1975	16.3	19.2	14.7	6.9
1980	15.6	20.1	15.8	6.9
1985	19.4	21.9	17.9	6.4
1990	18.6	20.6	17.8	7.2

Sources: Canadian Tax Foundation (various years); Advisory Commission on Intergovernmental Relations (various years).

cial governments were spending about the same amount of money, again expressed as a percentage of GDP. In the U.S. the trend is rather different. In the 1950s the federal government outspent the states by a ratio of 5 to 1 (17.5 percent of GDP compared with 3.5 percent). By the 1980s the states were spending comparatively more, but the federal government's share of expenditures was still three times what the states' was. Where Canadian provinces now spend almost as much the federal government, American states spend only a third of what Washington spends. To put it slightly differently, American states are now in roughly the same fiscal position with respect to Washington that the provinces were in with respect to Ottawa forty years ago. Moreover, these data almost certainly understate the contrast between the two countries. In both Canada and the U.S., provincial and state governments depend on transfers or grants from the federal government to meet their policy responsibilities. The large difference, though, is that where in Canada most of these transfers come with few strings or conditions attached, a far greater percentage of fiscal transfers from Washington to the states come with specific conditions attached that constrain the state government's freedom to act as it chooses. In Canada, the relative absence of conditions on federal grants gives provinces greater freedom or autonomy; the widespread existence of conditions on federal grants in the U.S. gives the federal government another source of leverage over the states.

These observations fit well with the evolution of constitutional federalism, the broad outlines of which we surveyed above. The courts have given Congress broad authority to make policy under the commerce clause and other parts of the Constitution. Similarly, they have given Congress essentially free rein in raising money through taxation—and in spending it. The upshot is that Congress has enormous constitutional resources to deploy if it so chooses. It doesn't always choose to do so because, for a number of reasons, members of Congress want the states to retain power and independence. But Congress has on many occasions accepted the invitation to act, and this is one of the reasons that it remains the dominant partner, both constitutionally and fiscally, in the American federal system.

Can the Canadian data be interpreted in a similar way? Broadly speaking, the answer appears to be yes, for the differences in relative fiscal power between Canadian provinces and American states parallel important differences in the way Canadian and American courts have interpreted the federal division of powers in their respective countries. Where American courts have given broad, almost limitless, authority to the federal government to pursue national objectives, Canadian courts have tended to try to maintain a balance between federal and provincial governments. For instance, while most of the Fathers of Confederation expected and wanted the federal government to be overwhelmingly powerful, the Judicial Committee of the Privy Council in Britain (which served as the final court of appeal for Canadian constitutional cases until 1949) tended to be more sympathetic to the principle of "provincial autonomy"—the idea that there is a constitutionally protected sphere of power in which provincial governments may pursue their own objectives without fear of federal interference. And since 1949, the Supreme Court of Canada seems to have bent over backwards to ensure that neither federal nor provincial governments will become too powerful. Sometimes the Court has decided in favour of the federal government, sometimes in favour of the provincial governments, and sometimes it has found ingenious ways of splitting the difference between them. Many of these decisions have been criticized on the grounds that they lack coherency, that is, that they are not logical or that they cannot be squared with past decisions. But, as Peter Russell has argued, there may be a larger political logic that informs the Supreme Court's federalism jurisprudence. In Russell's view, there is one basic principle that runs through the federalism cases that have been decided by the Supreme Court of Canada, and that is "balance."[2] The Supreme Court believes it has a duty to ensure that neither the federal government nor the provinces can overwhelm the other.

From this comparative judicial perspective, then, it is hardly surprising that the federal government in the U.S. outspends the states and attracts most of the attention from observers and citizens alike. Nor is it surprising that, in Canada, provincial and federal governments are much more evenly matched fiscally and more competitive politically. In both cases there is a plausible constitutional or judicial explanation for the respective patterns of centralization and decentralization.

INSTITUTIONAL FACTORS

Thirty or forty years ago, this sort of constitutional or judicial approach to understanding politics dominated political science, especially in an area like federalism. Gradually, however, dissatisfaction grew with the attempt to explain complex political arrangements solely, or primarily, on the basis of constitutional frameworks and judicial decisions, and other explanations began to be taken much more seriously. The case of Canadian federalism is a good example. For years, most of the scholarly work done on the development of Canadian federalism focussed on the role of the Judicial Committee of the Privy Council (JCPC) and the Supreme Court of Canada. Yet, as Alan Cairns put it in a famous article, it is hard to believe that a small group of judges sitting in London deciding a few cases a year could really have single-handedly shaped the Canadian federation. Cairns went on to suggest that there were a number of other factors having little or nothing to do with judicial decisions or the Constitution that needed to be added to the Canadian "story."[3] In other words, Cairns argued that the constitutional explanation fails because it does not, and cannot, explain as much as it claims to. Constitutional cases may be part of the explanation for why the Canadian federation has evolved and developed as it has, but they are at best one factor among several.

Looking at this question from a comparative perspective is especially helpful here, because from a comparative perspective the problem with the constitutional explanation is not that it doesn't explain enough but just the opposite—that it explains too much. Recall the basic outlines of federal development in the United States. We have seen that the Supreme Court has given the federal government such wide latitude to legislate under the commerce clause that there is almost nothing, no matter how local, that the federal government may not touch. If the constitutional explanation were sufficient, we would expect the states to have no legislative or policy-making manoeuvrability at all. Yet this is clearly not the case. The figures in Table 1 show clearly that while the federal government is the dominant partner in the relationship the states still act (and spend money) in ways that are significant. The federal government *may* act, but that does not necessarily mean that it actually *does* act. The constitutional explanation, in this sense, explains too much. To provide a fuller and more nuanced explanation of federalism, then, we need to look more closely at how and why it is that the federal government, in both countries, acts aggressively in some policy areas and not in others. And to do that, we need to understand how different political institutions in the United States and Canada produce deep differences in federalism.

Two institutional factors are especially crucial in shaping a different politics of federalism in the two countries. Take, first, national political institutions in the United States. The

American system of separate institutions sharing power was created with the explicit intention of dividing power among three institutions (legislative, executive, and judicial), fragmenting legislative or congressional power by giving the Senate and the House of Representatives co-equal legislative authority, and diffusing power within the House of Representatives. The last point is especially important. Because party discipline in Congress is not necessary to keep the president in power, power tends to be widely dispersed—especially in the House of Representatives. The most important locus for policy-making in Congress is in the many legislative committees and subcommittees, where individual members of Congress or (small groups of them) can have an enormous influence on what policies see the light of day and in what form. This pattern has extremely important implications for federalism because it means that regional issues will often get played out in these congressional committees. In the 1980s, for example, there was significant pressure on Congress (including pressure from the government of Canada) to reduce the toxic industrial emissions that cause acid rain. Legislation that would have established much stricter emission standards was introduced into Congress but was bottled up in one of the House committees for almost a decade by a coalition of legislators—some Democrats, some Republicans—who represented the states most affected by the proposal. Former speaker of the House of Representatives Thomas "Tip" O'Neill used to say that "all politics in the United States is local politics." The simple but extremely important point is that the diffuse and fragmented nature of power in Congress facilitates this "localism" in national policy-making.

The institutional logic here is important: Because national policy-making is so diffuse in the United States, it creates opportunities for regional representation in Congress that profoundly affect the dynamics of federalism in the United States. In some cases regional representation is formal. For instance, each state, no matter how large or small, sends two senators to Congress. Under the original terms of the Constitution, those senators were actually appointed by the state legislature, so there could be no doubt that they were really representing the interests of the state from which they came. That is, of course, no longer the case. Since the Seventeenth Amendment was passed in 1913, senators have been elected directly by the people of their state, and it is usually said that this has contributed to creating a more "national" and less "local" outlook. Still, the fact that the smallest state sends as many senators to Washington as the largest contributes to the idea that regional concerns will get a lot of attention.

The most important sort of regional representation that occurs in Congress, however, is informal. In some cases, as in the acid rain example, members of Congress who share a similar regional interest come together, issue by issue, and vote as a bloc. Over the last decade or so, this has developed to the point where members of Congress who come from the same region, the Sun Belt, for instance, now meet on a regular basis to exchange information and discuss common objectives and strategy. Nor is this sort of regional representation practised only *within* Congress. States, cities, and other regional interests have understood that if they are to protect their interests in Washington they have to be able to make their case to members of Congress, agencies, and the administration directly. The result is that, again over the last decade or so, most states and major cities have established offices in Washington whose purpose is to ensure that their views are heard and their interests are taken into account in Congress—and wherever else decisions that affect them are made. In other words, states and cities have begun to act like other interest groups in the American political system, trying to use various techniques of lobbying to affect policy-making. Just as there is a "business lobby" and an "environmental lobby," there is now an "intergovernmental lobby."

The success of this intergovernmental lobby is predictably unpredictable. In the early 1980s, Ronald Reagan, who resolved publicly time and again to return power to the states, nevertheless sponsored legislation that had the effect of establishing 21 as the uniform, national drinking age in the U.S. On the other hand, a few years later the states succeeded in dismantling policy that had effectively created a national speed limit of 55 miles per hour, so as to allow individual states to set their own speed limits. The basic point, then, is simply this: Regional interests are not absent in American politics by any means. But more often than not they are expressed in and through national political institutions such as Congress. The American federal system, therefore, is what some commentators call an example of "*intra*state federalism" because so much that bears on federal or regional concerns occurs in the context of national politics.

The politics of federalism in Canada are quite different. Where power in the congressional system is highly diffused, power in a parliamentary system is concentrated in the prime minister (or premier) and cabinet. And where states are formally and informally represented in Congress, provinces (and regional interests more generally) often complain that they do not have adequate representation in Parliament. Certainly the Senate is not presently constructed to play the role of regional broker (which is the basic reason why the idea of a Triple-E Senate has become popular), and party discipline very much constrains the creation of the sort of regional blocs that are so visible in congressional politics. The upshot is that in Canada the politics of federalism are dominated by provincial-federal bargaining. The concentration of authority within governments means that provinces *can* negotiate with Ottawa with confidence; the weakness of regional representation within the federal Parliament means that provinces *have* to negotiate to protect their interests. So that where the Americans have created an *intra*state federal system in which regional, state, and local issues are typically represented *within* national political institutions, Canadians have created an *inter*state federal system, in which provincial interests are most often represented *to* the federal government.

There are, of course, important exceptions to this general rule. State governors sometimes will take issues that are important to them directly to the president, and sometimes there is even the sort of interstate bargaining that is usually associated with the Canadian system. By the same token, Americans do not have a monopoly on intrastate federalism; there are elements of intrastate federalism in the Canadian federal system as well. For instance, virtually every prime minister since John A. Macdonald has attempted to construct the cabinet in a way that ensures regional representation where the most important decisions are being made, and the party caucus often serves as a vehicle to articulate regional interests. Still, it is clear that Canadian federalism is characterized to a much greater extent than American federalism by executive-to-executive bargaining—by what has come to be known as "executive federalism" or "federal-provincial diplomacy."

SOCIOCULTURAL FACTORS

Thus far we have concentrated on the ways in which constitutions and political institutions shape federalism in the United States and Canada, and we have seen how regional interests get processed differently in the two federal systems. But where do these "interests" come from? In the Canadian case, some argue that the institutions themselves are largely responsible for generating the interests, and out of them the conflict, that characterizes modern Canadian federalism. Individual Canadians, the argument goes, are quite content to think of themselves both as Canadians and as citizens of a particular province, and they see no great problem in reconciling these two distinct loyalties. Conflict arises, rather, when governments get involved and for their own purposes and through their own institutional means take uncompromising positions. This argument has sometimes been made, for example, about the rise of Quebec nationalism. By this account the people of Quebec are by and large eager to remain Canadians as well as Québécois; it is the Parti Québécois government that, over the years, has hardened the alternatives and consciously adopted a more conflictual position of Quebec versus Ottawa.

There are several problems with this sort of argument, however. One difficulty is that it can't explain the political dynamics of the last two major constitutional initiatives—the Meech Lake Accord and the Charlottetown Agreement. Both initiatives were designed by the federal and provincial governments working together. Both were hailed as compromises that did justice to national and provincial perspectives. And both ran into considerable public opposition and were ultimately repudiated.

The larger problem with this sort of institutional or "state-centred" explanation, though, is that it may get the causal linkages wrong. The institutional explanation would have us believe that it is the institutional configuration that produces different patterns of conflict and co-operation in the two federal systems. But maybe it is just the other way round. Maybe the patterns of conflict and co-operation have their roots in social or cultural patterns, and these sociocultural factors then work themselves out through political institutions. To put the point very starkly, could it not be that the distinctive institutional patterns we have noted are the effect rather than the cause of social and cultural conflict in federal systems?

Here again a comparative perspective is helpful because the most important social and cultural conflicts or cleavages have been quite different in the two countries and have given rise to quite different political patterns. In the United States, race has been the most fundamental social division from the time the country was founded. The existence of slavery brazenly contradicted the ideals of the Declaration of Independence and the Constitution, and the attempt, in the mid-nineteenth century, to extend slavery westwards as far as California was one of the factors that precipitated the Civil War. For someone trying to understand the evolution of federalism in the U.S., the great significance of the Civil War is that it took what had been a regional issue and transformed it into a national one. Why? For one thing, the abolition of slavery meant that African-Americans could move about freely (at least in theory), so that they were not bound to live in those southern states that had permitted slavery. For some, economic opportunities in the North appeared attractive, and when most of the former slave states passed laws that legalized racial segregation, this created another powerful incentive for black Americans to move away from the South. Many did, with the result that for most of the twentieth century race has not been identified simply as a regional issue; racial divisions did not simply translate, as they had before the Civil War, into regional conflict between North and South because the black population was now dispersed throughout the whole country.

The Civil War was important for nationalizing racial politics in the United States in another way as well. The Civil War produced three amendments to the Constitution, including one, the Fourteenth, which established the "equal protection of the laws" as a fundamental constitutional principle and which has subsequently been interpreted by the courts to "nationalize" the Bill of Rights. This has been a hugely important development because it made it possible to talk in terms of certain national (rather than merely regional) ideals, and it gave the federal government a strong mandate to take the actions necessary to realize these ideals. However adequate or inadequate those actions have been over the years, there is no doubt that the politics of race are considered to be a national, rather than an exclusively regional, question.

In Canada, the most significant social and cultural cleavage has not been race but language and religion. And in Canada, unlike the United States, this conflict has deepened the sense of regionalism over time, not lessened it. The Confederation settlement of 1867 was achieved with a keen recognition among all concerned that the French-Canadian minority within British North America needed protection, that this minority was concentrated within a discrete geographic space (i.e., Quebec), and that federalism, which guaranteed local control over local affairs, was therefore the best way of providing protection within a larger Canada. Since 1867 this basic demographic fact has not changed; indeed, it is now truer than ever before that most French-speaking Canadians live in Quebec. And since 1867, predictably, the call for political autonomy as a way of protecting language and religion, whether within a federal Canada or in a sovereign Quebec, has become more insistent. In short, where the politics of race in the United States have been nationalized, the politics of language in Canada have been provincialized.

Where does this leave us in attempting to explain the differences (and similarities) between Canadian and American federalism? We have examined three different sorts of variables commonly employed in comparative politics—constitutional, institutional, and sociocultural factors—and assessed their explanatory power. What is perhaps most striking here is less that one factor is so obviously superior to the others than that all three variables appear to lead in the same direction. That is, all three factors provide reasons and evidence why the American federation should be more centralized than the Canadian federation. In this sense, then, the important point to take away from this study is that, in studying complex political phenomena, it is usually impossible to isolate a single "cause" for a single "effect." Rather, as in this case, causation is more often than not complex and multifactored. Many causal factors are at play in understanding a phenomenon like federalism, and many of these factors actually reinforce each other, which is one of the things that makes social science interesting, challenging, and, occasionally, frustrating.

AMERICAN FEDERALISM REBORN?

Having argued that Canadian and American federalism feature quite different levels of centralization, it is important to take note of some critical recent developments in American federalism that suggest a significant, if gradual, trend to greater decentralization and a more vigorous role for the states. First, in 1995, the U.S. Supreme Court, for only the second time since 1936, struck down part of a congressional act that had been defended as a valid exercise of the commerce power. In the case *U.S. v. Lopez*,[4] the Supreme Court held that a federal law that prohibited individuals from carrying firearms into schools or onto schoolyards was unconstitutional because it exceeded Congress's authority under the commerce clause. The federal government had defended the law by arguing that possessing a firearm in a local school zone "substantially affected" interstate commerce. The Court, though sharply divided, responded that this argument stretched the meaning of commerce too far. If carrying a handgun in a schoolyard in Texas had a substantial effect on interstate commerce, then almost anything could be construed to affect commerce. While the commerce power is broad, one member of the Court said, it did not and could not grant Congress "a blank check." Whether *Lopez* will be a blip on the Court's screen or the beginning of a new trend is difficult to say, but it does mean that questions of federal-state jurisdiction are back in court.

More important for the future of federalism in the U.S. are political developments, especially in Congress. Over the last several years, Congress has moved towards a major restructuring of the way in which social programs are defined and delivered. Nowhere is this more evident than in the area of welfare policy. For more than sixty years, the cornerstone of welfare policy in the U.S. has been a piece of New Deal legislation known as AFDC (Aid to Families with Dependent Children). Over the years, AFDC has expanded and contracted and the role of the states (which often administer or help administer federally funded programs) has waxed and waned. But the basic principle—that there should be a national welfare safety net with enforceable national standards—was bedrock. The important recent development, therefore, is that in the summer of 1996, U.S. President Clinton signed legislation pressed by a Republican Congress to replace AFDC with a new, leaner and "more flexible" welfare system that gives states considerable room to define who is eligible to receive welfare, for how long, and under what conditions. Whereas in the past states received money from the federal government in a "categorical" (or conditional) grant that was tailored to meet the state's welfare needs as defined by the federal government, the new approach would transfer money to the states in what are called "blocks," where there are fewer strings attached and where the states have much more discretion about how this money should be spent.

The legislation gained support for a number of related reasons. For some, the basic purpose of the reform was to dismantle a "liberal" program that, in their view, had obviously failed. For others "off-loading" welfare onto the states was the only way to keep federal spending in check. For still others (including the National Governors' Association, an important member of the "intergovernmental lobby"), welfare reform was a way of redressing the federal imbalance and returning an important area of social policy to the states. The reform would thus allow state governments to run welfare programs in ways that take into account the distinctive needs, characteristics, and choices that inevitably vary from state to state. Whatever the precise combination of reasons, it is now clear that the states will have a far greater role in developing welfare policy in the near future than has been the case for most of this century.

Finally, and most speculatively, the larger forces of economic globalization may allow (or force) states to become more important and visible political actors in the United States. As such things as national tariff barriers have receded in importance, states have become increasingly entrepreneurial and competitive in attempting to lure large companies to locate in their state. As Richard Simeon and Elaine Willis point out, this level of entrepreneurialism among the states is reminiscent of the era of "province-building" in Canada that attracted considerable attention in the 1970s.[5] Indeed, American states, like Canadian provinces, have become dynamic, outward-looking, and increasingly competitive economic and political actors. Where precisely this will lead American federalism is, of course, difficult to know, but it seems that, both among scholars and among politicians on the ground, federalism in the United States is being rediscovered. And what is both important and exciting is that in the United States, as in Canada, federalism is connected to some of the most basic questions of politics. As Samuel Beer has argued, "federalism is not a humdrum matter of public administration but a serious question of political philosophy"[6]—which is as it should be.

NOTES

1. *Daniel v. Paul*, 395 US 298 (1969).

2. Peter H. Russell, *The Judiciary in Canada* (Toronto: McGraw-Hill Ryerson, 1987).

3. Alan C. Cairns, "The Judicial Committee and Its Critics," *Canadian Journal of Political Science* 4 (1971): 301–345.

4. 115 S. Ct. 1624 (1995).

5. Richard Simeon and Elaine Willis, "Democracy and Performance: Governance in Canada and the United States," in Keith Banting, George Hoberg, and Richard Simeon, eds., *Degrees of Freedom: Canada and the United States in a Changing World* (Montreal and Kingston: McGill-Queen's University Press, 1997), 150–186.

6. Samuel H. Beer, *To Make a Nation: The Rediscovery of American Federalism* (Cambridge, Mass.: Harvard University Press, 1993), 21.

LIBERTY, EQUALITY, FRATERNITY ... AND FEDERALISM

Samuel LaSelva
and Richard Vernon

Federalism is often pictured as a halfway house between a *unitary state* with a single central authority, and a *confederation*, an alliance between states that retain their separate identities. Historically, federations arise when groups of political societies experience a need for some integration but refuse to give up their distinct existence entirely. The founding of the United States provides an example: problems such as financing the Union, or pacifying the western frontier, dictated integration of the states, while the distinct interests of those units made it impossible to absorb them within a unitary nation-state of the kind that had become familiar in Europe. The federation, or *compound republic,* was the solution.

Sometimes, observers of federalism draw the conclusion that because federations spring from compromise it is pointless to examine them in terms of political principle; since they are pragmatic in origin, it makes no sense to examine them in the light of broad questions about justice, liberty, and so on.[1] But this does not follow, for we can distinguish between *origin* and *value*. The European monarchies owed their origins to conquest, fraud, and dynastic interest; but that did not prevent political theorists from developing arguments about what made monarchy valuable. Democracies owe their origins, in part, to class warfare, fears of revolution, and the competition among elites for popular support; yet it makes perfect sense to think in a principled way about democratic values. Why should we not think about federalism in the same kind of way—about what makes it worth having, about its connection with other political beliefs, and about whether, and why, it is right or wrong? Moreover, why should we think of *compromise* as something purely pragmatic or unprincipled, as though compromise could not sometimes be a way to realize a particular kind of ideal?

Here we want to examine the idea of federalism in the light of three values that will be immediately recognizable as essential to modern polities: "liberty, equality, and fraternity"—the slogan adopted by the democratic revolution in eighteenth-century France. Our conclusion will be a mixed one. We cannot make a simple link between federalism as an ideal type and any one of these three values; but for particular federations, the link between their federal character and one of these three values may be very strong. In particular, we stress the importance of fraternity to the way in which the Canadian federal system should be understood.

LIBERTY

Does federalism provide for liberty in ways in which unitary states cannot? If so, its capacity to do this must have something to do with its dividing of powers between centre and province. But unitary states, too, can divide powers in this way. There is no large unitary state that does not have a system of local government; and there are theories of democracy that make the case that *all* democracies need to have multiple levels of government.[2] So if federations are to claim any advantage in this respect, it must arise from their *constitutional protection* of divided power. Although unitary states can and usually do establish lower levels of power or administration, they can and do unmake them too. In Britain, a country in which the value of local self-government is often celebrated, a recent Conservative government unilaterally dissolved the Greater London Council, the largest municipal entity in the country. The Canadian federal government could not in the same way dissolve the independent legal and political existence of Prince Edward Island, the smallest provincial component of the Canadian federation.

So if liberty is advanced by the division of powers between centre and province, federations may have a claim to do it better over the long term. Why, though, might such a division advance the value of liberty? An eighteenth-century French political theorist, the Baron de Montesquieu, may have been the first writer to connect federation with liberty. Book 9 of Montesquieu's *Spirit of the Laws* (1748) examines a problem faced by small "republics," that is, small societies that govern themselves. Being small, they run the risk of being destroyed by foreign enemies. Becoming large is no solution, for large societies lose the spirit of self-government: they will lose the "virtue" specific to republics and become societies of a different type—monarchies or despotisms. But there is a middle way, that of the "federative republic." The small republics agree to become a "society of societies," which is, as it were, *one* society for the purpose of conducting foreign and military affairs, while remaining *many* societies for domestic purposes. "This kind of republic, able to resist external force, can remain large without corruption within: the form of this society averts both problems."[3]

The issues here, however, are not those that a twentieth-century reader expects. When Montesquieu speaks of *liberty* he means two (related) things. First, there is the freedom from *external* control, that is, the capacity of a political society to govern itself without undergoing domination by larger political societies. Second, there is the *virtue,* or spirit, of self-government that Montesquieu identifies with republics: the capacity of citizens to accept private loss for the sake of public gain, and thus to form part of a society that can manage its own affairs, without *internal* domination by a king or despot.

The provinces or states that make up modern federations are not republics in Montesquieu's sense, that is, political societies recalling the city-states of the ancient world, devoted primarily to the activities of war and politics. When we think about the freedom that modern federations might provide, we do not think first of political independence, or the spirit of self-government. Rather, we are likely to think about the ability of people, individually or in association, to live their lives as they wish without being constrained by government or by each other. Freedom in this sense is sometimes called *modern* liberty, as opposed to the *ancient* liberty of which Montesquieu was thinking in the passages mentioned above.[4] The idea that modern liberty is the value of federalism was first developed by the authors of *The Federalist Papers* (1787–88). This remarkable work, indispensable to understanding the American political system, was written by James Madison, Alexander Hamilton, and John Jay in the months of debate and negotiation leading up to the ratification of the Constitution. It makes a case for adopting a *federal*, or *compound*, republic, a "more perfect union" than the loose form of confederation that the states had entered into thirteen years before, in their fight for independence; and the case that it makes depends heavily on the claim that a federal republic will safeguard freedom.

When the authors of *The Federalist* write about freedom, they have two main concerns.[5] One is the fear that *factions,* or self-interested groups, will use the powers of governments to promote their interests at others' expense. The other is the fear that government itself will become oppressive. The risk of faction is greater, they argue, in local or state politics, and so the solution is to include the states within a larger political society capable of sheltering individuals and minorities from factious majorities at the state level. As for the risk of governmental oppression, this is to be met in two ways: by separating the legislative, executive, and judicial powers of government from one another, in order to minimize the influence that they might exercise over each other; and by dividing jurisdictions territorially, some being exercised by the federation, others remaining with the states.

If the danger of faction is greater at the state level, it could be met at least as well, surely, and perhaps better, by eliminating the states altogether and having a single, large, national political society (unattainable though this was at the time). The second argument, from the division of power, is more relevant to federalism. It is certainly true that a government that has incomplete jurisdiction can exercise a less complete oppression than a government with no restrictions on its scope. If states have a role in, for example, education or broadcasting, if they have independent legislative powers in areas of social policy, or if they serve as alternative employers, this diminishes the capacity of a federal government to dominate society.

As has often been pointed out, this only happens if state and federal governments are not working in concert.[6] If state governments go along with the federal government's projects, the fact that power is divided between them means nothing; if both levels are propelled by anticommunist hysteria, for example, their victims will be no better off than in a unitary state. But perhaps there is a partial answer to this in another suggestion about the value of federalism, not made by *The Federalist*, but by the English political scientist Lord Bryce. If states have an independent political life within the larger polity, they may serve as laboratories in which "experiments" can be made with novel projects.[7] Bryce's point was that this makes federations politically creative, with states able to learn from each others' successes and failures; but his idea may also be important for the question of liberty, for to the extent that the states come to contain diverse kinds of politics, there is less risk that they may become mere allies of the federal government, and the argument from the division of powers retains some strength.

There is, however, another dimension to the argument of *The Federalist*, which raises different questions. This is the sense that liberty is not just a matter of ensuring that government is nonoppressive, but also, and no less important, a matter of ensuring that it is limited in its scope. *The Federalist* certainly invites us to think that the harder it is to mobilize power, the more liberty we enjoy. Repeatedly we are assured that the combined effect of the federal division of jurisdiction and the separation of powers is to place huge obstacles in the path of movements that want to impose policy on a national scale. A century and a half later, political scientists were to complain that the American federal system did just that. But they did not think that this enhanced liberty; rather, they thought that the complexity of the system, and the difficulty of securing concerted action, was making it impossible for the American people to tackle their social and economic problems.[8] For those who think this way, it is not enough to see liberty as freedom from government. Some liberties may be denied us by social and economic arrangements, and to respond to this denial we would want a responsive system of government, not one designed for inertia. This disagreement hinges on a long-standing dispute about the political meaning of liberty, and at some point the evaluation of federalism would have to enter into that dispute.[9] Is it meant to provide *negative* liberty (the freedom to act with few impediments) or, rather, *positive* liberty (the freedom to take part in determining the laws that one must obey)?

EQUALITY

At first sight, nothing may seem to connect the idea of federalism with equality at all. Yet there is one interesting text that tries to do so: *The Principle of Federation* (1863), one of the last works of the French socialist theorist Pierre-Joseph Proudhon.[10] Proudhon calls for the dissolution of existing nation-states, such as France, into federations of *provinces*: this dissolution, he believed, was the necessary political complement to the kind of socialism that he favoured. In place of large enterprises owned by the owners of capital, he advocated an economy of small worker-owned enterprises trading with one another according to a principle of just exchange. There appear to be two main links between Proudhon's socialism and the federalist political project that he turned to in the last years of his life. The first is that he saw a natural alliance between concentrated financial power and concentrated political power, inclination and necessity driving the bankers and the politicians together to form a single ruling elite. Socialism would destroy one part of this elite, by taking economic power out of the bankers' hands, and federalism would destroy the other, by devolving power to locations closer to the people themselves. The second link is Proudhon's fear of mass politics. He observed that, taken in large numbers, people have a diminished sense of responsibility and of reality, and fall easy prey to Napoleon-like figures (such as Napoleon III, who took power in 1851); so to get rid of such dictators, we must get rid of the large states that make them possible. It is Proudhon's assumption that in smaller groups, where people can more easily grasp the consequences of their actions, more rational politics will prevail—almost exactly the opposite, interestingly, of the position taken by *The Federalist*.

Proudhon's book raises a host of questions about economics, ethics, and political psychology, but we need not tackle these here. Although some have seen a Proudhon-like socialist federalism in the former Yugoslavia,[11] by and large Proudhon's model is too remote from existing federations to be directly useful. There is no anarcho-socialist economy for Proudhonian federalism to complement. Even if it were true that small political units behave more rationally than large ones, the provincial units of existing federations are typically not small enough. Ontario and California are big polities, by world standards, and certainly big enough to sustain mass political behaviour of the kind that worried Proudhon.

Proudhon's concern is with *social* equality, something that we have no reason to expect federations to be especially good at promoting. Suppose we change the focus to *polit-*

ical equality: do federations promote that? One's first answer is likely to be negative. Political equality requires us to give everyone equal political power; when a vote takes place, everyone's vote has to be counted and given equal weight; and giving each vote equal weight means that we make decisions by majority rule—letting the minority win would mean giving the votes of members of the minority more weight than the votes of members of the majority, which would violate equality. So the majority principle is a basic requirement of political equality; but federalism is one of the most important ways in which the majority principle, in countries such as Canada, is *not* adopted. For many political and constitutional purposes, we give weight to provinces; and since provinces are very unequal in size, this means that we are giving more weight to the members of smaller provinces than we are to the members of larger ones. Moreover, in most federations (Canada being a notable exception) provinces or states are given equal voting weight in a second legislative chamber or Senate[12]—an even sharper departure from strict political equality.

Now we can think of circumstances in which treating people equally might not mean giving them equal weight. For example, it may be that a 40 percent minority feels very intensely about some issue while the 60 percent majority does not feel strongly at all. Letting the majority win would produce only slight satisfaction among the 60 percent while causing acute distress among the 40 percent.[13] Might we not decide that it would be fairer to weight the minority's vote more heavily, on the grounds, perhaps, that we are trying to weight *interests* equally, and the minority has much more of an interest than the majority? Again, a minority might face special disadvantages just because it is a minority, for example, it may have to take special steps to preserve its language, whereas the majority's language is safe just because it is the language that tends to dominate. If we take the view that both the minority and the majority have the right to live in their own language, would the principle of equality itself require us to allow special measures to the minority, measures that are necessary if they are to enjoy only the same right as the majority?

If equality does not always mean treating people in the same way, but, rather, treating them in ways that allow them to enjoy equal advantages, how might this topic apply to federalism? A well-known essay by the Canadian philosopher Charles Taylor suggests an answer.[14] Let us suppose that we want to ensure that people enjoy equal respect and whatever follows from that. One political tradition tells us that it means treating individuals as having equal dignity, none of them having special privileges, and all of them enjoying equal rights. We should, as it were, be "blind" to the differences between people; or, if we take account of difference, that is only as a special measure to enable the disadvantaged to exercise their rights effectively. Another tradition, however, tells us that we are not treating people with equal respect unless we respect their cultures; not to give weight to their differences is to deny them respect; and this is not just a matter of temporarily compensating for disadvantages, it is a matter of giving permanent, institutional recognition to cultural identity. This second idea of equality is brought into play if some provinces within a federation attach importance to preserving their own identity in the face of a majority culture that threatens it. To give respect to their members' identity it is not then enough to grant them the same rights as other members of the federation enjoy; to leave it at that would be to deny who they are.

These two ideas of equality can of course come into conflict, if the steps taken to protect a culture place limits on the rights that protect individual equality. Taylor does not pretend that the solution to this conflict is easy. He strongly defends special measures to protect the Québécois identity within the Canadian federation. He believes that this is compatible with the core of the other, individualist tradition, as long as certain individual rights still have priority. He mentions "rights to life, liberty, due process, free speech, free practice of religion, and so on" as "fundamental."[15] Other rights, such as the right (if it is one) to "commercial signage in the language of one's choice," may have to give way to the legitimate need of a group to express its identity and secure its future.

Obviously there is fertile ground for disagreement here. While there would be little dispute in a modern democratic state about the rights that Taylor lists, there certainly is dispute about the *interpretation* of basic rights; indeed, the whole effect of Taylor's paper is to make the idea of a "right to equal treatment" contentious. The importance of his argument, however, lies in showing that there is no simple opposition between federalism on the one hand and equality on the other, for federalism can sometimes be defended as protecting a particular idea of what equality requires.

FRATERNITY

As an element of federalism, fraternity is discussed even less often than equality.[16] Part of the reason for its neglect is that federalism, as we have already suggested, is normally connected with political expediency or is regarded as an instrumental value to be abandoned as soon as circumstances allow. But there are also deeper reasons for the neglect: some of them relate to the concept of fraternity, others spring from the fact that nationalists have attempted to constrict the meaning of fraternity and have used it for their own purposes. After noting that "political theorists have written ... hardly at all about fraternity," Eric Hobsbawm suggests that, unlike liberty and equality, fraternity is exceedingly difficult to translate into even partial practice. There is, he adds, an air of fantasy in attempting to legislate fraternity, if only because love is not something that can be compelled.[17] A similar view was expressed by J. F. Stephen in a classic book on the subject. "The real truth," he said, "is that the human race is so big, so various, so little known, that no one can really love it."[18] The implication seems to be that fraternity has no place within a realistic theory of government and society.

But such a conclusion is both unwarranted and troublesome. Fraternity is unquestionably a difficult concept to analyze precisely and an enormously difficult ideal to realize satisfactorily; yet it is not easily dispensed with, at least not by those who wish to come to terms with the most important social and political events of the modern world. A thinker who has recognized its importance is Isaiah Berlin. As he suggests, the significance of fraternity arises in part from its connection with nationalism. "No political movement today," he writes, "... seems likely to succeed unless it allies itself to national sentiment."[19] Nationalism derives its present power from the important, but neglected, notion of belonging. Men and women are made miserable, Berlin explains, not only by poverty and disease, "but also because they are misfits or outsiders or not spoken to, ... liberty and equality are nothing without fraternity."[20] Other thinkers have spoken of the nation as the motherland or the fatherland, and have described citizens as brothers and sisters. It is this imagining of fraternity that has made it possible for millions of people willingly to die for the nation.[21] If nationalism is important, then so is fraternity.

But nationalism also has a darker side, which has led some political theorists to call it "the starkest political shame of the twentieth century."[22] Much the same view was expressed a century earlier by Lord Acton. In a famous essay, he wrote that the modern theory of nationality was a retrograde step in history, and its course would be marked with material as well as moral ruin. If the nation was conceived as an ideal unit founded on the perpetual supremacy of the collective will, then it would overrule the rights and wishes of the inhabitants and absorb their divergent interests in a fictitious unity. Moreover, a nationalist state, Acton warned, would reduce practically to a subject condition all minority nationalities and cultures that may be within its boundaries.[23] To many students of nationalism, the verdict of Lord Acton has seemed "prophetic, temperate, and just." The attempt to remake so much of the world on nationalist lines, surmised Elie Kedourie, has not produced greater peace and stability. "On the contrary, it has created new conflicts, exacerbated tensions, and brought catastrophe to numberless people innocent of all politics."[24]

The critics of nationalist politics not only expose its darker side but also offer alternatives to it. If humanity is to free itself from the evils of nationalism, then it is necessary, they suggest, either to embrace cosmopolitanism or to redefine the nation as a unit that uses legal rather than ethnic criteria as the basis of citizenship. In their view, a country should be a civic nation, which implies that—in addition to using legal criteria to determine membership—emphasis should be placed on the instrumental features of social institutions, and utilitarian considerations should provide the ties that bind individuals to the social order and to each other. But civic nationhood encounters its own difficulties. Missing from it is the important notion of belonging. What Rousseau said of cosmopolitanism has been also urged against civic nationhood. The cosmopolitan, Rousseau complained, will talk about the public good but will think only about himself. Those who share such a concern attempt to meet Lord Acton's criticisms of nationalist doctrine by distinguishing between a chauvinistic nationalism that degrades the other and a sane nationalism that sustains its members and cherishes their cultural achievements. The challenge, they believe, is not to create a world without nationalism but to ensure that nationalism flourishes in its best form.

But even if the distinction between chauvinistic and sane nationalism is accepted, difficulties remain. Take the case of Herder, who is usually regarded as the father of sane (or cultural) nationalism. His image of the world was not unlike a garden of diverse national plants, each flowering according to its own distinct nature and exhibiting a unique development. Moreover, Herder despised the state and believed that a natural community such as a Volk had no need for a sovereign authority exercising supreme power. One difficulty with Herder's views is that much of the world is simply too diverse and too ethnically mixed to fit within his scheme of cultural nationalism. Polyethnicity and ethnic friction are a cost of participating in the modern world. Another difficulty is that the nationalist argument unnecessarily constricts the idea of fraternity. When nationalists describe their country as their fatherland or motherland, they imply, as we have seen, that citizens should treat each other as brothers and sisters and their implicit appeal is to the ideal of fraternity. But the concept of fraternity is richer than nationalists seem willing to allow. In fact, nationalists fail to notice that the concept of fraternity looks two ways. It looks to those who share a way of life, but it also looks to those who have adopted alternative ways of life. The greatest fraternity is the brotherhood and sisterhood of all people. Moreover, it may not be possible to restrict fraternity in the way that the nationalist program presupposes. "If fellowship," it has been asked, "is morally compelling in part because it connotes respect and concern for others ..., is it not compromised when confined in expression to a particular group of people?"[25]

Such a question has a special significance for Canadians and provides a clue about the way in which the Canadian federal system differs from the American. Students of American federalism have often glimpsed aspects of the difference. "Canadians ...," wrote Carl Friedrich, "had a very special problem to deal with which found no parallel in the American experience: that was how to arrange a federal system that would satisfy their French-speaking citizens."[26] The problem was even more difficult than such a view appears to suggest. French and English had been described by Lord Durham as two nations warring in the bosom of a single state. There was also the problem that, in the years immediately preceding Canadian Confederation, was best exemplified by the Maritimes: how to accommodate a strong sense of local identity and firm belief in a distinct provincial destiny. Critics believed that such problems were unsolvable; they predicted the early demise of Confederation or warned of the creation of a country that would be nothing more than a weak association of groups, incapable of developing a common citizenship. Americans had confronted no comparable problem because virtually everyone agreed, including the antifederalists, that the United States was one nation. What they disagreed about in 1789 was the kind of government that would best establish republican liberty.

All the great questions of Canadian Confederation were somehow connected to the difficult problem of nationhood. Confederation would not work if French and English had come together merely to war with each other; it would be equally unacceptable if it attempted to create a monolithic nationalism. But if Canadians were so different among themselves, what would hold them together? Canadians still address this question. In 1867 it was Georges-Etienne Cartier who provided the most compelling answer to it. Cartier had to demonstrate, in other words, not only that federalism was desirable, but also that a Canadian nation could exist. His solution was to articulate a federalist theory based on the twin ideas of multiple identities and political nationality. Canada, he believed, would be a great nation, but it would be a nation sustained by federalism. Far from presupposing the nation, Canadian federalism created it.

Not only was Cartier the pivotal figure in the achievement of Confederation, but his ideas provided the moral and conceptual basis for a distinctively Canadian federalist theory. His most basic assumption was that by joining in Confederation French and English agreed both to live apart and to live together. Moreover, although he did not use the word *fraternity*, his discussion of a Canadian political nationality presupposes it. Of course, it could be only a partial fraternity and could not require intense emotional bonds or demand a complete identity of interests between French and English. What the Canadian fraternity did suppose was that peoples with distinctive ways of life could possess goodwill towards each other, participate in common endeavours, develop and sustain common allegiances and common sentiments, and operate political institutions for the welfare of all. Cartier spoke of such things but left them nameless. There is, however, a neglected tradition of Canadian federalist thought—to which Cartier appears to belong—that explicitly connects federalism and fraternity. "The fatherland, for us," wrote Henri Bourassa, "is the whole of Canada, that is a federation of distinct cultures and provinces." French and English are separated by language and religion, he added, "but united in a sense of brotherhood."[27] Pierre Trudeau appealed to the same tradition of Canadian federalist thought when he insisted that British Columbians could "go it alone" but had agreed to pay taxes to the federal government so that some of the money could be used "to help the less fortunate provinces." Regional economic inequalities, he added, can lead to disunity "if we are not willing to consider that we are our brother's keeper in all of Canada."[28]

But fraternity is an enormously difficult ideal to realize, and Canadians have sometimes not attempted to achieve it at all. A well-known image of Canada conceives of it as a country of solitudes, such that peoples with different cultures and distinct identities live side by side, having little interaction and virtually no understanding of each other. This view, which is sometimes known as consociational democracy, supposes that Canada is held together by elite accommodation and passive tolerance. Not only does consociational democracy not attempt to achieve fraternity through federalism, but its implicit assumption is that close contact between peoples with different cultures will lead to strain and hostility. Nationalist thinkers share many of the same assumptions, but have drawn different conclusions from them. They have insisted that a federal state such as Canada—which brings together peoples with different ways of life—is both conceptually incoherent and morally pernicious. If Canada is an intriguing country, part of the reason is that Canadians profoundly disagree about the requirements of nationhood. So long as this is the case, Canadians cannot avoid reflecting on the claims of nationalists, many of whom appear committed to dismantling federalism. But the strength of nationalism is also its weakness. Ultimately, nationalists base their program on the powerful ideal of fraternity, yet fraternity looks beyond nationalism and provides a compelling justification for federalism, at least in Canada.

NOTES

1. For a sceptical view of the value of federalism, see William H. Riker, "Six Books in Search of a Subject: or Does Federalism Exist and Does It Matter?" *Comparative Politics* (1969): 135–46.

2. See Robert A. Dahl and Edward R. Tufte, *Size and Democracy* (Stanford: Stanford University Press, 1973).

3. Montesquieu, *The Spirit of the Laws*, Eng. trans. (New York: Hafner, 1949), 126–28.

4. See Benjamin Constant, *Political Writings* (Cambridge: Cambridge University Press, 1988), 309–28.

5. See *The Federalist Papers* (New York: Mentor, 1961), especially Letters 10 and 51.

6. See especially Franz Neumann, *The Democratic and the Authoritarian State* (New York: The Free Press, 1957), 216–32.

7. James Bryce, *The American Commonwealth* (New York: Macmillan, 1907), vol. 1, 353.

8. See Harold Laski, "The Obsolescence of Federalism," *The New Republic* 98 (1939), 367–69.

9. Some of the most useful recent discussions are collected in David Miller, ed., *Liberty* (Oxford: Oxford University Press, 1991).

10. For an English translation, see Richard Vernon, ed. and trans., *The Principle of Federation by P.-J. Proudhon* (Toronto: University of Toronto Press, 1979).

11. See Branko Horvat et al., eds., *Self-Governing Socialism* (White Plains, NY: International Arts and Sciences Press, 1975), 11–15.

12. See K. C. Wheare, *Federal Government*, 3rd ed. (London: Oxford University Press, 1946), 92–96.

13. This is known as the "intensities problem." See Robert A. Dahl, *A Preface to Democratic Theory* (Chicago: Chicago University Press, 1956), 90–119.

14. "The Politics of Recognition," in Amy Gutmann, ed., *Multiculturalism* (Princeton: Princeton University Press, 1994), 25–73.

15. Ibid., 59.

16. The value of *fellowship* is prominent in the work of the German theorist Johannes Althusius (1557–1638): see the English translation of his *Politica* (Indianapolis: The Liberty Fund, 1995). But Althusius departs from the mainstream federalist tradition in advocating multiple governing levels—as does Proudhon—and in giving political status to nonterritorial units.

17. E. J. Hobsbawn, "Fraternity," *New Society* 3 (1975), 471.

18. J. F. Stephen, *Liberty, Equality, Fraternity* (Cambridge: Cambridge University Press, 1967), 241.

19. Isaiah Berlin, *Against the Current* (London: The Hogarth Press, 1979), 355.

20. Isaiah Berlin, *Vico and Herder* (London: Chatto and Windus, 1980), 198.

21. Benedict Anderson, *Imagined Communities* (London: Verso, 1991), 7.

22. John Dunn, *Western Political Theory in the Face of the Future* (Cambridge: Cambridge University Press, 1979), 55.

23. Lord Acton, *Essays on Freedom and Power* (Cleveland: Meridian, 1962), 168.

24. Elie Kedourie, *Nationalism* (London: Hutchinson, 1969), 138–39.

25. Caroline McCulloch, "The Problem of Fellowship in Communitarian Theory," *Political Studies* 32 (1984): 447.

26. Carl J. Friedrich, *The Impact of American Constitutionalism Abroad* (Boston: Boston University Press, 1967), 60–61.

27. Quoted in Ramsay Cook, Canada, Quebec, and the Uses of Nationalism (Toronto: McClelland and Stewart, 1986) 190.

28. Pierre Elliott Trudeau, *Conversation with Canadians* (Toronto: University of Toronto Press, 1972), 207–08.

FEDERALISM AND
REGIONAL ALIENATION
Roger Gibbins

It is important to begin with the obvious: regional differences and hence regional conflict are inevitable in a country of Canada's size and complexity. The regions—be they provinces, the northern territories, or more abstract amalgamations such as the West and Atlantic Canada—differ substantially in their economic foundations, sociodemographic composition, and political cultures. Therefore regionalism—the intrusion of territorially based interests, values, and identities into national political life—is unavoidable. We can no more purge regionalism from the political system than we can purge conflict among classes or between linguistic communities; regionalism and some measure of regional conflict are facts, although by no means simple facts, of political life. However, we can and should ask to what extent our political institutions *moderate* or *exacerbate* regional conflict and regional alienation. Have those institutions been reasonably successful in handling and containing regional conflict? Or have they exaggerated and intensified such conflict? In short, have our political institutions been part of the solution or part of the problem?

To answer these questions we must turn to the relationship between federalism and regional alienation, a relationship that is complex, inconsistent across the country, and fluid over time. It is also a relationship that takes on a unique coloration in the Canadian experience, reflecting the particular way in which parliamentary government and federalism have been institutionally married in this country. Therefore, in order to come to grips with the manner in which *Canadian* federal institutions moderate and sometimes foster regional alienation, we need first to understand the more generic relationship between federalism and regionalism.

REGIONALISM AND FEDERALISM

Regionalism is an inherent, almost primordial, element of federalism, for contemporary federal states were constructed from the building blocks of regional communities. Now, admittedly, not all provinces or states preceded the construction of the federal state. Alberta and Saskatchewan, for example, were products rather than founding members of the Canadian federal state that came together in 1867, and thirty-seven of the fifty American states that joined the Union were in fact created following the War of Independence in 1776. Yet the point remains that federal states at their founding pulled together pre-existing regional communities, or separate colonies as was the case in Australia. In the Canadian case, where it is argued by many in Quebec that the founding federal elements were national rather than regional communities, the Maritime colonies were well-established before 1867 and cultural duality had assumed regional expression in Quebec. Thus Canadian federalism provided new institutional forms for pre-existing regional communities and new structures of national governance within which communities such as Alberta and Saskatchewan could emerge and prosper.

It is here that we find the complex interplay traced out by Alan Cairns in his 1977 presidential address to the Canadian Political Science Association.[1] Regional communities provide the societal foundation for federalism and for the provincial governments that in turn protect and promote regional communities in the face of homogenizing pressures from the national community. Just as regional divisions led to the adoption of federalism in the first place, the provincial governments which were thereby created go on to sustain and sometimes even to promote regional divisions in the national society. Citizens think politically in provincial terms because their lives are structured largely by provincial institutions and surrounded by provincial symbols such as drivers' licences, car plates, flags, and distinctive forms of social services. Politically, we come to see ourselves as British Columbians or New Brunswickers rather than in terms of class, ethnicity, or gender because our political institutions push us in this direction.[2] This also means, and not incidentally, that regional communities lacking governmental structures are less significant than those that have governments to support and promote them. The "West," for example, or for that matter even the prairie West, lacks institutional or governmental structures—there are no *regional* political offices or bureaucracies, networks of social services, or elections and there is no flag, driver's licence, or car plate. The West is a "region of the mind" rather than one knit together by political institutions and public services.[3] True, there are the Western Canada Summer Games, the annual meeting of the western premiers, and the Canada West Foundation, but these are small potatoes indeed compared with the institutional, programmatic, and symbolic resources of the region's constituent provincial governments. As a consequence, the West is a less significant factor in citizen identities and regional conflict than are the individual western provinces. The whole in this case is much less than the sum of its parts.

There is a broader point to make here, and that is that federalism recognizes and sometimes even celebrates a particular form of diversity. It is the recognition and protection of *territorial diversity* that are central to the federal creed. Thus we find in Canada today an acceptance that patterns of public policy will inevitably vary, indeed should vary, across provincial boundaries.[4] We expect provinces to differ one from another, and would be disappointed if they did not. Social programs are molded, at least to a degree, to fit idiosyncratic provincial conditions, and economic programs are expected to reflect the nuances and needs of the provincial economy. The contemporary push for greater decentralization, the continued existence of interprovincial trade barriers, and the nationalist movement in Quebec all reflect federalism's respect for diversity, or at least for diversity that is territorially defined.

At the same time, it is by no means clear that federal states are any more respecting of *non-territorial diversity* than are unity states. National minorities that are also minorities in the provinces or states, minorities such as African-Americans, aboriginal peoples in both Canada and the United States, and the gay and lesbian communities, may find that federalism per se works to their disadvantage.[5] Certainly this was the case in the United States in the 1960s when state governments in the South sheltered policies of racial discrimination from civil rights legislation emanating from Washington, D.C.

In a more innocuous fashion, federalism may crowd out the mobilization of nonterritorial forms of political identity by strengthening the centrality of regional identities in the political realm. We can only take on so many political identities at a time, and the omnipresent nature of regional identities provides stiff competition for other identities based on class, gender, ethnicity, or even ideology. Canadian socialists have often argued, for instance, that the fragmentation of social classes by provincial boundaries and the salience of regional identities have made the orchestration of class-based political action difficult. (Some, of course, might see this as one of the virtues of federalism and the regionalism it sustains.) Only regional identities, or at least provincial identities, have governments dedicated to their maintenance. Transboundary identities, such as those associated with feminism and environmentalism, lack similar forms of governmental support.

However, respect for territorial diversity is only one face of the federal coin; the other is the desire to transcend diversity, to create an overarching national community greater than the sum of its parts. As the American motto says, *e pluribus unum*: "from the many, one." The political experience of federal states has been concerned as much with nation-building as with the protection of constituent regional communities. Federal states, therefore, seek a balance between protecting and transcending regional diversity. It is not an easy balance to strike in terms of institutional design or political practice, and it is hardly surprising that failure in both respects at times fosters regional alienation in federal states such as Canada. The balance between the protection of regional diversity and the promotion of national integration is to be found largely in the constitutional division of powers between the national and provincial governments. In essence, although far from neatly in practice, the powers essential to the protection of regional diversity are assigned to the provinces, and those essential to national integration are assigned to the federal government.[6] Thus we find, for example, that the Constitution Act of 1867 assigned jurisdiction with respect to education, social services, and property to the provinces, and jurisdiction with respect to trade and national economic management to the federal government.

Yet the constitutional division of powers alone cannot meet the integrative aspects of federalism. A critical question remains: how well are the various regional communities treated by and within the national government *in areas of federal jurisdiction*? In short, how well do they fare within the national community? If regional alienation is to be moderated and contained, regional communities must have not only protection through the constitutional division of powers; they also must have an effective voice within national political institutions. The real test here comes not from the largest of the regional communities, such as Ontario, for they have sufficient economic and electoral clout to ensure their interests are heard; formal protection within the institutions of the national government is seldom an issue. The test comes instead from the regional communities to the west of Ontario, to the east of Quebec, and, in a complex way, from Quebec itself. Do these communities feel sufficiently protected from the political weight of the national majority?

To summarize the discussion to this point: federalism provides two basic forms of protection for regional communities and the territorial diversity they are thought to embody. The first comes from the constitutional division of powers, and through the provincial governments created by that division of powers. This basket of protections is generally referred to as *interstate* federalism. The second form of protection comes from the design and operating principles of national institutions such as Parliament. Protections embedded within national institutions are generally referred to as *intrastate* federalism. A closer look at these two forms reveals some of the problems Canadians have had in dealing with regional alienation and discontent.

INTERSTATE FEDERALISM

The term *interstate federalism* encompasses two forms of protection that federal systems provide to regional communities. The first and most fundamental protection comes from the federal division of powers between, in the Canadian case, the national and provincial governments. This division of powers is sketched in by sections 91 to 93 of the 1867 Constitution Act. The legislative domain of the provinces is protected from the political weight of the national majority by the division of powers, provided of course that those matters of concern to the regional community fall within the provincial legislative domain. The importance of this proviso can be seen in the different regional experiences of Quebec and the West.

When the Canadian federal state was established in 1867, matters of particular concern to French Canada were assigned to the legislative domain of the provinces. These included education, property, and civil rights, and many areas of contemporary social policy. The expectation was that this division of powers would provide a first line of defence, although by no means the only line of defence, for Catholic francophones within Quebec. Thus the division of powers effectively walled off the majority of the Catholic-francophone community, a majority encompassed by the boundaries of Quebec, from the national majority, which was predominantly Protestant and anglophone. As noted above, francophones outside Quebec, who were both national and provincial minorities, were not similarly protected.

For the first eighty years after Confederation, this form of interstate federalism worked reasonably well for French Canada, or at least for those French Canadians who formed the provincial majority in Quebec. The primary task of the Quebec government was to ensure that the federal government respected the constitutional division of powers. However, this task became increasingly difficult after the end of the Second World War when the federal government began to use its spending power to invade provincial areas of jurisdiction. Federal-provincial shared-cost programs with respect to health care, social assistance, post-secondary education and interprovincial transportation greatly blurred the constitutional division of powers and encroached upon the legislative autonomy of the provinces. With the onset of the Quiet Revolution in the early 1960s, the Quebec government began to argue for the withdrawal of Ottawa from provincial fields of jurisdiction, and also for an expansion of the provincial domain. This combined argument for withdrawal and expansion challenged the interstate underpinnings of the Canadian federal state and became, at the extreme, an argument for Quebec's independence. Thus the pre-eminent federal question of the last three decades has been whether a stable equilibrium can be found that will satisfy Quebec's quest for greater autonomy while at the same time meeting the essential conditions for national integration. It is a question that remains in search of an answer.

The protection of regional interests through the constitutional division of powers never worked particularly well for western Canadians, or at least failed to do so until quite recently. The primary interests of the West, particularly in the early period of agrarian settlement, were economic rather than social or cultural. More importantly, they were not ones that could be assigned logically to the legislative domain of the provinces. For example, western Canadians in general and particularly those involved in the prairie grain economy were very concerned with international trade, interprovincial trade, interprovincial transportation, national tariff policy, regulation of the financial sector, and national fiscal policy relating to interest rates. Legislative powers in these respects could not be delegated to the provinces, and thus the central issue for western Canadians was how to achieve effective influence *within the national government*. The founding slogan of the Reform Party—"The West Wants In"—nicely captured this long-standing western Canadian quest. Interstate federalism through the constitutional division of powers was of little relevance in addressing the region's traditional basket of economic grievances. Unfortunately, and as we will discuss in a moment, intrastate federalism offered little more by way of assistance.

Perhaps the best example of the failure of interstate federalism comes from the National Energy Program (NEP), introduced by Pierre Trudeau's Liberal government in 1980. The NEP was designed to address rapidly escalating world oil prices and their impact on the Canadian economy and regional equalization; this was to be done by setting Canadian energy prices below world market levels, increasing the rate of energy taxation by the federal government, and encouraging oil exploration on "Canada lands."[7] The public policy dilemma arose from the fact that energy resources were not evenly distributed but were overwhelmingly concentrated in the West and, within the West, in Alberta. As a consequence, the NEP was necessarily redistributive in its effects; its costs and benefits were not shared equally by all Canadians. Although the constitutional division of powers protected Alberta's *ownership* of its natural resources, ownership did not equal control. The interstate line of defence proved to be of little use in the face of the federal government's taxation policies, and its constitutional clout with respect to international and interprovincial trade. The outcome of the NEP for Alberta was the loss of approximately $50 billion in provincial revenues to the federal government and, through lower energy prices, to Canadian consumers.

The point here is not to bemoan Alberta's loss, or to debate the pros and cons of the NEP. Rather, it is to illustrate that interstate federalism may fail to provide adequate regional protection unless it is coupled with effective intrastate representation in the national government. In the 1980 federal election there were no Liberal candidates elected in Alberta, and indeed only two Liberals were elected west of the Ontario-Manitoba border. To western Canadians, and particularly to Albertans, the NEP starkly demonstrated the limitations of interstate federalism and the need for intrastate reform.

Support for interstate federalism is now enjoying growing support in western Canada. In part, this revival may simply reflect the lack of headway with respect to intrastate reform. Interstate reform may not be the preferred option, but it appears to be the only option in play, which is to say the only option acceptable to soft nationalists in Quebec who have no interest in strengthening the legitimacy of parliamentary institutions in Ottawa. However, the growth of regional support for interstate federalism also reflects the dramatic transformation that has recently taken place in the economic sphere. The implementation of the North American Free Trade Agreement (NAFTA) and the larger context of economic globalization have meant that the federal government's powers with respect to international trade and monetary policy are becoming increasingly constrained. If globalization means anything, it means that national governments are less able to shield their economies from international market forces. As a consequence, regional power at the centre becomes less important as the national government's power to shape the economy diminishes. Thus, as control over tariffs, international trade, monetary policy, and investment drifts more and more to international agreements, or drifts out of the hands of governments altogether and into the hands of markets, decentralization and interstate federalism make more sense. Here we see, then, a potential convergence between western Canadian visions of the federal state and nationalist sentiment in Quebec. Both favour decentralization, although by no means to the same degree or with the same ends in mind.

As mentioned above, a second and important interstate line of regional defence comes through the participation of provincial governments in national politics. Of particular note here is the role played by provincial premiers. This role has been enhanced by the constraints that party discipline places on intrastate representation by MPs (discussed below), and by the fact that senators are not taken seriously as regional representatives. Although MPs and even senators may be effective advocates for regional interests behind the closed doors of caucus and cabinet, they are not *seen* to be effective. As a consequence, premiers often have the stage to themselves when it comes to vigorously defending regional interests *in the public forum.*

The premiers' federal role is strengthened by the nature of parliamentary government, which concentrates political power in the hands of the executive and, more specifically, in the hands of premiers and prime ministers. Because premiers control their cabinets, and because cabinets seldom face any effective challenge from provincial legislatures, the premiers can speak with authority on behalf of their province on the national stage. They can wheel and deal with other premiers, and with the federal government, and can do so with the confident expectation that any agreement they might conclude will be supported by their cabinet and, if necessary, ratified by the provincial legislature. This expectation is not always met, as the Meech Lake debacle showed. However, Meech was truly an exception to the general rule that premiers, and for that matter the prime minister, command the loyalty of their cabinet and caucus, and therefore encounter few if any significant legislative constraints. This combination of the *federal division* of legislative powers and the *parliamentary concentration* of legislative powers has produced a unique brand of executive interstate federalism, a brand epitomized by the first ministers' conference.

It is a brand of federalism, however, that often seems to be characterized by sustained intergovernmental conflict, which in turn takes on the coloration of regional conflict and appears to feed regional alienation. The question can be raised, therefore, whether the intergovernmentalism that is so characteristic of interstate federalism can be directed into less acrimonious channels. In many ways, the contemporary proponents of greater decentralization are trying to do just that by recommending that provincial governments be formally incorporated into the establishment and monitoring of national social programs and their accompanying standards. It has been frequently suggested, for example, that a new House of the Provinces be established, staffed by provincial delegations and charged with responsibility for federal programs in areas of provincial jurisdiction, for the use of the federal spending power, and possibly for national economic management. Whether such interstate reforms to Canadian federalism would significantly reduce regional conflict and alienation is by no means clear. The answer may well depend on what, if anything, happens with respect to intrastate reform.

INTRASTATE FEDERALISM AND PARLIAMENTARY GOVERNMENT

The intrastate routes of regional influence are to be found *within* the institutions of the national government, and particularly within Parliament. It is, therefore, the representative performance of MPs and senators that is of particular importance; although the methods by which justices are appointed to the Supreme Court has also been a matter of debate, the representative *behaviour* of those justices has been less at issue. The general argument that has emerged in the Canadian political science community, especially among political scientists in western Canada, is that intrastate federalism often works poorly, and that in this respect parliamentary institutions are maladapted for the regional nature of the country. In short, parliamentary institutions do more to cause regional alienation than to resolve it. To understand and assess this argument, we have to look first at the nature of parliamentary government, and then at the performance of specific institutions.

When the Canadian federal state was formed in 1867, the founding fathers attempted to replicate British parliamentary institutions that had evolved in a small, island country without Canada's geographic and linguistic complexity. As a British colony we retained the crown, although the crown-in-Canada was represented by the governor general in Ottawa, and by lieutenant-governors in the provincial capitals. The Canadian House of Commons was a faithful replication of the British model. It was elected on the same basis, and its internal operations were molded by British norms of responsible government whereby the political executive (the cabinet) remained in office only so long as it enjoyed the confidence of the House. As a consequence, strict party discipline came to prevail in the House. Indeed, party discipline was, if anything, tighter in Canada than it was in the United Kingdom. While the British House has adopted more relaxed standards of party discipline in recent years, party discipline has been strengthened in Canada. As recent parliamentary debates over gun control have illustrated, dissent from government backbenchers is not tolerated even when the legislative majority of the governing party is not at risk.

The central, defining role of party discipline in the Canadian House of Commons has had important repercussions for regional representation. If, for example, a western Canadian MP on the government side of the House disagrees with a cabinet decision, if he or she concludes that its regional impact is unwarranted, the MP can only voice that disagreement behind the closed doors of cabinet or caucus. Within the House itself, the MP has no alternative but to toe the party line. As a result, voters back home have no evidence that their MP understands their concerns or has spoken out on their behalf. Instead, they see their elected representative faithfully following a party line that might well reflect the regional interests of central Canada rather than their own. A House divided on party lines, and operating according to strict party discipline, has difficulty providing for the public expression of regional differences and regional discontent.

The House, of course, was not designed to be a *federal* institution, although it does accommodate federalism at the margins. For example, smaller provinces tend to have more seats in the House than they would be entitled to by population alone. Nova Scotia has one more, New Brunswick two, Prince Edward Island three, Saskatchewan three, and Manitoba two. The northern territories have three seats in the House, although their total population amounts to less than that for a single riding in southern Canada. However, these departures from strict representation by population have not been the subject of serious critical debate in

TABLE 1:	Regional Distribution of Seats in the House of Commons, 1996				
	Atlantic	**Quebec**	**Ontario**	**West**	**North**
% 1995 population	8.2	24.9	37.4	29.2	0.3
% Commons seats	10.8	25.4	33.6	29.2	1.0
% difference	+2.6	+0.5	−3.8	0.0	+0.7

Canada. As Table 1 shows, moreover, they have not contributed to significant regional discrepancies.

The cabinet, which is drawn almost exclusively from the House, is considered to be the most important *federal* institution in Parliament. Generally, all provinces are represented within the cabinet, provided there are elected MPs from each province on the government side of the House. When there are not, senators are sometimes appointed to the cabinet to fill in the provincial holes. The cabinet, therefore, is chosen to look like a territorial microcosm of the national population; all provinces are in, the larger provinces have greater cabinet representation than do the smaller provinces, and even regions within the larger provinces are represented. Cabinet ministers from Ontario, for example, would never be drawn exclusively from Toronto, nor, if possible, would British Columbia ministers be drawn exclusively from Vancouver. However, cabinet deliberations are shrouded in secrecy, and the cabinet speaks publicly with a single voice. Therefore, cabinet ministers face the same constraints that MPs from all parties face in the House; regional representation is neither seen nor heard. Public displays of regional representation are left to provincial premiers, or to opposition MPs far removed from the exercise of effective political power.

Frustration with the public face of regional representation in the House and cabinet has frequently been mobilized by western Canadian protest parties. In the early 1920s, much of the electoral appeal of the Progressive Party of Canada stemmed from the Progressives' adamant opposition to party discipline, and to what they saw as the nefarious influence of political parties broadly defined. More recently, the Reform Party has campaigned on the need to relax party discipline, and to make MPs more accountable to their constituencies and less accountable to their party. However, none of this protest has had any effect; party discipline in the House and secrecy in cabinet are as strict today, if not stricter, than they have ever been. While loosening party discipline in order to provide more effective, or at least more visible, regional representation in the House has long been a staple of opposition rhetoric, it has never been of any appeal to governing parties even at times when regional alienation has been a matter of acute concern, as it was in the late 1970s and early 1980s.

Given that the House is designed only at the margins to reflect federal principles, and that regional representation within cabinet takes place behind closed doors, the Senate assumes great *potential* importance as a federal institution. It was in the Senate that the 1867 marriage of parliamentary government and federalism was to be consummated. In the initial design of the Senate, furthermore, Canadians were not constrained by British institutional precedence. We could not have replicated the British House of Lords even if we had wanted to do so because Canada lacked a landed aristocracy, and therefore we were able to use the Senate as a federal body to represent the regional communities. In this instance, and in this instance alone, we opted for American rather than British precedence. Unfortunately, from the outset the Senate was badly designed as a federal chamber, and it only got worse with time. Equal representation of the provinces (the American model, and subsequently the Australian model) was rejected in favour of regional equality for the Maritimes, Quebec, and Ontario. This decision led in turn to an erratic pattern of provincial representation. Ontario and Quebec each have 24 senators, New Brunswick and Nova Scotia have 10 each, the four western provinces and Newfoundland each have six, Prince Edward Island has four, and the Yukon and Northern Territories have one each. As Table 2 shows, this inequality of provincial representation in the Senate has not been offset by an approximation of representation by population. In fact, the two provinces that are the most underrepresented in the House, Ontario and British Columbia, are also among the most underrepresented in the Senate. Thus the distribution of Senate seats reflects neither federal principles nor representation by population. In terms of institutional design, it resembles a dog's breakfast more than the federal chambers in Australia and the United States.

It should be stressed that the distribution of Senate seats has been the subject of less critical commentary than has been the method by which senators are selected. Senators are appointed rather than elected, and therefore their legitimacy as regional representatives has been fatally eroded in a mature, democratic society. Perhaps worst of all, senators, who are supposedly regional representatives, are appointed not by the provincial governments but by the federal government. Thus, in virtually all respects, the Senate fails as a *federal* institution.

The Senate has come to be seen as a home for retired party loyalists and bagmen, an institution of little relevance to the operation of contemporary Canadian government, and a complete waste of institutional potential with respect to regional representation. In many ways, this description may be too kind, although on some recent issues (the GST, the Free Trade Agreement, abortion, and constitutional reform with respect to denominational schools in Newfoundland), the Senate has shown sparks of legislative life. What is emphatically

TABLE 2:	Ratio of Population to Senate Seats	
Province or Territory	**Number of Senate seats**	**Population per senator (1995)**
Newfoundland	6	95,000
Prince Edward Island	4	32,000
Nova Scotia	10	89,000
New Brunswick	10	72,000
Quebec	24	287,000
Ontario	24	420,000
Manitoba	6	182,000
Saskatchewan	6	165,000
Alberta	6	424,000
British Columbia	6	547,000
Yukon	1	28,000
Northwest Territories	1	58,000

clear nonetheless is that the Senate has failed to consummate the institutional marriage between parliamentary government and federalism. As the supposedly federal chamber, the Senate has been a dismal failure.

Given this assessment of the Senate, and given the above-noted constraints on the House with respect to regional representation, it is hard to avoid the conclusion that intrastate federalism has not been a Canadian success. Certainly this is the story that western Canadians have been prone to tell, although here it is also important to stress that western Canadians have been far more united in their diagnosis of the intrastate problem than they have been in their recommended solutions. Over the past 80 years, western Canadians have pushed for reduced party discipline, nonpartisanship, new political parties altogether, electoral reform, Senate reform, and now decentralization. The lack of a consistent remedy has not helped the western quest for intrastate reform, although it has not been the only obstacle.

In theory, one might expect that the critique of intrastate federalism that has so animated western Canadian politics would also be found in the Atlantic provinces. After all, the same conditions apply: Atlantic MPs are as constrained by party discipline as their western counterparts, and Atlantic senators, while relatively more numerous than western senators, are still federally appointed politicians with little public profile or credibility. (There are 30 senators from Atlantic Canada, and 24 from the West.) However, the critique of intrastate federalism is far less pervasive in Atlantic Canada where the institutional status quo, if anything, has worked to the region's advantage.[8] This regional difference simply reflects reality; federal programs including equalization, regional economic development, and employment insurance have worked more to the advantage of Atlantic Canada than to the advantage of western Canadian provinces. And maybe western Canadians, with close to four times the population of Atlantic Canada,[9] just expect more and are therefore more easily dissatisfied.

Less surprisingly, the western Canadian critique of intrastate federalism has failed to take root in the two most populous regions, Ontario and Quebec. While the lack of enthusiasm in Ontario is not surprising, the Quebec case is more complex. Certainly there have been situations in the past where the interests of Quebec residents have been seriously compromised by the actions of the federal government; the case that comes most immediately to mind is the imposition of military conscription in the First and Second World Wars, an imposition that was vigorously but ultimately unsuccessfully resisted in Quebec. Mention could also be made of Ottawa's growing use of the federal spending power in areas of provincial jurisdiction in the decades following the Second World War, a use hotly contested in Quebec. However, given the dominance of Quebec-based prime ministers over the past 30 years, it has become more difficult to argue that parliamentary institutions have some inherent bias against Quebec interests. The empirical evidence suggests that the regional interests of both Quebec and Ontario have not fared badly within the context of parliamentary government. As a consequence, there has been little interest in intrastate institutional reform. While there has been a persistent demand by Quebec for a reduction in Ottawa's role in the Canadian federal state, a demand recently picked up by Ontario, there has been no support for parliamentary reforms designed to strengthen regional representation within national institutions.

The western Canadian vision of intrastate reform to enhance regional representation within parliamentary institutions has largely fallen on deaf ears, and recently support for this strategy has begun to fade even in the West. Some of the most ardent supporters of Senate reform, including former Alberta premier Don Getty, have disappeared from the provincial stage, and have been replaced by leaders such as Ralph Klein who attach much less importance to institutional reform. Even the Reform Party has started to downplay its initial emphasis on intrastate reform; the early focus on a Triple-E Senate (equal, elected, and effective) has been replaced by an emphasis on decentralization as the party trolls for support in vote-rich Ontario.

LOOKING AHEAD

As we noted at the outset of this chapter, regional differences in interests, values, and beliefs are inevitable in a country of Canada's size and complexity. So too are regional identities, conflicts, and alienation. It would be unrealistic to hope that regionalism could be banished from Canadian political life, and indeed our political life would be poorer as a consequence. Rather, the central question to ask is whether Canadian political institutions do a reasonable job in maintaining the federal balance between the protection of regional interests and the promotion of national integration. Is the level of regional alienation in *political life* greater than we should expect given the territorial diversity of Canadian life?

If an answer is to be found, it is to be found in the nature of federal institutions. In trying to address the regional dimensions of political life, Canadians have relied upon federalism as the master solution. More specifically, they have relied upon the federal division of powers, the active participation of provincial governments in national politics, and the representation of regional interests within the institutions of the national government. Of these three solutions, the third has clearly been the least successful, and weakness in this respect has contributed to a growing emphasis on interstate federalism. This shift from the search for intrastate reforms to a reliance on interstate federalism is reinforced by the nationalist movement in Quebec, which is emphatically interstate in its orientation to the Canadian federal state.

In the years ahead, the growth of interstate federalism should ensure that one side of the federal challenge, the protection of territorial diversity, is met. If there is less and less that Ottawa can do, then there is less and less harm it can inflict on regional interests. What remains to be seen is whether the other side, the promotion of national integration, will also be met. Here there may be greater cause for concern as the Canadian federal state enters the twenty-first century.

NOTES

1. Alan C. Cairns, "The Governments and Societies of Canadian Federalism," *Canadian Journal of Political Science*, 10 (1977): 695–726.

2. This point was originally made by Richard Simeon, "Regionalism and Canadian Political Institutions," in Richard Schultz, Orest M. Kruhlak, and John C. Terry, eds., *The Canadian Political Process*, 3rd ed. (Toronto: Holt, Rinehart and Winston, 1979), 294.

3. David Smith nicely captures this sentiment: " . . . it is at the level of public consciousness that the region [the Prairies] has achieved its lasting identity. Visually, to anyone travelling between the rim of the Shield and the foothills of the Rockies across a thousand miles of 'black soil sliding into open sky,' the Prairies merge as one vast land. For those who have never seen the Canadian plains but know their history and literature, the region is myth, of the mind . . . ." David E. Smith, "The Prairie Provinces," in David Bellamy, Jon H. Pammett, and Donald C. Rowat, eds., *The Provincial Political Systems: Comparative Essays* (Toronto: Methuen, 1976), 46.

4. If there is an exception here, it is with respect to health care and the constraints of the Canada Health Act.

5. For example, see William H. Riker, *Federalism: Origin, Operation, Significance* (Boston: Little, Brown, 1964).

6. There is an interesting cultural difference in the terminology applied to the government in Ottawa. English Canadian scholars such as myself are prone to refer to the *national* government, or to use the terms *national* and *federal* interchangeably. However, Quebec scholars argue that because Canada is composed of two national communities, Ottawa should be referred to as the *federal* rather than the *national* government.

7. "Canada lands" were those whose mineral rights were owned by the federal government and not the provinces. The NEP thus encouraged a shift in exploration from the three western provinces to the North and offshore.

8. The Maritime Rights Movement in the 1920s was a clear exception to this conclusion. For a discussion, see Ernest R. Forbes, *The Maritime Rights Movement, 1919–1927: A Study in Canadian Regionalism* (Montreal: McGill-Queen's University Press, 1979).

9. At the time of writing, approximately 29.2 percent of the Canadian population reside in the four western provinces, compared to 8.2 percent in the four Atlantic provinces.

P a r t

FEDERALISM AND POLITICAL INSTITUTIONS

Federalism's influence is felt among our political institutions. Governments are structured along territorial lines. Parties work carefully in crafting appeals to both provincial and national electorates. Institutions of representative government are shaped by federal values (diversity amid unity, importance of subnational communities, etc.) and constitutional divisions of power. Courts have been entrusted with the task of sorting out jurisdictional conflict. Canadian structures of government show clearly the results of federal beliefs and pressures.

Note that institutions are not simply neutral government machines churning out results. They are sites for political mobilization as citizens work through these structures in hopes of attaining desired ends. There are rules and conventions about how the institutions should operate, but political dynamics are always at play. Without assertive provincial governments prepared to challenge federal government plans in court, or without national and provincial wings within various parties, or without elected assemblies at both the national and provincial levels, the pressures of centralization and uniformity might have triumphed. Canadian history is replete with instances where federal structures were used for furthering the ambitions of particular communities and governments.

Rand Dyck focusses on the interrelationship of federalism and the operation of political parties. Parties are vehicles of representation, political socialization, citizen mobilization, and policy debate. Throughout our history, partisanship has been a key factor shaping life in the public arena. Parties have framed choices for voters. In doing so they have had to adapt to the opportunities and the perils offered by federalism. The various parties have responded in different ways to this challenge. Understanding these variations and their significance to the parties involved is important.

Nathalie Des Rosiers offers an illuminating overview of federalism and its legal ramification. Courts with their interpretation of the division of powers are critical players on the federalism playing field. In Canada the interpretive handiwork of the British and Canadian courts has had far-reaching implications. Even in a rights-based environment rooted in the 1982 Charter of Rights and Freedoms, federalism remains a critical influence on court structure, precedents, and jurisprudence.

DISCUSSION QUESTIONS

1. Why might political parties have an interest in issues of federalism? Why might federalism facilitate regional divisions?

2. Should parties have special provincial and federal elements in their structure? Why or why not?

3. Compare and contrast the responses of Canadian parties to federalism and the corresponding political divisions. Which parties have responded most effectively? Why?

4. What challenges await a party attempting to operate on a highly centralized basis?

5. Does your province need (or deserve) its own political party? Why or why not?

6. How important are the courts in the Canadian federation? Why?

7. What values do you think should guide the courts in adjudicating federal matters? Why?

8. Explain and outline the evolution of judicial interpretation of cases involving federalism and/or federal-provincial disputes.

9. In what ways do the Canadian courts reflect federal realities?

10. Which level of government do you think should appoint the members of Canada's highest court, the Supreme Court? Why?

11. Why do some political parties operate at both federal and provincial levels, and others only at one?

12. Identify and explain the differences in the formal federal-provincial links of the Liberal, Progressive Conservative, and New Democratic parties.

13. What are the advantages and disadvantages of close federal-provincial party links?

14. What factors influence the informal relationships between federal and provincial parties?

15. Why do federal-provincial party links appear to be weakening?

16. What are the implications for Canadian unity of increasingly autonomous federal and provincial parties?

FEDERALISM AND
POLITICAL PARTIES

Rand Dyck

Federalism in Canada not only affects the formal institutions of government; it also complicates the life of entities that emerge to operate within and around these institutions, such as political parties. Federalism offers political parties the option of seeking power at either the national or the provincial level of government, or both. Some Canadian parties contest only federal elections; some, only provincial; but historically, most have taken advantage of this dual opportunity to control the policy and personnel of government. In addressing the impact of federalism on political parties, therefore, it is instructive first to inquire into why such differential patterns exist; second, to examine how federalism affects the formal structure and organization of political parties; and third, to decipher the complex informal relations between national and provincial branches of parties, whether of the same name or not.

TWO POLITICAL WORLDS OR ONE?

Although some historical exceptions can be found, as a general rule Canadian political parties until recently operated at both federal and provincial levels of government. This is certainly true of the three parties that dominated the scene for the 30 years following 1960— the Liberals, the Progressive Conservatives, and the New Democrats. In the 1990s, however, the Reform Party and the Bloc Québécois functioned exclusively in national politics, while the Parti Québécois and Reform Party of British Columbia[1] were unique to those two provinces.

It will help to unravel these differential patterns by beginning with a common definition of political parties: "organized, autonomous groups that make nominations and contest elections in order to influence the policy and personnel of government."[2] If a party aims to maximize its influence on policy, it would seem logical to contest elections at every available level of government that makes such policy. Such a strategy would also make sense even if the party merely wanted to place its supporters in positions of power or public remuneration. The virtual absence of organized party activity at the level of municipal government in Canada is an obvious exception to this expectation, but that can probably be explained by factors beyond the scope of this chapter.

For a political party that desires to influence policy, the widely overlapping jurisdiction between federal and provincial governments would also recommend itself to contesting elections at both levels. In the era of "co-operative federalism" since 1945, the two levels of government have come to share jurisdiction in so many policy fields—especially through the raising and spending of money—that the formal division of powers has become almost irrelevant. Both have major roles, for example, in social policy, including health, education, and welfare; the justice system; environmental protection; transportation; industrial development; and almost everything else. Any party with a distinctive approach to any or all policy fields would almost *have* to operate at both levels of government to be fully effective. To try to influence most policies at only level would be like a boxer fighting with one hand tied behind his back. Thus even parties with relatively low ideological orientations like the Liberals and Progressive Conservatives find it useful to be able to use both hands, or to be in the two rings at once.

Since it is so logical and usual for a political party in Canada to be involved simultaneously in federal and provincial battles, it is the behaviour of parties that are abnormal in this respect that requires explanation. The Reform party, the Bloc Québécois, and the Parti Québécois offer practical reasons for such abstention. The Parti Québécois, like several earlier parties in Quebec (especially the Union Nationale), is only interested in governing that province, preferably as a separate country. It would *not* be logical for such a party to contest federal elections. On the other hand, its cousin, the Bloc Québécois, *only* runs candidates at the federal level and only in Quebec. The Bloc is an anomaly, however, originating from disaffected sitting MPs who were upset at the treatment Quebec received in the 1987 Meech Lake Accord. They justified staying in the House of Commons and running in the 1993 federal election on the grounds that they were needed there to protect Quebec's interests. Without the charismatic leadership of Lucien Bouchard, they would not have done so well, and when he (logically) moved to become head of the PQ and premier of Quebec, their voice was significantly muted.

The fact that the Reform party does not contest provincial elections is not as easy to explain, but three main reasons seem to be involved. First, as a new party, it decided that it had only enough resources to fight in a single forum, the national one. Second, Reform leader Preston Manning (the person who essentially made this decision) wanted to be in complete control of the party and did not want to have to deal with lieutenants, let alone equals, at the provincial level. Third, as it turned out, the party's ideological appeal was so great that most provincial Conservative parties—especially in Alberta and Ontario—began to appropriate Reform party policies, so that Manning's party could influence policy without even contesting provincial elections. Indeed, to have split the right-wing vote would have been counterproductive. The mere threat that Reform might run provincially was usually enough to get provincial Conservative governments back on the "right" ideological track.

Thus, Canadian political parties usually operate in two political worlds. Those that restrict themselves to the provincial level or to representing a single province at the federal level (the PQ and BQ) simply have no interest in the rest of the country. Those that restrict themselves to the federal level but not to a single province are either too weak to mount two sets of campaigns, have too authoritarian a leader, or, ironically, are so influential that they do not need to.

IMPACT OF FEDERALISM ON PARTY STRUCTURE AND ORGANIZATION

As noted above, the Liberal, Progressive Conservative, and New Democratic parties generally seek to maintain branches in all provinces as well as at the national level. That does not mean, however, that they all possess the same kind of formal organization. In fact, not only has federalism affected the parties differently, but not one of them even has a uniform relationship between its national and provincial organizations. This can be seen by examining party constitutions, structures, membership, offices, and finances.

The federal Progressive Conservative party returned from the 1993 federal election in a severely weakened state, but it is strong in most provinces except British Columbia, where it is virtually nonexistent, and in Quebec, where it became defunct in 1935–36. The national PC party and the provincial PC parties are essentially independent organizations, but two formal links exist. First, by virtue of the fact that they sit on the national PC Youth Federation, provincial youth presidents have a seat on the party's National Council. Second, the federal party's bylaws provide for the representation at national PC conventions of elected members of provincial legislatures, current and past provincial party leaders, and provincial party presidents, women's presidents, and youth presidents. Since the party no longer elects its leader at such a convention, however, these links are rather insignificant.

Reflecting this independence, a complete set of federal riding associations and executives co-exists with provincial constituency organizations. In many cases, however, federal riding association constitutions provide for executive representation from overlapping provincial constituency associations, and many of the same people sit on both federal and provincial executives at the local level. In general, federal and provincial party memberships are also separate. In some cases, provincial party executives contain federal party representatives, and in some provinces, joint federal-provincial suborganizations (youth or women) exist. On occasion, the federal and provincial parties have shared staff or office space, but provincial party offices ordinarily do not serve the federal party.

Although federal and provincial PC parties were once linked financially, the provincial PCs in the West became fully self-sufficient by the mid-1970s, and today the two wings of the party are also totally separate in this respect. While it rarely transfers cash, as such, the federal party sometimes helps provincial parties at election time, primarily through the provision of personnel and services. Such electoral co-operation is often a two-way street, however, as the federal party draws on the expertise of its provincial cousins. The federal party has also lent staff to provincial parties for the organization of general meetings or leadership conventions, especially if most of the provincial personnel were busy working in individual candidates' campaigns. Provincial parties do not contribute to the federal party's budget, and there are virtually no joint fund-raising events in any province. Consistent with common sense, however, federal and provincial parties usually consult each other in order to avoid conflicting dates in organizing fund-raising dinners and such.

The national New Democratic Party was also crushed in the 1993 federal election and has never been uniformly strong across the country. It has by far the most integrated organization of the three main Canadian political parties, however, and the federal party constitution provides for an autonomous provincial party in each province except Quebec. In 1989, after many years of discord, the federal NDP completely severed ties with the provincial party there. While provincial parties, as such, are not represented on the federal executive, this body does contain two representatives from each region. The federal council, on the other hand, does include two representatives (table officers) of each of the provincial and territorial sections. These key officials thus formally interact with each other and with their federal counterparts at least twice a year. In addition, in some cases, federal council members automatically sit on the provincial council in the province of their residence.

One joins the NDP at the provincial level, but this entails an automatic membership in the national party as well, almost as if the federal party is an afterthought. Generally speaking, the provincial riding associations have traditionally been the party's centres of gravity. Federal constituency associations are strongest in ridings traditionally held by the party, federally or provincially, which are mostly located in the five provinces or territories where it has held power—Manitoba, Saskatchewan, British Columbia, Ontario, and the Yukon.

Provincial party executives, councils, and conventions in the NDP demonstrate a federal-provincial integration, although they naturally have a provincial orientation. A provincial convention, for example, always has a federal item on the agenda—a report from the federal leader, president, secretary, caucus, or chair of the election planning committee. In each case the secretary of the provincial party is also head of the federal party in that province. The provincial office of the party serves both levels, a situation that does not ordinarily present a problem because efforts at one level reinforce those at the other. This joint office probably does an average of about 75 percent of its work for provincial purposes.

Despite the generally harmonious and mutually supportive federal-provincial party relationship, federal party officials and others have been concerned about this strongly provincial orientation of the party. The first response, about 1990, was to establish a Council of Federal Ridings in each province to combat the dormancy of the federal party at the provincial and constituency levels between federal elections. Such councils, containing MPs, nominated federal candidates, and a representative of each federal riding association, were supposed to meet once a year. Only a few are of any significance, however, largely because they have no independent financial resources. This continuing concern to make the federal party a more distinct entity led to constitutional restructuring of the federal executive and council at the 1995 convention.

The NDP is also uniquely integrated in its finances. To a large extent, the federal party is financed by its provincial wings, and the latter are obliged to send the former 15 percent of all provincial monies received, plus 60 percent of union affiliation fees. In some cases the membership fee is split among federal, provincial, and constituency parties, but legislation in such provinces as Ontario, New Brunswick, and Alberta prohibits the direct cross-level flow of funds.

Although funds in the NDP flow primarily from the provincial to the federal level, the national NDP in turn assists provincial parties, especially in Atlantic Canada and the North, as well as the federal wing in Quebec. These parties get "subventions," which usually take the form of debt forgiveness or cash. Joint fund-raising events are rare, partly because some provincial laws require a strict separation of federal and provincial party finances. Nevertheless, the annual statement of contributions and expenses that the federal party submits under the federal Election Expenses Act includes the accounts of the provincial sections.

The constitution of the Liberal Party of Canada provides for several formal links between the national and provincial or territorial associations. The twelve provincial and territorial party presidents sit on the national executive, and the provincial leaders are entitled to attend such meetings as nonvoting members, although they rarely do so. A representative of each provincial and territorial association is entitled to sit on the federal party's standing committees on policy development, organization, and communications and publicity, and several provincial and territorial party officials are automatic delegates to national party conventions: the leader, the president and three other members of the executive, and the president of the youth and women's commissions. In addition, each provincial and territorial executive can select ten other delegates.

The Liberal party's situation is complicated, however, by combining two different federal-provincial constitutional relationships. In six provinces and the territories the structure is integrated (it is called *unitary* or *joint*) and the provincial organization functions in unison with the federal party, somewhat as in the NDP. In the four "split" cases, a separate federal party organization coexists with the provincial party: the Liberal Party of Canada (Quebec) and the Parti Libéral du Québec; the Liberal Party of Canada (Ontario) and the Ontario Liberal Party; the Liberal Party of Canada in Alberta and the Alberta Liberal Party; and the Liberal Party of Canada (British Columbia) and the B.C. Liberal Party. The nature of these relationships is closer to those found in the PC party.

In these four split cases, there are separate federal and provincial Liberal party memberships, separate federal and provincial executives and conventions, separate federal and provincial offices and staff, and separate federal and provincial riding associations. From the provincial point of view, the advantages of separation are that the provincial party can take distinctive policy stands, is less burdened by the potential of an unpopular national government or leader, can raise and spend its own money, employ staff for provincial purposes, do its own candidate recruitment, and generally establish its own image or identity. On the other hand, overall costs are increased; the number of creative, talented people available is usually limited; and in spite of attempts to forge a separate identity for the provincial party, the electorate may not make the desired distinction.

Constitutional amendments passed at the June 1990 Calgary convention facilitated the taking out of individual federal party memberships. Now, besides joining a federal constituency association directly, a person can become a member of the federal Liberal party by joining a unitary provincial party or a youth, women's, or aboriginal club, and their members are assigned automatically to a federal constituency association.

The financial relations between the federal Liberal party and its provincial counterparts have always been complex. The national Liberal party has different arrangements with each provincial wing of the party with respect to revenue-sharing and expenses. Every year the federal chief financial officer sits down with each provincial party counterpart to work out an arrangement for the forthcoming twelve months. In most of the cases, the federal party provides provincial wings with some of their annual budgetary needs which are supposed to cover the *federal* political efforts of the joint organization. The proceeds of major joint federal-provincial fund-raising dinners are sometimes shared, while in Ontario, where the federal and provincial wings each hold major fund-raising dinners every year, they consult one another on timing.

INFORMAL FEDERAL-PROVINCIAL PARTY RELATIONS

If the formal, constitutional relationship between the federal and provincial branches of the three "national" parties differs within and among them, their informal relations are even more varied. To a large extent, of course, such relations centre around supporting each other in their respective election campaigns. At one extreme, a party can demonstrate all-out support; at the other, total indifference. Occasionally, a party can even have contact with a party of a different name at the other level of government.

The strength of the federal-provincial relationship depends in part on whether either or both branches of the party are in power. A strong federal government party headed by a leader inclined to help his or her provincial counterparts as much as possible (e.g., the Mulroney Conservatives 1984–93) can offer more assistance to provincial branches than a weak federal opposition party (e.g., the Charest Conservatives, 1993–97). Similarly, a strong provincial government party (e.g., McKenna's New Brunswick Liberals) has the resources to help the federal party, or even take over the federal branch of the party in the province. On the other hand, a party that forms a provincial government might be so obsessed with its own re-election that it ignores the fate of the federal party in the province. In some cases, for example, a provincial NDP party far from power has had closer links with the federal party than a provincial NDP party in government. A provincial party may also try to distance itself from an unpopular federal government party, as the Ontario Liberals did in 1976 and the Alberta PCs in 1991.

A second factor in the federal-provincial party relationship is the financial status of the respective parties. If the federal party is well endowed financially, it can offer assistance to its provincial branches in a variety of forms. It can also afford to establish its own offices in provincial capitals. If unable to do so, it may have to ignore its provincial partners or else rely on them for help. Once again, the experience of the Conservatives and NDP before 1993 contrasted sharply with that in the post-1993 period, as the former closed its regional offices. Similarly, an affluent provincial party can help its federal counterpart more than one that is strapped for funds.

Affluence alone, however, is no guarantee of an intimate federal-provincial party connection. The relationship is also affected by the personalities of federal and provincial party leaders. Where such leaders have close personal relations, they generally direct their whole respective party organizations to help each other as much as possible. Examples include Ontario premier Bill Davis's support for federal PC leaders Robert Stanfield in 1972 and Brian Mulroney in 1984, as well as David Peterson's close relationship with federal Liberal leader John Turner (1984–90). When such leaders did not care for each other personally, they have often let their party organizations know that they should concentrate on their own affairs. Examples of such frosty relations include Bill Davis and Joe Clark (1979–80), Mackenzie King and Ontario premier Mitch Hepburn (1935–45), and Lester Pearson and Saskatchewan premier Ross Thatcher in the 1960s.

This distant relationship between federal and provincial party leaders is sometimes founded merely on personality differences; sometimes it is based on pure political opportunism (i.e., where there would be no advantage in supporting the party at the other level); but it may also be influenced by ideological differences. Part of the reason the Harris provincial PCs distanced themselves from the federal Charest PCs in the mid-1990s was that the federal party pursued a more moderate ideological agenda. Similarly, around 1980, Bill Davis in Ontario and Richard Hatfield in New Brunswick felt closer to federal Liberal constitutional and energy policies than to those of their own federal party. The 1993 election saw a chill in relations between the federal and Ontario NDP because of the Bob Rae government's social contract legislation. This situation was somewhat reminiscent of the discord, based on different constitutional perspectives, between the federal NDP and the Alberta and Saskatchewan wings of the party around 1980. In the 1990s, the Chrétien federal Liberals and the Daniel Johnson provincial Liberals have often been at odds over strategies to combat Quebec separatism.

A final factor of some significance is the migration of personnel from one branch of the party to the other. This is now relatively rare at the level of elected politicians (Brian Tobin's move from the federal cabinet to the Newfoundland premiership being a recent exception), but it is still frequent among the staff of all three parties. Many examples could be cited of such personal relationships helping to knit the federal and provincial branches of a party together.

Federalism also raises the possibility of the provincial branches of a party co-operating with each other. A certain amount of such co-operation exists within the provincial branches of the Liberal and Conservative parties, but it has been more pronounced and even somewhat institutionalized within the NDP. This includes lending election organizers to each other in their respective campaigns, a process that also involved the federal party, which paid the airfare of out-of-province organizers. It also includes assisting with creative graphics, polling, and other professional services and skills. In fact, smaller provincial and territorial parties are actually twinned with larger ones for just such purposes.

On the other hand, where there is no provincial branch of the party, or where it is so weak as to be inconsequential, the federal party has sometimes collaborated with a party of a different name. For example, the federal PC party developed informal links with the Social Credit party in British Columbia in the 1950s and again in the 1970s and 1980s, much to the chagrin of its fledgling PC provincial counterpart. Also in the 1980s, Brian Mulroney repulsed efforts to create a provincial PC party in Quebec, preferring to develop an informal alliance with anyone in that province opposed to the federal Liberals—whether from the Union Nationale, the Parti Québécois, or even the provincial Liberal party. On the federal Liberal front, the party has interacted at various times with non-Liberal parties in at least four provinces (Ontario, Quebec, Alberta, and British Columbia), and occasionally, provincial Liberal parties have been disloyal to the federal party, especially in the Hepburn and Bourassa eras.

Like so many other aspects of federalism addressed in this book, then, federal aspects of political parties exist to a large extent in the realm of informal relationships that supplement what is provided for in constitutions, organization charts, and laws. In this case, much federal-provincial contact is maintained by individuals who are active at both levels of the party and who carry information between them. To cite only one example, the office of the federal Liberal party in Ontario is located down the hall from the office of the provincial Liberal party, with much daily interchange between them. Even so, it is probably true to say that such informal relations mirror the formal structure of the different parties to some extent, and that in both respects, the PC party is least integrated, the NDP is most integrated, and the Liberals occupy an intermediate position.

CONCLUSION

Federalism naturally gives rise to the existence of political parties at two levels of government. It does not, however, demand any particular relationship between the federal and provincial branches of such parties. Most parties in Canada have historically operated at both levels, but in the 1990s two of the five represented in the House of Commons did not have provincial branches, and at least two provincial parties did not contest federal elections. In general, Canada appears to be experiencing a growing separation of federal and provincial politics, for even when a party operates at both levels, the two branches are increasingly autonomous of each other. Laws often require them to keep separate accounts; voters are less and less inclined to identify with the same party at both levels of government; and new election campaign technologies reduce the necessity of maintaining traditional party organizations that could help each other. Given that political parties are one of the few agents of integration in this highly divided society, the autonomy of federal and provincial parties is probably not conducive to keeping the country together.

FURTHER READING

Carty, R. Kenneth. "The Federal Face of Canadian Party Membership," in Campbell Sharman, ed., *Parties and Federalism in Australia and Canada*. Canberra: Federalism Research Centre, Australian National University, 1994.

Dyck, Rand. "Links Between Federal and Provincial Parties and Party Systems," in Herman Bakvis, ed. *Representation, Integration and Political Parties in Canada. Vol. 14 of the Research Studies, Royal Commission on Electoral Reform and Party Financing*. Toronto: Dundurn Press, 1991.

Dyck, Rand. "Relations Between Federal and Provincial Parties," in A. Brian Tanguay and Alain-G. Gagnon, eds. *Canadian Parties in Transition*, 2nd ed. Scarborough: Nelson Canada, 1996.

Smiley, Donald V. *Canada in Question: Federalism in the Eighties*, 3rd ed. Toronto: McGraw-Hill Ryerson, 1980.

Smiley, Donald V. *The Federal Condition in Canada*. Toronto: McGraw-Hill Ryerson, 1987.

NOTES

1. A party with an identical name and similar ideology to the federal Reform party, but with no organic links to it.
2. Rand Dyck, *Canadian Politics: Critical Approaches* 2nd ed. (Scarborough: Nelson Canada, 1996), p. 369.

FEDERALISM AND JUDICIAL REVIEW

Nathalie Des Rosiers

In Canada, there is no tradition of an elected judiciary. When nonelected judges declare statutes to be unconstitutional, legislation enacted by democratically elected representatives is defeated and relegated to history. Why would a democracy accept, and even encourage, such a role for its judiciary? This essay discusses the role and the scope of judicial review in constitutional matters in Canada. I evaluate the strategies and rationales used by judges to justify, on the one hand, an aggressive intervention or, on the other hand, a more passive approach to constitutional questions. The essay first discusses the principle of the Rule of Law, which underpins much of the discussion with respect to judicial review (Part 1). I then assess the role and scope of judicial review in federalism issues, that is, in challenges to the authority of a government to enact legislation pursuant to the Constitution Act, 1867 (Part 2). In Part 3, a similar assessment is made in the context of questions arising out of the application of the Canadian Charter of Rights and Freedoms[1]. Finally, I offer some conclusions about possible ways to rationalize the role of the courts in constitutional litigation.

THE RULE OF LAW

The principle of the Rule of Law operates as a useful rationale for the power of the courts to overrule the will of the democratically elected. The essential nature of federalism is a division of legislative authority between the central and provincial governments. Therefore, there is a need for an arbiter of the boundaries between the two levels. This arbiter, the judicial power, ensures that only those empowered by law exercise power.[2] In essence, the principle of the Rule of Law mandates that persons exercising power do so because they are empowered by law, not by force.

Even prior to the enactment of the Charter, the principle of the Rule of Law provided justification for the role of the courts in constitutional matters. It is said to be included by implication in the words of the preamble of the Constitution Act, 1867 "with a Constitution

Whereas Canada is founded upon principles that recognize ... the rule of law (Preamble to the Canadian Charter of Rights and Freedoms)

similar in Principle to that of the United Kingdom." The principle of the Rule of Law also explains other aspects of public law that are inherent in Canadian constitutional law. For example, it defines the duty of a government official to act within his or her mandate and in pursuit of the statutory objectives (*Roncarelli v. Duplessis,* [1959] S.C.R. 121). Theoretically, it also requires the equal treatment of all citizens before the law *(Smith v. Rhuland*, [1953] 2 S.C.R. 95).

The principle of the Rule of the Law has justified certain considerations with respect to the remedy that courts may use. In the case *Re Manitoba Language Rights,* [1985] 1 S.C.R. 721, the Supreme Court of Canada ruled that all statutes adopted by Manitoba in contravention of its constitutional obligation to enact bilingual statutes, that is, since 1890, were unconstitutional. However, it suspended its declaration of unconstitutionality for several years, pending the translation and re-enactment of the statutes. The concern was that if Canadian society must obey the Rule of Law, there must be law to be obeyed. Finally, courts also rely on the Rule of Law to protect access of citizens to the courts and have therefore denied the right to picket in front of courthouses (*British Columbia Government Employees' Union v. British Columbia (Attorney General)*, [1988] 2 S.C.R. 214).

Seeing themselves as the protectors and the enforcers of the Rule of Law, courts will seek to evaluate the constitutional validity of legislation enacted by Parliament or the legislatures. This reviewing exercise is mandated by section 52 of the Constitution Act, 1982, and involves an assessment of compliance of legislation with all Constitution acts listed. As such, judicial review has been exercised to determine the appropriate division of powers between the two levels of government primarily defined in the Constitution Act, 1867.

JUDICIAL REVIEW AND DIVISION OF POWERS

In this section, I study the role of the courts when dealing with division of powers issues. My conclusion is that the courts do not view their role as safeguarding the integrity of the division of powers designed in the Constitution Act, 1867. The courts are, in reality, quite deferential towards legislation, particularly federal legislation. What interventionist stances they take can be explained on two grounds: first, a desire to protect individual rights, and second, a will to prevent aggressive redistribution of powers or constitutional amendment, that is, a will to preserve the rules of the game.

A Neutral Exercise?

The judiciary considers the review of the division of powers effected by the Constitution Act, 1867, as an exercise aimed simply at determining whether it is the right government that has enacted a given statute. In the words of the Privy Council

> In so far as they possess legislative jurisdiction, the discretion committed to the parliaments, whether of the Dominion or of the provinces, is unfettered. It is the proper function of a court of law to determine what are the limits of the jurisdiction committed to them; but, when that point has been settled, courts of law have no right whatever to inquire whether their jurisdiction has been exercised wisely or not. (*Union Colliery Co. v. Bryden* [1899] A.C. 580, at 585.)

Therefore, theoretically, the exercise does not involve an assessment or evaluation of the wisdom of legislation. On the contrary, the courts determine only what the "pith and substance" of the statute is; that is, what is its subject matter, its purpose, and effect. Having determined what is the subject matter of the statute, they then determine whether such subject matter is properly conferred upon the legislatures or Parliament pursuant to the Constitution Act, 1867. In the following two sections, I first examine how the process of judicial review has led to the adoption of an approach that ensures that political decisions are validated and that the constitution does not "get in the way" of policy. I study the examples of the peace, order, and good government power and the "double-aspects" doctrine. Second, I examine the few instances of what one might consider an interventionist attitude of the courts towards political powers; that is, an attitude in which the courts stop and curtail legislative pronouncements.

Empowering Government

Courts intervene and void legislative action when the "pith and substance" of such action is said not to be within the list of powers of a government. What are the concerns of the courts in exercising such power? Courts should be concerned about preserving the equilibrium between the two levels of government. Such equilibrium is, after all, a necessary element of the protection of the regional diversity of Canada. One could argue that courts should be particularly concerned about the potential for abusive invasive action on the part of the federal government. The Constitution Act, 1867, does not provide any mechanism for the provinces to stop abuse of power on the part of the federal government. It specifically provides tools for the federal government to control overly forceful provincial actions. The federal government may withhold its assent to a provincial bill (the reserve power) or boldly "disallow" provincial legislation (section 90 of the Constitution Act, 1867[3]). Furthermore, it may declare works wholly situated in a province to be to the "national advantage of Canada" (section 92(10)[4]). It may also enact paramount legislation in provincial subject matters, provided that it is for the "peace, order, and good government of Canada." Therefore, according to the document, the federal government is empowered to refute an unwise, abusive, or excessive provincial statute[5]. However, the provinces would not have any way of controlling excessive or unilateral action on the part of the federal government. Interestingly, controlling federal excesses has not been the focus of judicial review of federalism issues. Patrick Monahan has described the focus of judicial review of federalism issues from 1950 to 1984 as invalidating provincial statutes.[6] Based upon my analysis, this trend has continued[7].

Although the exercise of judicial review of federalism issues appears mechanical and devoid of value judgment, it is not always so. For example, one delicate aspect of constitutional interpretation is to give meaning to words that may be purposefully vague. According to the Constitution Act, 1867, Parliament has the authority to make laws "for the Peace, Order, and good Government of the Dominion" (introductory paragraph of section 91 of the Constitution Act, 1867, hereafter, POGG). One would hope that all laws aim at peace, order, and good government. What scope should be given to this federal power? The Privy Council recognized early on that too generous an interpretation of the POGG power could render meaningless the list of provincial powers in section 92. Nevertheless the POGG power was interpreted as giving the authority to the federal government to act in times of emergency, even economic ones (*Reference Anti-Inflation,*[1976] 2 S.C.R. 373). Courts have also accepted that the federal government has the power to act in cases of "national concern". This includes the power to regulate for new subject areas that could not be assigned in 1867 such as aeronautics (*Johannesson v. Municipality of West St. Paul*, [1952] 1 S.C.R. 292). The national concern aspect could also derive from the apprehension that the provinces might be unable to deal with the problem if one of them refused to act. This argument, dubbed the provincial inability argument,[8] has led the courts to recognize the power of the federal government to regulate marine pollution (*R. v. Crown Zellerbach Canada Ltd.*, [1988] 1 S.C.R. 401) or to deal with nuclear energy (*Ontario Hydro v. Ontario (Labour Relations Board)*, [1993] 3 S.C.R.)

In determining whether a statute enacted by the federal government in a field that does not come under any of the jurisdictional headings of the Constitution Act, 1867, is a proper exercise of the POGG power, courts evaluate the possible encroachment upon provincial powers. However, they do not seem to find it very often.[9] The federal government's winning streak in the context of its POGG litigation is, I suggest, part of a larger trend in which courts have become less interventionist in federalism issues. This trend is exemplified by the rejection of the "watertight-compartment" philosophy and the whole-hearted endorsement of the "double-aspect/ancillary-effects" model of constitutional interpretation.

In "discovering"[10] the pith and substance of a statute, courts often realize that although a government is generally empowered to legislate in this area, it has used mechanisms normally within the other jurisdiction's powers. For example, the federal government may create a private right of action in pursuit of general trade and commerce objectives.[11] What should the courts do? On the one hand, a strict approach to the constitutional division of powers might justify a refusal to endorse a back-handed extension of the powers by a government: if the framers of the Constitution had wanted the federal government to create private rights of action, they could have provided it with such a power.[12] On the other hand, the Constitution should not always be an impairment to governmental policy: there is a danger in reading a document too strictly and hence preventing the evolution of the country. A flexible vision allows governments to fulfill their agenda when it is generally within the confines of their powers.

During the era of constitutionalism, as it has been called, courts referred to sections 91 and 92 as "watertight compartments." This metaphor served to limit legislative action, particularly provincial legislative action. However, the "watertight theory" now has been discarded and the flexible view currently prevails in the division of powers case law (*O.P.S.E.U. v. Ontario (Attorney General)*, [1987] 2 S.C.R. 2). This vision essentially allows one level of government to encroach on the other level's powers if the encroachment is necessary to the fulfillment of an otherwise constitutionally accepted objective under the Constitution Act, 1867.[13] Needless to say, this vision supports an expansion of each government's powers and must take care of its natural by-product, duplication. If two levels of governments are entitled constitutionally to use tools that may affect each other's jurisdiction, there will be situations when two validly enacted provisions apply. In *Multiple Access v. McCutcheon,* [1982] 2 S.C.R. 161, the Supreme Court considered the provisions against insider trading in both the Canada Corporations Act and the Ontario Securities Act, which were identical. Should the provincial legislation be "suspended" because the federal law occupied the field? No, concluded the courts, both statutes should be applicable. The principle of paramountcy of federal legislation is applicable only when there is a real conflict, when the two statutes cannot be obeyed at the same time. Such a narrow view of paramountcy rules is compatible with the expansive view of the list of powers supported by the Court.

In summary, the courts have continued to adopt a view of federalism issues that may render meaningless the initial distribution of powers defined in 1867.[14] An expansion of the role of the federal government might ensue from this movement, but, if applied fairly, the "double aspect" theory may also encourage provincial governments to pursue their policy agenda without constitutional hindrance. There are exceptions, however, and they merit a close examination.

Restricting Government

Courts continue to override legislative action on federalism grounds; as we saw, they do this mostly to provincial legislation. Why? I suggest that the courts have two main concerns. First, the division of powers analysis is an instrument by which the courts can impose, indirectly, a set of values on Canada. Second, the courts are wary of radical changes that aim at redefining the initial constitutional bargain.

The Indirect Protection of Individual Rights

The Constitution Act, 1867, has been described as containing a "hidden Bill of Rights."[15] Both before and after the Charter came into existence, attempts by provincial governments to marshall a political agenda that the courts found incompatible with a "liberal" state were curtailed by judicial decisions on federalism. In *Reference re Alberta Statutes*, [1938] S.C.R. 100, an Alberta statute that obliged newspapers to publish government notices was struck down. The decision can be read as constitutionalizing freedom of the press. The decision in *Saumur c. Québec City*, [1953] 2 S.C.R. 299, where a municipal bylaw preventing the distribution of religious pamphlets was found to infringe upon Parliament's power over criminal law, looks like a guarantee of freedom of religion. As for freedom of expression, one might want to consider the following cases. In *Switzman v. Elbing*, [1957] S.C.R. 285, the Quebec Act to Protect the Province against Communistic Propaganda was ruled unconstitutional on the basis that it dealt with criminal law, a subject matter that the Constitution Act, 1867, reserves for the federal government. In *R. v. McKay*, an Etobicoke municipal bylaw preventing advertisement was ruled not to apply during federal elections; Mr. McKay was therefore allowed to advertise his NDP affiliation. For a more recent example of the use of a division of powers analysis to prevent limitations on a right to security of the person, one can refer to the case of *R. v. Morgentaler,* [1993] 3 S.C.R. 463, where the attempt by the province of Nova Scotia to prohibit private abortion clinics was forestalled because the Supreme Court considered that this was an attempt by the province to deal with the subject of abortion, a criminal law subject. However, this analysis of the protection of individual rights through federalism is far from reliable. One can also cite several cases where freedom of expression disguised as a federalism challenge failed. In *Nova Scotia (Board of Censors) v. McNeil*, [1978] 2 S.C.R. 662, the Supreme Court accepted that a province could censor the right to view *The Last Tango in Paris* under its "property and civil rights" jurisdiction. In *A.G. Canada and Dupond v. Montreal*, [1978] 2 S.C.R. 730, a 1969 municipal bylaw prohibiting the holding of assemblies for thirty days was upheld as coming under the provincial power to regulate matters of a local nature and was not an infringement of the federal criminal law power.

Besides this indirect and haphazard Bill of Rights protection, one would be remiss not to mention that the courts have attempted to play the role of "protecting the rules of the game" in our constitutional history.

The Rules of the Game

Courts saw and continue to see themselves as the protectors of the basic tenets of federalism. They objected to the attempts by Nova Scotia to delegate its powers to the federal government.[16] In the words of Chief Justice Rinfret:

> The Constitution of Canada does not belong either to Parliament, or to the Legislatures; it belongs to the country and it is there that the citizens of the country will find the protection of the rights to which they are entitled. It is part of that protection that Parliament can legislate only on the subject matters referred to it by section 91 and that each Province can legislate exclusively on the subject matters referred to it by section 92. (*Nova Scotia (Attorney General) v. Canada*, [1951] S.C.R. 31, at 34.)

A similar attitude can be found in the decision on the Patriation Reference (*Ref. Constitutional Amendment*, [1981] 1 S.C.R. 753) when the Supreme Court held that the unilateral action of the federal government to amend the Constitution without a substantial amount of provincial approval was legally constitutional but "conventionally" unconstitutional.[17]

Federalism issues continue to be subject to judicial pronouncements. However, since the judicial review of federalism issues in the past was often a cautious attempt at protecting individual rights, the advent of a direct means of addressing these concerns has narrowed the focus to the division of powers. The Charter is now the main focus of constitutional judicial review.

JUDICIAL REVIEW AND THE CHARTER

The criticism of the antidemocratic nature of the judicial review process is particularly virulent in the context of Charter issues.[18] If it is imperative to have an arbiter for disputes between the two levels of jurisdiction, there is not the same logical requirement to have a body to supervise legislative choices made between individual rights and the public interest. This supervisory role, thrust upon the courts by the Charter, could theoretically have more serious consequences than a mere conclusion that it is not the right level of government that has adopted a statute. A finding of unconstitutionality does not mean simply that it was the wrong government that adopted the statute. It may mean that *no* government can enact such a statute, except through the use of the notwithstanding clause in section 33 of the Charter.[19] Hence the criticism that judicial review may be dangerous and undemocratic.

There are, however, possible justifications for this role of the courts. First, the Rule of Law obviously justifies conformity with all constitutional documents, and one is the Charter. Second, even democratic ideals may justify a role for the courts. Barry Strayer proposes that at the core of the democratic ideal lies the concept of individual freedom and dignity.[20] In his view, the protection of individual freedom enhances democratic ideals and does not necessarily defeat them. In *Andrew v. Law Society of British Columbia*, ([1989] 1 S.C.R. 143), Justice McIntyre referred to the work of the American John Hart Ely[21] to suggest that access to justice for groups traditionally excluded from participation in democratic decision-making justified the attention of the courts. According to Ely's theory, democracy is about equal participation in the political process. When groups are and have been excluded from true participation in the political process, the courts should respond and curtail further attempts by the majority to oppress them. In the United States, the theory has justified an interventionist approach by the judiciary in the context of racist laws.

"in the absence of its natural defenders, the interest of the excluded is always in danger of being overlooked..."

(John Stuart Mill, Considerations of Représentative Gouvernant (Book III) cited by Wilson J., in R. v. Turpin, [1989] 1 S.C.R. 1296)

The mandate to protect "discrete and insular minorities" (Ely's description of oppressed groups) provided an added justification for an interventionist approach by the Supreme Court in the early days of Charter litigation. I now discuss three aspects of the Charter case law that illustrate the tensions between judicial activism and a more passive approach: the court's handling of preliminary matters that define access to the courts; its interpretation and definition of the scope of freedoms; and finally its understanding and appreciation of section 1.

Defining Access

Judicial review can be pre-empted by the imposition of legal barriers to being heard. Two of these barriers are studied below: the possibility that the court may declare itself "incompetent" to hear a matter (lack of justiciability) and the possibility that the court may find the speaker "incompetent" to speak (lack of standing).

In the decision *Operation Dismantle Inc. v. R.,* [1985] 1 S.C.R. 441, the Supreme Court was faced with a request by an environmental group objecting to the testing of cruise missiles in Canada. The federal government took the position that the question of whether Canada should agree to have nuclear testing on its territory was a "political question" outside of the Court's competence; that is, a question that was not justiciable. The Supreme Court dismissed the claim of the environmental group but not without expressly rejecting the argument put forth by the federal government. There would not be any distinction in Canada between political and legal questions. This rejection of the political questions doctrine enlarged the scope of judicial review—no legal question was beyond the Court's review.

However, while the Supreme Court was prepared to answer a "political question" that had a constitutional aspect, it was not prepared to let just anyone ask such questions. "Standing rules" define who is entitled to bring a question to court. Traditionally, only a person with an "interest" in the proceedings could be heard. An interest included both an economic and a legal interest. Accused persons whose freedom was at stake had an obvious interest in raising any issue relevant to their defence. More difficult issues arose when citizens sought to be heard by the courts to argue the unconstitutionality of a statute that they objected to, but were not affected by.

Interested in hearing the constitutional problems in the land, the courts adopted a test that recognized the interest of a publicly minded actor when "no other person could reasonably bring the issue to the court." Under that test, the Supreme Court began to adopt a flexible policy towards standing rules. A taxpayer, Mr. Thorson, got standing to argue the unconstitutionality of the Official Languages Act (*Thorson v. Attorney General of Canada*, [1975] 1 S.C.R. 138). McNeil argued his interest as a viewer to challenge the constitutionality of the censorship laws of Nova Scotia (*Nova Scotia Board of Censors v. McNeil*, [1976] 2 S.C.R. 265). Borowski was able to argue on behalf of the foetus, even if doctors performing the abortions or potential fathers could argue that they had a more compelling interest in the issue (*Canada v. Borowski*, [1981] 2 S.C.R. 575).

The tightening of the rules came when a group of churches wanted to argue that the immigration legislation that threatened to deport people on an expedited basis upon their arrival did not comply with Charter principles (*Canadian Council of Churches v. Canada (Minister of Employment and Immigration)*, [1992] 1 S.C.R. 236). The Court considered that the immigrants themselves could argue—albeit with difficulty, since they were on the verge of deportation—their constitutional challenge. Therefore the test of "no other person can reasonably bring the issue to courts" was not met and the churches could not argue the constitutional case.

Defining Rights

Early in Charter jurisprudence, the courts set out to give a liberal and generous interpretation to the rights protected in the Charter. In *Hunter v. Southam Inc.*, [1984] 2 S.C.R. 145, Dickson J., explained:

> A constitution ... is drafted with an eye to the future. Its function is to provide a continuing framework for the legitimate exercise of governmental power and, when joined by a Bill or a Charter of Rights, for the unremitting protection of individual rights and liberties. Once enacted, its provisions cannot easily be repealed or amended. It must, therefore, be capable of growth and development over time to meet new social, political and historical realities often unimagined by its framers. The judiciary is the guardian of the constitution and must, in interpreting its provisions, bear these considerations in mind. Professor Paul Freund expressed this idea aptly when he admonished the American courts "not to read the provisions of the Constitution like a last will and testament lest it become one."

Justice Dickson then referred to the famous quote from Viscount Sankey's decision in *Edwards v. Attorney-General for Canada,* [1930] A.C. 124, at p. 136:

> The British North America Act planted in Canada a living tree capable of growth and expansion within its natural limits. The object of the Act was to grant a Constitution to Canada.... Their Lordships do not conceive it to be the duty of this Board—it is certainly not their desire—to cut down the provisions of the Act by a narrow and technical construction, but rather to give it a large and liberal interpretation.

The generous interpretation school is usually associated with the case of *R. v. Morgentaler*, [1988] 1 S.C.R. 30. In that case, the Court recognized that the right not to be deprived of one's "security of the person except in accordance with principles of fundamental justice" (section 7 of the Charter) extended to the right of a woman to have access to an abortion. The Court considered that the therapeutic abortion model and the criminal sanctions that attached to a failure to obtain an abortion in a recognized manner threatened the right to psychological security of the person. Madam Justice Wilson went further and recognized that limits on the right to obtain an abortion might infringe the "liberty" aspect of section 7.

> ... the basic theory underlying the Charter, namely that the state will respect choices made by individuals and, to the greatest extent possible, will avoid subordinating these choices to any one conception of the good life.

Thus, an aspect of the respect for human dignity on which the Charter is founded is the right to make fundamental personal decisions without interference from the state. This right is a critical component of the right to liberty. Liberty ... is a phrase capable of a broad range of meaning. In my view, this right, properly construed, grants the individual a degree of autonomy in making decisions of fundamental personal importance. (166)

This expansive reading of the rights continued in the cases dealing with "commercial speech." The American experience with the constitutional protection of commercial speech had been criticized.[22] Many had suggested that the core of the protection of the Charter should be political and artistic speech, pointing to the dangers of extending protection to what is, after all, the action of powerful economic agents. The Supreme Court, in the case of *Ford v. Québec*, [1988] 2 S.C.R. 712, concluded without much hesitation that the right to advertise was protected by section 2 of the Charter.[23]

Section 15, which guarantees "equality before and under the law," presented a challenge for the generous interpretation school. Since all laws make distinctions, the equality provisions could lead to extensive reassessment of legislative policies. Which distinctions should be constitutionally prohibited? In *Andrews v. Law Society of British Columbia*, [1989] 1 S.C.R. 143, the Supreme Court initially embraced a broad concept of equality. The Court was willing to look at the effects of the statute as well as its intent. It was also willing to expand the grounds of discrimination by drawing comparisons with similar sets of circumstances. An example of this was discrimination based upon citizenship.

However, the next round of constitutional equality litigation proved far more conservative. In *Symes v. Canada*, [1993] 4 S.C.R. 695, the Supreme Court held that even if the business expenses deduction in the Income Tax Act affected single parents in a negative way, it did not constitute discrimination. In *Egan v. Canada*, [1995] 2 S.C.R. 513, although homosexuality was recognized as an analogous ground, the Court considered that defining spouses as a heterosexual couple for the purposes of providing benefits was legitimate. Finally, in *Rodriguez v. B.C.*, [1993] 3 S.C.R. 519, the discriminatory effects on the disabled of the Criminal Code provisions regarding aiding and abetting suicide were again justified. It seemed that after realizing the potential for change resulting from examining the effects of a statute on equality-seeking groups, the courts pulled back. It may be that the conservative appointments to the Supreme Court finally tipped the balance. After venturing onto the terrain of equality, the Supreme Court shied away, frightened of the necessary changes that a bold approach would bring. However, a timid interpretation of section 15 is no less an exercise of judicial power since it legitimizes the discriminatory language and effects of different statutes, thereafter symbolically clothed with the approval of the "court—protector of the Rule of Law."

An expansive reading of rights and freedoms can and should be justified because of the presence of section 1 of the Charter, which provides an avenue for the government to justify a statute that otherwise infringes upon citizens' rights and freedoms.

Defining Governmental Justification

Section 1 of the Charter provides that the rights guaranteed may be subject to "such reasonable limits prescribed by law as can be demonstrably justified in a free and democratic society." It is, in a sense, the opportunity for the courts to "constitutionally approve" governmental action that infringes upon the rights of citizens. In *R. v. Oakes*, [1986] 1 S.C.R. 103, the

Supreme Court elaborated a methodology that continues to be used to test an infringement upon a Charter right. The government must first establish that the objective sought is of sufficient importance to warrant overriding the constitutionally protected right or freedom. The second requirement is that the measures chosen to achieve the objective be proportional to the objective. The proportionality requirement has three aspects: the measures chosen must be rationally connected to the objective; they must impair the right as little as possible; and there must be proportionality between the deleterious effects of the measures and the salutary effects.

The most difficult requirement for governments to meet has been the necessity to prove that the legislative measures chosen "impair the right as little as possible." Must the government prove that it has chosen the "best" alternative possible? Must it prove that the measures chosen are the only ones that will accomplish the objective? Although courts agree that the evidentiary burden on the government varies according to the context, it is still unclear what level of scrutiny the courts will impose on governmental action. For example, in *R. v. Edwards Books and Art Ltd.*, [1986] 2 S.C.R. 713, the Supreme Court upheld the Retail Business Holidays Act, which obliged store owners of a certain magnitude to close on Sundays. The Court argued that the legislature had made a reasonable attempt to balance the freedom of religion of some with the public interest in having a designated day of rest. In *Irwin Toy v. Quebec*, [1989] 1 S.C.R. 927, the prohibition against directing advertisements at children under thirteen years of age, although an infringement of the freedom of commercial expression, was justified. No one could prove that thirteen was the age of recognition of the puffery of advertisement, but flexibility was given to the government, which undertook to protect children.[24]

Other cases raising similar issues of regulation of commercial speech produced different results. In *RJR-Macdonald Inc. v. Canada (A.G.)*, [1995] 3 S.C.R. 199, for example, the Supreme Court invalidated the federal Tobacco Control Act, which prohibited advertising tobacco products. The Court held that the statute infringed upon the freedom of expression and could not be justified because the government had not proven that other, less stringent, alternatives would not have been as successful in curbing smoking.

In the end, the case law under section 1 is not surprising. Balancing individual rights with collective interests is not more easily done at the judicial level than at the political level. The only advantage of the judicial role is that it provides an additional forum for discussion. The legal arguments advanced on behalf of the constitutionality or unconstitutionality of a statute may be different from the ones marshalled on the floor of the House of Commons. The constitutional legal discourse mandates a discussion and an assessment of governmental objectives in light of their impact on individual rights and fundamental values. The government must prove that it has sought one of the least problematic alternatives. The public value of this accountability should not be discounted. The debates surrounding abortion, euthanasia, and even antismoking policies may have been enriched by the debates in the courts.

> **"Section 1 of the Charter appears to invite the Court to second-guess the "wisdom" of the balance struck by the legislature."**
>
> *(P. Monahan (1987), p. 53)*

Courts have made and will make mistakes. They might too readily ignore a possible justification for a governmental policy. They might misconstrue the evidence supporting it. They might be swayed by the better lawyers as opposed to the better argument.[25] Nevertheless, the debates take place on a different basis, a structured and principled one.

A provincial or federal government may respond to the judiciary. It can use section 33 of the Charter to override the effect of the declaration by the Court. It may amend the statute to take into account the Court's concerns or return to the drafting table and try to find a better balance between individual and collective interests. One might view this process as a dialogue between the courts and the legislatures.[26] One would hope that through the evolution of the dialogue, a better legislative product would emerge.

CONCLUSION

Federalism review by the Supreme Court of Canada has played a minimal role in terms of protecting provincial autonomy. The courts rarely intervene to override legislation, and legislative projects may generally proceed unhindered by the constitutional distribution of legislative powers. Governments are stopped only in cases of serious and far-reaching impact on the very nature of federalism or if they detract from the Court's liberalism agenda. It is not surprising therefore that the courts have continued to promote individual rights when given the mandate under the Charter. The judicial review mandated by the Charter is not, in itself, problematic since it is simply a modern form of the earlier interventionist attitude of the courts. The advantage of the Charter is that it allows for a direct and principled approach to the issue of balancing individual rights and public interest.

However, the judicial forum for discussion is not without problems. Access to the courts is just as problematic, if not more so, than meaningful participation in the political process. The "discrete and insular minorities" are waiting at the doors of the courthouse just as they linger outside the political forum. Maybe it is simply better to have two entrances instead of one.

FURTHER READING

The issue of the proper scope of judicial review in a democracy is the subject of numerous debates. The present article attempts to give an introduction to this debate in the context of Canadian constitutional law. The reader is invited to consult, in addition to the authors cited in this paper, the works listed below.

Dworkin, Ronald. *Taking Rights Seriously*. London: Duckworth, 1977.

Tribe, Lawrence. *Constitutional Choices*. Cambridge: Harvard University Press, 1985.

On the Canadian side, again among others:

Manfredi, Christopher. "The Canadian Supreme Court and American Judicial Review: United States Constitutional Jurisprudence and the Canadian Charter of Rights and Freedoms," *The American Journal of Comparative Law* 40, no. 1 (1992): 213–35.

Morton, F. L., and Rainer Knopff. *The Supreme Court as the Vanguard of the Intelligentsia: The Charter Movement as Postmaterialist Politics* (1992), University of Calgary Occasional Paper Series, Research Study 8.1.

Russell, Peter. *The Judiciary in Canada: The Third Branch of Government*. Toronto: McGraw-Hill Ryerson, 1987.

NOTES

My thanks to my research assistant, Stephanie Ross, to my colleague Berend Hovius for his comments, and to the Law Foundation of Ontario for its financial support.

1. Schedule B to the Canada Act, 1982, U.K. 1982, c. 11, (hereafter the Charter).

2. A. V. Dicey, *Introduction to the Study of the Law of the Constitution*, 10th ed. (London: McMillan and Co., 1959), 181–311.

3. Neither of these powers are ever used now. The power of disallowance has not been used since 1943 and the reserve power since 1961.

4. Again, this power is rarely used. See *Ontario Hydro v. Ontario (Labour Relations Board)*, [1993] 3 S.C.R. 327.

5. This understanding of the Constitution Act, 1867, is not shared by several English-speaking Canadian authors. They argue that the centralizing features of the Constitution Act, 1867, should have been recognized by the courts and they denounce the "emasculation" of federal authority that, according to them, the Privy Council forced upon Canada. See Vincent C. Macdonald, "Judicial Interpretation of the Canadian Constitution," *University of Toronto Law Journal* 1, no. 2 (1935): 260–85; and, for a summary of the English-speaking writings, particularly during the 1930s to 1970s, see Patrick Monahan, *The Charter, Federalism and the Supreme Court of Canada* (Toronto: Carswell, 1987), 222–23. My view is that the same features could and should justify the approach of the Privy Council in order to protect the federalist nature of Canada. For an analysis of the Constitution Act, 1867, in light of federalism objectives, see André Tremblay, *Droit Constitutional: Principes* (Montréal: Les Editions Thémis, 1993), 137–84.

6. Patrick Monahan, "The Law and Politics of Federalism: An Overview," in *Making the Law: The Court and the Constitution*, eds. John Saywell and George Vegh (Toronto: Copp Clark Pitman, 1991): 280. Monahan has noted that in the 1950s and 1960s, "federal laws were virtually immune" constitutionally (p. 280): of the 20 challenges to federal statutes, only two were successful. Monahan notes greater severity towards federal legislation in the 1980s. From 1980 to 1984, there were 28 challenges to federal law and 12 were successful.

7. From 1984 to 1995, out of approximately 62 division of power challenges, fifteen focussed on federal statutes and only one was successful, *Clark v. Canadian National Railway Co.*, [1988] 2 S.C.R. 680.

8. Dale Gibson, "Measuring 'National Dimensions'" *Manitoba Law Journal* 7, no. 1 (1976): 15–37.

9. Andre Bzdera, "Comparative Analysis of Federal High Courts: A Political Theory of Judicial Review," *Canadian Journal of Political Science* 26, no. 1 (1993): 3–29. The POGG power is usually argued as a measure of last resort if no other power listed under section 91 can justify the federal statute enacted. See *Johannesson v. Municipality of West St. Paul*, [1951] 1 S.C.R. 292; *Munro v. National Capital Commission*, [1966] S.C.R. 663; *Re: Anti-Inflation Act*, [1976] 2 S.C.R. 373; *Contra: Labatt Breweries of Canada Ltd. v. Attorney General of Canada*, [1980] 1 S.C.R. 914.

10. Determining what is the pith and substance of a statute is often determinative of the results. For example, contrast Mr. Justice La Forest's definition of the pith and substance of the Tobacco Control Act in the *RJR- Macdonald Inc. v. Canada (A.G.)*, [1995] 3 S.C.R. 199 as the pursuit of health concerns sufficient to justify the use of the criminal law power with Justice Major's dissenting view on this issue, where he argues that the statute aims at regulating advertisement, a provincial subject matter.

11. *General Motors of Canada Ltd. v. City National Leasing*, [1989] 1 S.C.R. 641; *O.P.S.E.U. v. Ontario (Attorney General)*, [1987] 2 S.C.R. 2.

12. There were times when the courts used a strict approach to the division of powers provided in the Constitution Act, 1867. The "watertight-compartment" approach prevented the governments from using tools not provided for them in the Constitution Act, 1867.

13. Theoretically, the "ancillary-effects" doctrine applies equally to provincial and federal powers. It has been used to justify the British Columbia Heroin Treatment Act, which provided for the compulsory treatment and detention of heroine addicts (*Schneider v. British Columbia*, [1982] 2 S.C.R. 112.) See also *Irwin Toy Ltd. v. Québec (A.G.)*, [1989] 1 S.C.R. 927 for the upholding of the Québec prohibition of advertisement to children on television, traditionally a federal responsibility.

14. Monahan, 1991.

15. See the reference to the concept in *O.P.S.E.U. v. Ontario (Attorney General)*, [1987] 2 S.C.R. 2.

16. The rigidity of this position was tampered with by other cases that have allowed legislation "by reference" or "adoption," that is, where one level of government refers to and incorporates in its legislation a regulatory scheme adopted by the other level of jurisdiction: see *Coughlin v. Ontario*, [1968] S.C.R. 569.

17. Dale Gibson, "Founding Fathers-In-Law; Judicial Amendment of the Canadian Constitution," *Law and Contemporary Problems* 55, no. 1 (1992): 261–84. The Court later found that a "substantial amount of provincial approval" need not include the assent of the province of Quebec (*Ref. re: Amendment of Canadian Constitution*, [1982] 2 S.C.R. 793).

18. For examples see Michael Mandel, *The Charter of Rights and the Legalization of Politics in Canada* (Toronto: Wall and Thompson, 1989); Robert E. Hawkins and Robert Martin, "Democracy, Judging and Bertha Wilson," *McGill Law Journal* 41, no. 1 (1995): 1–58; and F. L. Morton, *Morgentaler v. Borowski: Abortion, the Charter and the Courts* (Toronto: McClelland and Stewart, 1992).

19. Jacques Gosselin, *La légitimité du contrôle judiciare sous le régime de la Charte* (Cowansville: Les Editions Yvon Blais, collection Minerve, 1991).

20. Barry Strayer, *The Canadian Constitution and the Courts: The Function and Scope of Judicial Review*, 2nd ed. (Toronto: Butterworths, 1983).

21. John Hart Ely, *Democracy and Distrust* (Cambridge: Harvard University Press, 1980).

22. Jonathan Weinberg, "Constitutional Protection of Commercial Speech," *Columbia Law Review* 82, no. 4 (1982): 720–50; see also Donald Lively, "The Supreme Court and Commercial Speech: New Words with an Old Message," *Minnesota Law Review* 72, no. 2 (1987): 289–310.

23. It indicated as well that the Québec Charter of Human Rights and Freedoms, R.S.Q., c. C-12, also protected commercial speech. It concluded that although the province of Québec had a legitimate objective in wanting to protect the French "visage linguistique" of Québec, it had not presented sufficient evidence that other alternative measures infringing less on the right of the English minority to advertise would not be equally successful in curbing the assimilation of the French language.

24. See also *R. v. Butler*, [1992] 1 S.C.R. 452, where the obscenity provision of the Criminal Code was upheld as a reasonable limit on the freedom of expression: again the court considered that the government needed only to prove that there might be a link between pornography and violence against women.

25. Philip Zylberberg, "The Problem of Majoritarianism in Constitutional Law: A Symbolic Perspective," *McGill Law Journa* 37, no. 1 (1992): 27–82.

26. Peter Hogg, "The Charter Dialogue Between Courts and Legislatures," *Law Times* (January 29–February 4, 1996), 10.

CONSTITUTIONAL POLITICS—Direct Democracy, the Legacy of Charlottetown, and Possible Separation

The central issue in any federation is the working out of the understandings and arrangements that constitute the political system. All countries are founded upon documents, conventions, core values, and legal interpretations that define the character and conduct of public life. These together determine the constitutional arrangements under which people live. Federations often pose special constitutional complications because of the complexities and sensitivities associated with such political fundamentals. Federalism speaks of nation-building amid province-building and diversity of political communities. Designing constitutional arrangements that allow for stable and accepted government is a daunting task. Furthermore, it is a task that political leaders and peoples return to periodically to resolve evolving controversies. Arriving at mechanisms by which this might be accomplished and reaching compromises which may endure are recurring challenges.

In Canada constitutions have traditionally been regarded as the preserve of the political elite. Patrick Boyer offers an argument for unpacking this elite notion and according a measure of constitutional sovereignty to the Canadian people. Canadians have not often had the opportunity to express themselves politically through the instrument of direct democracy. Boyer's spirited and thoughtful review of Canadian outlooks on popular involvement in constitutional change offers room for thought about citizenship, public involvement, and the evolution of our national political culture. As an experienced parliamentarian and author, his observations reflect extensive political experience.

Other essays in this section look to the Charlottetown Accord and to the possibilities of separation in the event of failure at constitutional reform. Martin Westmacott surveys the basics of the Accord and assesses the primary points of political contention. The Charlottetown Accord had various complicated elements and these are explained in the context of the associated political debate. Robert Young explores the complexities associated with the concept of political separation and its implications. Young's commentaries provide an insightful exploration of a concept that is elsewhere often superficially described. These essays contrast that which appears to divide us politically with the potential ramifications of that disagreement.

Students should understand constitutions and their reform as topics of relevance to all, not simply as territory reserved for politicians and experts in the esoteric realms of constitutional minutiae. The issues, debates, ramifications, and political instruments of change, are all part of the public domain. What is more, the consequences of these factors will be felt throughout Canadian society.

DISCUSSION QUESTIONS

1. What is meant by a referendum? Explain Boyer's arguments in favour of its use.
2. Why should people be cautious about leaving major constitutional and political decisions to government leaders or a social elite?
3. Assess the voting outcomes in the referendum on the Charlottetown Accord by looking at the voting among the different provinces and groups.
4. What, in your view, were the key issues in the Charlottetown Accord? Why?
5. Assess the main political divisions or cleavages produced by the debate over the Charlottetown Accord. Why might a document like the Charlottetown Accord be divisive?
6. If you had to draw up a "Canada Clause," what would be in it? What characterizes Canada as a political entity?
7. Aboriginal participation has been an element in recent rounds of constitutional reform. Examine the sections of the Charlottetown Accord dealing with aboriginal self-government.
8. Might separation occur as a political outcome even if it were not everyone's preferred political outcome? Why or why not?
9. How might the possible separation of Quebec affect your life? That of your family? That of your province? That of your country?
10. Assess the relations between political leaders in Ottawa and Quebec City. How do their mandates, objectives, and political support bases compare?
11. What are the principal reasons why people should vote in a referendum to ratify constitutional change?
12. What are the reasons that the use of direct democracy (through voting in referendums) is opposed in Canada? Is there valid reason for scepticism about direct democracy?
13. Has Quebec separatism been the driving force behind a reconsideration of the role of referendums in constitutional matters?

"WHOSE CONSTITUTION IS IT, ANYWAY?":

Democratic Participation and the Canadian Constitution

Patrick Boyer, Q.C.

As an attribute of our national character, the way we Canadians discuss and amend the Constitution is embarrassingly revealing. Casual and all-inclusive and relativistic in what we'll entertain as proposed changes to our country's charter document, we then become perversely formal and exclusionary and absolutist in the procedures we devise to screen out any of those proposals as amendments to it.

Worse still, this very style and approach to our Constitution and its remaking has emerged, as inevitably it should, as one of the treacherous challenges facing Canadian federalism—our system of government and the Constitution—itself. The reason is so basic. For in this realm of democratic participation and constitution-making, we soon come face to face with twin realities, which, if ignored, react lethally against the very basis of Canadian nationhood that the Constitution created in the first place.

CONSENT AND CONSTITUTION-MAKING

Of these dual realities, the first is a dynamic truism: democratic societies must, ultimately, be based upon the consent of the governed. When consent is neither achieved nor maintained, such failure in democratic fundamentals alienates people from the very system of government itself. In the process this alienation, or turning away, corrodes those invisible binding wires of Canadian nationhood that otherwise hold us together.

The second reality is a more static truism: constitutions govern the political process; the political process ought not to govern the constitution. We believe in the Rule of Law, not the Rule of Might, and the Constitution is the supreme law of Canada. The Constitution embodies our hard-bargained and historic agreement about the two most basic arrangements facing an organized society—where power resides, and how it is to be exercised.

The Constitution is intended, as a consequence of this agreement, to guide us through an extraordinarily complex web of volatile relationships. Accordingly, this blueprint document itself is not intended to become a topic of frequent revision, or to be the subject of agendas made up like the weekly grocery shopping list.

Steering Between Scylla and Charybdis

Failure to heed these two clamant truths about democratic government—that the governed must consent to fundamental change, and that the Constitution should govern us rather than we the Constitution—has repeatedly confounded the proposals, arrested the progress, and exacted a high political price from those who, lamentably, approached Canadian constitution-making without a healthy regard for democracy, or without reverence for their historic constitutional inheritance, and, sometimes, without either.

Anyone who would venture into these narrow waters must steer a most careful course, as mindful of destruction as those who, in Greek mythology, piloted their endangered ships through the narrow Straits of Messina hoping to pass between the two monsters, Scylla and Charybdis, one on either shore. Indeed, we have just passed through 30 years of unremitting constitutional drama, often with nail-biting intensity, aboard our Canadian "ship of state" on this voyage between two sources of destruction. The journey has proven largely counter-productive, even on its own terms—we seem to be getting nowhere. Separatism, which most of this passage was intended to avoid, is incomparably stronger than it was when we cast off from shore in the 1960s. Attitudes of regional and cultural alienation within Canada have been galvanized into powerful movements—some political, some attitudinal—for breaking the Constitution and dividing the country.

Yet in the process, this bad trip has also exacted the further harsh price inexorably demanded whenever these twin realities are not respected: alienation within the political system, and a Constitution regarded today less as a hallowed charter of nationhood and more as a draft document. The very category "constitutional discussion" in our country has become a talisman for trouble, and should properly come with a channel-marker warning: steer clear.

Too often those steering the ship, it should be added, just to complete this dismal travelogue, treated others on board as mere passengers, rather than working crew who could help spot dangers and redirect the course if only called upon to help. We have, in other words, the worst of both worlds. We suffered from a shortsighted lack of democratic participation in constitutional development, while those who had appropriated this exercise unto themselves saw virtually no limit on how they could tug and tinker with relationships, a role for which in truth they had neither mandate nor vision.

The whole lamentable exercise leads to one simple but hard question: "Who's Constitution is it, anyway?"

THE CONSTITUTION AS A "WORK-IN-PROGRESS"

We Canadians do approach the Constitution most earnestly. Yet our prevailing attitude in all this earnestness has now become, rather than one of respectful awe, that of busy engagement with a "work-in-progress."

It was once valid to observe that Canada had grown in size and changed in nature since 1867, when the present Constitution was first adopted, and that government had evolved to accommodate many new developments—from aviation and broadcasting to securities regulation and product testing. This original insight was about our operational flexibility within the framework of the Constitution and our occasional specific amendment of it—such as to create a national unemployment insurance program in 1940, or in 1951 to give Parliament scope for Canada's old age pension plan, or in 1982 to confirm and strengthen provincial powers over natural resources.

Yet somehow this observation became transformed into a much looser and highly contemporary notion, then even corrupted by some into a virtual doctrine, that the Constitution should be as much amended as adhered to. Certainly the prevailing wisdom came to be, during the past three decades, that the Constitution of Canada should be as changing and flexible and as dynamic as Canadian society itself. Even Pierre Trudeau—often misperceived by his acolytes as a constitutional hard-liner—opened the gates wide to fundamental re-ordering through the Constitution with the Charter of Rights and Freedoms, which stood traditional Canadian jurisprudence about civil rights and individual liberties on its head, and reversed the inherited balance of accountability and policy-making between the courts and the legislatures. Moreover, that was only half of Mr. Trudeau's proposed constitutional re-ordering. The other half of his policy, which he failed in his effort to implement, was intended to "entrench the economic union in the Constitution."

Drastic revision of Canadian constitutional basics had, from the Sixties on, in fact come to be seen as perfectly in order, quite normal as a central topic of Canadian public discourse, absolutely natural in the political ordering of things. In a surrealistic sense, it was almost as if we had no existing constitution at all.

We would make the Constitution conform to the political impulses of the day, rather than the other way around. The force of this new conventional wisdom ran to its extreme limit and eventually became expressed in a written form that will forever endure as a political artifact to record for all time the zenith of amendment mania once reached in Canada—the Charlottetown Accord of 1992.

Relativistic Approaches to Absolute Relationships

Ours is a relativistic age. On the profound level of science, it began with the unsettling promulgation of Einstein's theory of relativity, which not only shook and supplanted the fixed absolutes of measurement in time and space provided for by classical Newtonian theory, but coincided with public reception of Freudianism and a totally different way of looking at human behaviour, early in this century. By the 1960s, with the advent of "situation ethics" (where one personally and individually decided each moral question in the context of what one considered right in the specific situation faced at that moment, rather than according to some overriding predetermined and absolute code of ethical conduct), we were beginning to see the necessary implications—not only for science but also for society—of fixed standards in a relativistic world.

The Sixties was also an activist age. Times were exciting. The "winds of change" sweeping across Africa and elsewhere brought an end to colonialism. On all fronts it became a time of alternatives, of counterculture, of civil rights issues and protest against war and nuclear weapons, of student rebellion on campuses, of new directions in music, and open relations in sexuality and human community. It was a time to challenge, and change, the Old Order.

In politics and government, especially as reinforced by our quirky Canadian Oedipus complex to Mother Government, these new forces of relativistic judgment and social change came to be channelled in two new primary directions. First, we developed a peer-pressure regulatory impulse in our use of state power ("There oughta be a law..."), which turned our legislatures into year-round law-making factories and the spawners of vast new regulations and countless regulatory agencies to administer and enforce them. Second, we elevated into a moral principle of political society our relativistic attitude that if we encountered a law we did not like we'd rather disregard or change that rule than obey it.

At the extremes little changed. Canadians in poverty who got caught still went to jail. Rich Canadians continued as they always had to pay lawyers and accountants directly, and politicians indirectly, to find loopholes or obtain exemptions. Yet it was in the vast centre where new action took place: the large and politically dominant Canadian middle class lobbied government, through their countless and ever-expanding organizations, to make both government and its laws increasingly reflect their specific interests. Neither *discipline* nor *direction* (as in obedience to higher loyalties, or in simply following the rules and pattern of more traditional and orthodox societies, or even in subservience to laws of economics or to the laws of nature) were defining watchwords for most Canadians in this era of relativistic standards and public excesses during the last 30 years.

This profoundly changed Canadian political culture. We managed to build up—through our government and its increasing subservience to short-term impulses—a life-style that was not sustainable, either environmentally or economically.

In these very same times, unfortunately, Canadian interest and attention turned also to the long-term governing order of things: the Constitution. It, too, soon fell victim to a tide of rising expectations that would eventually prove to be as unsustainable as they were insatiable.

Politicization of the Constitution

With just a few changes in the constitutional document, some of our political leaders and academic authorities began to argue, at first tentatively, then with greater assurance and volume of voice as others found the song-sheet and joined the chorus, that the great ills of the nation—such as the consternation of Quebecers in their relationship with the non-French elements in Canada—could be solved.

In 1965, in a published manifesto entitled *Egalité ou indépendance¹*, Quebec Premier Daniel Johnson demanded "equality" for Quebec within Canada, as the alternative to Quebec "independence" from Canada. This opened a path which, in perhaps the most costly political misjudgment of Canadian history, was erroneously seen by some in the political elite to lead through the woods of constitutional discussions and thence onward into some sunny upland of blissful Canadian unity. They would unify the country, and overcome fears and misunderstandings between French- and English-speaking Canadians, not by a cultural re-Confederation, which had never yet been attempted, nor by a political accommodation, which had been the reasonably successful pattern of the past, but instead by having politicians talk about and tinker with the Constitution.

One of the most notable early prophets of this secular political religion was Ontario's premier John Robarts. In 1967, he convened a Confederation For Tomorrow conference.

Prominently present was Quebec premier Johnson. Smiling and accounted for, too, were the other eight premiers of provincial governments. Notably absent was the prime minister of Canada, the Rt. Hon. Lester B. Pearson, who had not exactly been invited.

Not through such mundane terrain as revisions to Ontario's school curriculum to better teach the province's youngsters the French language and Canadian history, or tedious changes to regular statute laws of all provinces to end interprovincial trade barriers, or sustained mental effort for political and cultural and legal innovations, would these provincial leaders take us. That course was not bold enough. Rather, something grander was called for. They would lead us through changes in the very Constitution itself. Such an approach was, of course, in full harmony with the mood of the times.

The pretentious high-mindedness of these premiers gathering in Toronto with Premier Robarts that year, even as the rest of the country joyously celebrated the 100th anniversary of our existing constitution, was demonstrated by the fact that Centennial intoxication made them want to play statesman. It was displayed equally by their unctuous insult to the realities of a federal state, in convening a conference on new constitutional directions for Canada without the government of Canada or the prime minister in attendance.

Thus was the Constitution of Canada "opened up" for discussion in a way it never had been before, and in a time and a context that politically were utterly unlike any other period in our history. The mad excursion on the wrong course had begun.

For the three decades following 1967—and certainly during the formative years of anyone now attending university—constitutional experts would become the high priests of Canadian political culture. In moments of difficult navigation, it was they who guided not only the nation, but the very leaders of the nation. They composed secret memorandums for Cabinets about constitutional stratagems, some of which made Machiavelli look timid (as we found out when these documents were embarrassingly "leaked"). They clustered, smooth hands cupped over their whispering mouths immediately behind the ears of prime ministers and premiers, at federal-provincial conferences. It was as if some Congress of Europe, with heads of state and plenipotentiaries to-ing and fro-ing, was being perpetually re-enacted in a Canadian setting. Television and news cameras portrayed such scenes, for years, to the people who meanwhile kept working and kept the country going. Never did a Canadian image speak more eloquently about the elite nature of this constitution-making enterprise.

With knowledge to spare, these same high priests also addressed a population increasingly finding itself in a fog of disconnectedness, through timely appearances on television screens, at never-ending conferences, between the covers of books, and on the op-ed pages of daily newspapers. They could be found eagerly interpreting arcane constitutional scriptures and dogmas, immersing us in deeper understanding of the mysteries of the Compact theory, that some claimed lay behind the origins of section 92, shedding new light on the yet-unfulfilled promise of section 91, even attesting to the remarkable prowess of "the federal spending power." With falling church attendance in these years, the religious void was filled by these scribes and scholars who divined and then revealed higher constitutional truth.

Today, in consequence, the number of Canadians considered constitutional "experts" is legion. We even export surplus ones. Some of our constitution-crafters are sent abroad at the behest of the United Nations, while others ship out on missions organized by the Canadian government on a bilateral basis. These constitutional emissaries—our legal equivalent to military peacekeeping forces—are supported annually by several millions in Canadian tax dollars. Drawing on extensive domestic experience, they advise other countries contemplating new constitutional provisions.

Indeed, by now we have all bathed so long in this topic and soaked it up through our skin that just about every Canadian considers himself or herself at least some kind of unappointed authority on matters constitutional, in the same natural way Americans know all about baseball, or citizens of France about wine.

Constitutionalization of our Politics

Within our country, we have thus been especially busy—in truth, preoccupied—with discussing and amending the Constitution. In the process, we have rather mindlessly converted the three-hundred-year-old political and cultural quest to achieve common community between French-speaking and English-speaking North American peoples into, of all things, a most dangerous constitutional issue.

It came upon us with a double dimension, this new era of "constitutional accommodation." For although the constitution was "opened up," it was primarily a process for political leaders and their policy advisers in government. The "opening" had been of the document, not the process. The inevitable result was that, in time, Canadians began to protest against such inappropriate exclusiveness in the discussion and planning of new basic arrangements for our country.

The second dimension of this era was that this newly created arena for constitutional debate—itself very much a separate and politically unaccountable world exclusive to prime ministers, premiers, constitutional experts, and public policy commentators—increasingly removed the major items on Canada's political agenda from the legislatures and placed them, instead, into this newly emerged first ministers' forum. The inevitable result, on this front, was the constitutionalization of our political agenda.

Large public questions and important political issues, which, in any other democratic country, would be discussed and debated week-in week-out, one by one, in their parliaments or congresses, were here in Canada increasingly "off limits" to accountable elected representatives in the legislatures. Most certainly they became untouchable for the broader body of Canadians themselves. The people were simply asked for their opinions by a plethora of pollsters who swamped news reports with percentage rankings more and more, while Parliament as a forum to crystallize and synthesize the opinion of the nation performed this function less and less.

When constitutional packages were devised through negotiations of first ministers, addressing real and fundamental aspects in the ordering of Canadian public affairs, even the elected representatives (never mind the people themselves) were told there was no scope for their input, no possibility of change. Prime Minister Brian Mulroney typically described one such constitutional package as "a seamless web." Translated, this meant no one part of it could be changed without affecting all the rest, so the constitutional proposals had to be received and accepted as they were—hopefully with gratitude, certainly with no real debate.

All in all, this revealed the crippled nature of a Canadian political system that incessantly sings its own praises to the democratic way of life, but in truth works a rather different reality.

Addiction to Constitutionalism

This perverse constitutional journey seemed unstoppable. Each time it failed to produce results, which increased the risk of separatism, governments sought to soften that very risk by attempting, yet again, a series of constitutional amendments that would "renew" Confederation.

Failure to obtain approval for the Meech Lake Accord led to the Charlottetown Accord. This agreement by political leaders combined, by far, the most far-reaching package of constitutional changes ever proposed in a single stroke since 1867. Going for broke, this was the comprehensive approach pushed to its limits. The very apogee of constitutionalized politics, this inexorable process of first-minister federalism, it now seemed obvious from our experience since Confederation of Tomorrow in 1967, nothing could stop or derail. It became almost perverse. Each time this constitutional locomotive faltered, more cars would be added to its train, pulling even more freight, additional issues, new proposals. What crashed on October 26, 1992, when 18 million votes in the Charlottetown Accord referendum were counted, was that all-in approach. Nothing more, nothing less.

It finally took a referendum—in which Canadians had a direct say on what they thought about the workings of first-minister federalism and its products—to derail this process. Like a runaway train barrelling along tracks of an endless siding, the Constitutional Express finally overturned when it crashed with spectacular force into a solid wall of ballots. Only this stopped it. For the very first time in our history, Canadians had become partners in this complex process of attempting fundamental constitutional change. It was none too soon.

Up to that point, the would-be architects of a new constitutional order for Canada had been so enmeshed in the inner wheels and mechanisms by which they kept turning out changes and new balances to the document itself that they had come to believe that that was the hard part. They forgot to keep an eye out for those perilous dangers on the rocky shores. The real balance had to come, not in the document alone, but equally between the document and the people whom it was to govern.

Many of the designers of the extensive Charlottetown Accord for constitutional amendment felt it was too complex for the people to grasp, so resisted to the bitter end the need to obtain their consent. They saw themselves as tragic heroes, even martyrs, in the cause of Canadian unity. Many others saw them as paternalistic, even arrogant, in their approach. By the fall of 1992, the process of constitution-making in Canada had become a lose-lose proposition. It was the referendum that revealed this truth.

Restoration of Balance

The endless first-minister constitutional conferences, and their attendant media coverage for 30 years, had, by this point, been quite enough. Canadians welcomed a respite from the hype of the constitutional wars. Most indeed looked forward to a cessation, following Prime Minister Brian Mulroney's statement, on the night of October 26, that "The Charlottetown Accord is now history."

After a thirty-year addiction, though, it has understandably proven difficult to kick the habit. In fact, more than a major mental shift is required to break free. Part IV of the Constitution itself, reflective of the default position in first ministers' behavioural patterns in recent times, as amended during this recent era, calls for nothing less than a constitutional conference. So immersed had first ministers become in the constitutionalization of our politics that they even entrenched this lose-lose formula in article 37 of the Canadian Constitution.

Free from problems of the magnitude besetting many other countries, Canada invented a domestic political escapism that allowed senior political leaders to appear to be dealing with high matters of state—the Constitution of the country itself—while in fact the country continued on, largely unchanged by their repeated failures. "The land is strong," intoned Pierre Trudeau in one of his election campaigns, unwittingly pointing out to us all how Canada was able to prevail even as he and most other political leaders indulged themselves in the theatrics of constitutional posturing. It was our luxury issue.

Yet luxuries carry a big price tag. The main cost was the loss of opportunity to actually deal with real problems, less spectacular but more consequential. These lost opportunities would show up in the cumulative result of inattention to accountable public financing—the national debt of $600 billion was still climbing. Another direct but not quantifiable cost was the exhaustion of goodwill in the relationship between Canadians, especially along the linguistic fault-line running through our country.

Even those involved in the process, such as New Brunswick's shiftable premier, Frank McKenna, who had played no small role in earlier scuttling the reasonable Meech Lake Accord, recognized the political message in the October 26 verdict from the Canadian people. The all-inclusive approach to constitution-making must be permanently abandoned. McKenna declared, after the referendum, that henceforth any suggested changes to the Constitution would have to be "incremental, modest, and less threatening."

The people's heartfelt imperative to deconstitutionalize our political agenda was one result of October 26. A second lesson from Canadians about our method of government was that in future no profound constitutional change will ever be attempted without first referring the matter to the people in a direct vote.

If balance had been restored, it was as the good result of a long and exasperating quest.

QUEST FOR DEMOCRATIC PARTICIPATION IN CONSTITUTION-MAKING

Our most salient political slogan to emerge in the past decade—"Constitutions Belong to People—Not Politicians!"—was certainly understandable in light of these increasingly unpalatable conditions which spawned it. The idea that changing constitutional fundamentals should involve those who live under that constitution, and require their assent, has been, by all evidence, a radical concept. Not in Australia, to be sure, nor in many other democracies, but here in Canada.

A quest for such participation has been under way a long, long time. *Quest* is the only way to describe it. The resilience of entrenched opposition to this democratic idea has been enduring, effective for more than a century in thwarting this aspiration, whenever and wherever expressed. In the process, suppressing any role for public involvement became in turn another factor contributing to our often forlorn and tentative Canadian sense of national identity.

The implicit message in denying popular participation was always clear: the Constitution in Canada is a matter for governments, not the people. The subtext here was the issue of sovereignty, expressed in ambiguous contradictions in a parliamentary democracy that is simultaneously a constitutional monarchy.

The government of Canada would be prepared to spend millions of dollars giving a birthday party for the flag, or distributing fireworks for July 1, in efforts to manufacture forced feelings of national pride. Yet something always seems fabricated about such moments, serving as they must as a substitute for that deeper patriotism which could otherwise more easily flow from a direct connection which people have with this country. Perhaps this would not have struck such a tinny note of artificiality had these same Canadians not, for several decades, watched political leaders disdainfully exclude them while toying with their Constitution. Patriotism is no more divisible into compartments than religion is into days of the week.

It was one thing, moreover, to be left standing on the sidelines, quite another to be spectators to failure. What had made the spectacle even more destructive of patriotism was that, in most cases, these political leaders emerged from their constitution-making efforts producing, not just failure, but real setbacks that hardened feelings of division within the country and diminished our positive feelings about a common Canadian future.

Insipid Democracy from the Start

This picture emerges from the very outset. Efforts to allow citizens at large to vote on the new Constitution at the time of Confederation in 1867 were thwarted by the powers on high.

The year before, the issue erupted over whether to let the people vote on having a new country, when 20 members of Parliament from Canada East (today, Quebec) addressed a "remonstrance" to the secretary of state for the colonies in London. This 1866 petition of complaint was an attempt to stop implementation of Confederation until the various governments in British North America had received a mandate from their people to create a new country with a new constitution.

This episode reveals a dominant attitude—present from our earliest days, and clearly lingering with us still—about how an appeal to the people is "unstatesmanlike." As important, these events from 130 years ago also demonstrate that unexpressed views do not simply fade away. They instead go underground, and get channelled elsewhere, waiting for a chance to resurface. If people are denied an opportunity to participate, the force of their convictions will, sooner or later, find alternate forms of expression.

Back in 1866, about a third of the elected representatives of Canada East declared that the people had "not yet consented to the sweeping changes in their institutions, and in their relations to the other Provinces or to the British Empire, contemplated by this scheme of Confederation." The people had "never had an opportunity of pronouncing a decision upon the question." A "proper regard for their rights," and "every principle of sound statesmanship," the MPs argued, required postponement of the final decision by London until it could be shown that "the measure be a good one and the people are really in favour of it."

No Mandate for the New Constitution

The MPs noted the irony of how all those who had lately come to advocate Confederation had previously spoken against it. The perverse logic implicit in this situation meant that while political leaders were allowed to change their minds in the face of changing circumstances, the people themselves could not be trusted to go through a similar mental process.

Since the Confederation plan had not been mentioned during either the 1861 or 1863 elections, it could be concluded there was no mandate from the people—no consent—to proceed with such fundamental change. The crux of this argument, in practical terms of democratic process, was that the elected parliament of the day for both Canada East and Canada West (later, Ontario) would expire the next summer in 1867, and likewise the existing assembly in Nova Scotia would be dissolved the following spring. These pending general elections should accordingly be allowed to take place, the 20 MPs argued, noting that the campaigns would primarily turn on the question of Confederation. That way, a full debate could unfold, both on the desirability of political union and on the conditions that would be acceptable under a new constitution. The result, said the MPs, would be "an election of Parliaments representing the settled convictions and the matured purposes of the people."

The decisions of parliaments elected under these circumstances, they reasoned, if favourable to Confederation, would go far to ensure the success of a system that at best could still only be regarded as an experiment. Creating a new country and constitution should only be attempted under the most favourable conditions—which would include the consent given by electors in positive mandates in the pending general elections. If the voting results proved adverse to Confederation, however, these MPs pointed out, "that fact alone would demonstrate the wisdom of the delay for which we plead."

They felt that promotion of the new constitution and union could be traced to "the party or personal exigencies of Canadian politicians, and not to a spontaneous or general desire among the people for fundamental changes in their political institutions, or in their political relations." The details of the new constitution had not been considered, they said, in the sense in which the clauses of a bill are considered, in any of the provincial parliaments; that in neither Canada nor Nova Scotia had the people had an opportunity to express themselves on either the principle or the details; and that in New Brunswick, where an election had recently taken place, "the people cannot be said to have assented to the Quebec scheme" (which was the only definite plan of union under consideration at the time of the New Brunswick election).

"We seek delay," they explained, "not to frustrate the purpose of a majority of our countrymen, but to prevent their being surprised, against their will, or without their consent, into a political change which, however obnoxious or oppressive to them it might prove, could not be reversed without such an agitation as every well-wisher of his country must desire to avert."[2]

"Consistent Reluctance" to Seeking a Popular Verdict

This effort to bring about a direct vote by the people on the new constitutional arrangements encountered, however, what Canadian political scientist R. McGregor Dawson would later describe as "the consistent reluctance to submit the question of federation to any popular verdict."[3]

Lost in the mists of time, and concealed by our present-day mythology about the Fathers of Confederation who created a new constitution and country in 1867, is any memory of how one of the most memorable of those men, John A. Macdonald, forcefully expressed that "consistent reluctance." Although Macdonald had himself once spoken against the idea of Confederation, he, like the others, subsequently changed his mind. Yet he ironically maintained a belief that the "fickle" public could not be relied upon. "The course of the New Brunswick Government in dissolving their Parliament, and appealing to the people [in an election on the issue of Confederation]," wrote Macdonald, "was unstatesmanlike and unsuccessful, as it deserved to be . . . Whatever might have been the result in the legislature, the subject would have been fairly discussed and its merits understood, and if he [the Premier] had been defeated, he then had an appeal to the people."[4] In short, Macdonald saw voting by the people on constitutional proposals only as a very last resort, something one might be forced into only if and when all else had failed.

Major Premise—You Cannot Trust the People

This point must be grasped well. For not only did Macdonald represent the scepticism about democracy that many in his day shared, but more significantly, he laid down a policy line with a political value and a point of view that still endure to this day. That policy has become the inarticulate major premise of his many disciples who are with us yet, and who almost instinctively—and evidently without clearly thinking the matter through—oppose popular endorsement of constitutional proposals.

Asked whether the Confederation scheme should be ratified by the electorate in a referendum, Macdonald stated, with the same bluntness we too often still hear today: "As it would be obviously absurd to submit the complicated details of such a measure to the people, it is not proposed to seek their sanction before asking the Imperial Government to introduce a Bill in the British Parliament."[5] This desire to avoid an election or to hold any form of nonbinding referendum, explains Dawson, "was conveniently explained as being in accord with British ideas of the functions of a representative legislature; but it also sprang from a shaky belief in the solid virtues of popular government."[6] The point to appreciate here is not only that a quest for direct popular endorsement of Confederation existed and was denied, but also that exclusion of the general public from a role in ratifying constitutional change in our country goes back a long, long way.

Even more important, perhaps, is to recognize and accept that failure to provide for public participation—this denial of any need for consent on fundamentals—comes at a price. Even by the time of the Meech Lake constitutional accord in 1987, Canada's political leaders had still failed to grasp this truth that unexpressed views never dissipate but instead get channelled elsewhere. It's a pity, since one of the benefits of having a history is to learn from it.

Costs of Exclusion Are Tangible

The denial of any direct vote on the constitutional issue of Confederation, for example, meant that contending views had to be channelled through the second-best procedure—a general election campaign. That, indeed, was all that the 20 MPs from Canada East had ever sought.

The case of Nova Scotia is instructive of the problems inherent in using such a blunt device as an election (rather than a referendum) to decide a precise constitutional question. Nova Scotia premier Charles Tupper, elected in 1863, and enjoying the five-year life span of the provincial assembly, did not need to go to the polls again in a general election until after Confederation came into effect on July 1, 1867. So he did not. In the ensuing election of September 1867, however, he reaped the whirlwind: candidates opposed to Confederation captured 36 out of 38 seats in the Nova Scotia House of Assembly, and in the voting for MPs to Canada's new Parliament in Ottawa, anti-Confederate candidates swept 18 of Nova Scotia's 19 seats.

Historian Peter B. Waite, noting how it had been fortunate for Confederation that Tupper did not "test his electorate" until after the new constitutional arrangement had taken effect, subsequently read this election result as if it had been a referendum. "Then, too late, it was clear that 65% of Nova Scotians opposed Confederation," concluded Waite, broadly assessing voting returns in that general election as a specific verdict on a single issue, and making the dubious assumption that a single factor—Confederation—influenced every vote cast.[7]

This mind-numbing mistake recurs frequently in Canadian experience, when a general election is subsequently interpreted as being a decision on a single matter alone (reciprocity in 1911, for example, or free trade in 1988). In reality, voters in the all-inclusive phenomenon of a general election (contrasted to an issue-specific referendum) were, as always, influenced by many factors besides the dominant issue of Confederation, including considerations of party, personality, local politics, and the general mix of prejudice and principle.

Opposition to Confederation within Nova Scotia was strong, based on the conviction that the maritime community had a natural affinity to Britain and historical ties with New England. These feelings of opposition were doubtless fanned hotter by the deliberate absence of any avenue through which to express them. Confederation meant a re-orientation of commercial life towards the interior of the continent, an unattractive prospect for those whose prosperity was based upon international commerce and shipping. Britain, with a larger military and economic context in mind, however, was simply unwilling to allow Nova Scotia to secede. So when the compelling separatist leader of those times, Joseph Howe, "accepted the inevitable," as historian Colin Howell notes, and agreed to enter Sir John A. Macdonald's government in return for an increased provincial subsidy in 1869, "the anti-Confederate protest collapsed."[8]

Brokering Among the Power Elite

Thus, in the Canadian pattern of brokerage politics and elite accommodation, the matter of acquiescence to new constitutional arrangements for Nova Scotians had been quietly settled by the powers-that-be, through negotiation, generous transfer payments, and exercise of brute political power. As for the people who actually had to live with the consequences of these decisions, they were left with no recourse but to retaliate after the event, in the context of a general election, and even then only when the government of the day could no longer postpone its day of reckoning.

By 1886 the Nova Scotia secession movement had re-emerged, led this time by Liberal premier William S. Fielding. Campaigning in a provincial election on the issue of repeal—while stressing, as an alternative to rejecting the constitution and quitting Confederation, the need for increased subsidies to the province from Ottawa (a script later picked up by Quebec provincial nationalists and separatists)—Fielding's party won 29 of 38 seats. It was a strong position from which to negotiate. Yet Nova Scotia voters, like their latter-day counterparts in Quebec, knew about hedging their bets (or what today is called *strategic voting*). This second repeal movement also collapsed when the Conservative party won 14 of 21 seats in Nova Scotia during the national election the following year on February 22, 1887.

No Clear Channel to Carry the People's Voice

The point is that such constitutional struggles and debate were all being funnelled through the political party and general election vortex, which, as anyone who has ever campaigned knows, brings in a lot of other elements as well. The issue of Confederation—first as a proposal for union, later for secession from that union—had never once been simply and directly put to the people of Nova Scotia. Not only had there been no clear opportunity to ratify the Constitution (which is why the issue proved so enduring), or to subsequently vote on the hard and clear choice of staying in Confederation or leaving, but just as unsettling—and so inevitable in such circumstances—the interpretation of what the people had really consented to, or rejected, remained always a subject of secondary analysis, extrapolation, and explanation.

In these pioneering times, the instruments of democracy being employed in Canada were still rather blunt and crude tools. The means to fashion a more responsive, and responsible, political system by blending representative democracy with direct democracy on occasions when transcending issues arose—such as joining Canada, or seceding from it—had not yet been appreciated. By the century's end, however, the experience with referendums had become considerable—primarily over the contentious issue of prohibiting the sale and consumption of alcohol. The people of Canada themselves had become direct participants in these rounds of decision-making through voting on ballot questions about liquor at municipal and province-wide levels and, by 1898, nationally as well.

FINDING A "FORMULA" TO AMEND THE CONSTITUTION

Although Canada had a constitution, something essential was still lacking: an acceptable procedure for amending it when the need arose. Given the major premise upon which most Canadian governments and political leaders operated, it was predictable that any effort to devise such a procedure would give short shrift to any role for the people. It was just as predictable, too, that if left to governments and power-broking politicians alone, the procedure would become complex. Indeed, so many elements and factors were introduced into the procedure that they had to start referring to it as a "formula" for amending the Constitution.

From the 1920s on, intermittent efforts had been made to convert the Canadian Constitution from a statute enacted by the British Parliament into a document that could be amended directly here in Canada. Our Constitution, known then as the British North America Act, could only be changed by Parliament in Britain enacting amendments to it at the formal request of Canada. This bothered the British, as it meant they still had to do work for a country that had ostensibly become fully self-governing. It troubled many Canadians, too, because the arrangement still evoked all the formalities of an enduring colonial status. There seemed every reason to change.

The endeavour to do so was dubbed "repatriation" of the Constitution. It sputtered along, however, never reaching a conclusion, for only one reason. No agreement could be reached on the amending formula—that is, the process to be followed, and the level of support required, and the possibility of a veto, for changing provisions in the Constitution.

No Dimension for Public Participation

Significantly, this arid debate lacked the necessary dimension of public participation. Not in the superficial sense that people failed to become keenly enthusiastic about it, but rather in the deeper sense that proposals for referendums that would allow the people to ratify or reject constitutional amendments simply were not even on the agenda. Canadian political leaders only contemplated various permutations and combinations of votes *by legislatures* in their formula for achieving adequate consent for a constitutional amendment.

This was especially strange, given that the kin-like country of Australia as early as 1900 had adopted a provision, which thereafter was being regularly used, requiring any proposed amendment to the country's constitution to be ratified *by referendum*. In our Canadian closet, however, we did not hear much about this idea until the 1960s. Referendums were considered briefly in the course of federal-provincial discussions during that decade when the Fulton-Favreau Formula for amending the Canadian Constitution was devised. Yet even in the new mood of the sixties, this approach for democratic participation was not greeted enthusiastically by many members of the country's governing political establishment. Like John A. Macdonald a century earlier, they saw no need to share their power with the people on matters constitutional. The Fulton-Favreau Formula, as a result, entailed no role for the people in changing the country's Constitution.

Referendum as an Exercise in Statecraft

By the next decade, the Liberal government of Prime Minister Pierre Trudeau proposed several forms of referendum procedures. First, on October 19, 1977, the prime minister announced in the Commons that the government of Canada would introduce its own legislation to permit and control national referendums. This move towards public participation had little to do with any sudden conversion, or any deep conviction that it was the right and proper thing to do in a democracy. It was, rather, just another aspect of statecraft. The Trudeau referendum plan was part of an arsenal of legal procedures whereby a referendum on separation in Quebec might be countered by a federally conducted vote on the same question. The people would be paraded on-stage simply as foot soldiers in the battle for the separatist hearts and the federalist minds of Quebecers. Director of the production, commander-in-chief for the battle, would still be the prime minister.

Mr. Trudeau, indeed, was at pains to point out how limited his approach to public participation was. He told the Commons that the proposed enabling legislation for referendums "would not be intended to change in any sense our parliamentary system." He believed that "the responsibility for legislation and policies should rest in Parliament." Accepting that Canadians live under a form of representative democracy and not seeking to change that, he clarified that his government "would not want enabling legislation which would permit any government at any time to come forward with referendums to solve problems that the House of Commons or the government find too hot to handle." Rather, direct voting "would be a tool used perhaps only for a limited number of years to permit us to deal with constitutional questions and questions of national unity."[9]

Democratic Participation a Casualty of Constitutional Negotiations

However, the constitutional accord as finally signed on November 5, 1981, by Prime Minister Trudeau and premiers of all provinces but Quebec—then duly enacted by the British Parliament, signed into law by Queen Elizabeth in Ottawa on April 17, 1982, and made part of the Constitution of Canada—ruled out the use of referendums as a formal part of a constitution-amending procedure. It was, the prime minister would say, to his "everlasting regret" that he had been forced to drop his proposal for a referendum.[10] That sounds like a touch of revisionist hyperbole, in light of Trudeau's earlier writings and speeches on the limited role of referendums. In any event, drop it he had. In his statement at the time of the accord being reached, the prime minister at least gave posterity a nice quotation, when formally placing on record his disappointment "that we have not kept in the amending formula a reference to the ultimate sovereignty of the people as could be tested in a referendum."

In the run-up to the November accord, however, use of a referendum as part of the amending formula had certainly seemed a distinct possibility. With the premiers of fully eight provinces opposing the prime minister's constitutional proposal, extraordinary steps were contemplated for demonstrating some other basis of support for the Trudeau government's plan. At various times a number of senior government officials and politicians publicly suggested that a referendum would be appropriate in the circumstances.

The pressure on Trudeau to drop the idea of a referendum came from two fronts: a group of premiers who never much liked the idea, led by Richard Hatfield of New Brunswick and William Davis of Ontario, usually his two staunchest allies; and his own closest political supporters, Intergovernmental Affairs Minister Marc Lalonde and Justice Minister Jean Chrétien. Neither Chrétien, Trudeau's chief constitutional negotiator, nor Lalonde, his strongest minister and Quebec chief of Liberal party affairs, liked the idea of institutionalizing a referendum in the Constitution, having just exhaustingly battled through the No campaign on the sovereignty-association referendum in Quebec in 1980.

Trudeau took Lalonde's and Chrétien's advice seriously. Doing so was reasonable, moreover, because he was simultaneously confronting opposition from his strongest supporters among the premiers. At the Ottawa Conference Centre, Hatfield spoke against Trudeau's idea of a tie-breaking referendum, after the prime minister had insisted on holding one. The New Brunswick premier simply did not like direct democracy. Indeed, in this he reflected his province's political culture, for he represented the only province in Canada never to have held a referendum.

Late on the evening of November 4, 1981, Trudeau and Davis spoke at length by telephone, as the premiers were pressing ahead to work out a compromise based on the so-called kitchen accord, which had been developed by Ontario attorney general Roy McMurtry, Saskatchewan attorney general Roy Romanow, and Jean Chrétien. The three shared an intense and constructive discussion about how to solve this impasse, and like many a heartfelt and productive exchange, this one had taken place informally as the three men stood around in a kitchen at the conference centre. Davis calmly conveyed the ultimatum that he would be unable to continue supporting Trudeau if the prime minister did not agree with the deal these three were then working out. If there was to be any hope of success, he needed Ontario's support. "Trudeau realized," according to Clarkson and McCall, that "Davis's dictum on the telephone meant giving up the idea of the referendum."[11]

Amending Formula Ends Up Governmental, Not Participatory

This "explicit denial of any referendum role for the people" in amending the Constitution, as political scientist Alan Cairns of the University of British Columbia astutely put it, meant that the 1982 formula was governmental.

"The formula," Cairns said, "reflected the traditional assumption that the constitution was about federalism, that federalism was about governments, and that accordingly it was necessary and appropriate for the formal amending process to be dominated by governments. After all, they dominated the intergovernmental arena by means of executive federalism, and the practice of responsible government sustained by party discipline meant that the premiers and cabinets were considered to be in effective control of their home turf, and thus capable of delivering the goods." In retrospect, Cairns concluded, "it is evident that the assumptions on which the formula was based were backward looking."[12]

GETTING TO THE 1992 REFERENDUM ON CONSTITUTIONAL CHANGE

At that point in Canadian history, it might reasonably have appeared to any observer that the quest for democratic participation in the process of constitutional change had been fully and finally thwarted. To answer the question, "Whose Constitution is it, anyway?" one could presumably get full marks for replying, "The governments'!"

Yet one decade later, on October 26, 1992, Canadians went to the polls for the first time in a nationwide referendum on fundamental constitutional change. Moreover, that event established a precedent that will henceforth mean no significant constitutional change in Canada will ever again be carried through without a referendum to ratify it.

What caused this sea change? It is a story that proves how dynamic Canadian political life can sometimes be.

Elected in 1984 with a strong majority, Progressive Conservative prime minister Brian Mulroney saw a great opportunity to complete the unfinished work of bringing Quebec into the new constitutional arrangements, where, with a separatist government in Quebec in 1982, Pierre Trudeau had failed. For in 1985 Liberal Robert Bourassa, with whom Mulroney had forged a close political alliance, was returned to office in the province, having campaigned on a specific five-point program for re-integrating Quebec into the constitutional order.

Quebec's adhesion to the Constitution, which had been fundamentally changed under Prime Minister Trudeau in 1982 over Quebec's expressed opposition (including that of the Liberal members of the Quebec National Assembly), could now take place on this basis: (1) explicit constitutional recognition of Quebec as a distinct society, (2) constitutional guarantee of broader powers in the field of immigration, (3) the limitation of federal spending power with respect to programs falling under Quebec's exclusive jurisdiction, (4) changes in the constitutional amending procedure enshrined in the 1982 act, and (5) Quebec's participation in appointing judges from Quebec to sit on the Supreme Court of Canada.

No Referendum on Meech Lake Accord

Since Mulroney's political career had been built upon "winning Quebec," he took up the project with enthusiasm. At last the perpetual question "What does Quebec want?" had been answered. It seemed an agreement to embody Quebec's five clear, specific, and demonstrably justifiable points—so recently consented to by a majority of Quebecers in an electoral mandate—would now be a formality.

By 1987 an agreement on the Constitution, reflecting the terms of the Meech Lake Accord between the government of Quebec, the government of Canada, and the governments of the nine other provinces with respect to the five conditions set forth by Quebec and several additional items sought by other provinces which Mulroney could not resist, was the culmination of this process. The eleven governments were in unanimous agreement. Yet the Meech Lake Accord was never ratified. Following three attenuated years of public debate and partisan manoeuvring, inept political handling, and, above all, inexcusable timidity in failing to put the matter swiftly and cleanly to the people directly in a ratification referendum, full ratification by the provincial legislatures had not been completed when the deadline under the new made-in-Canada amending formula ran out. It was more than lamentable; it was a heartbreaker.

True to form, most political leaders did not even contemplate as a possibility the value of early direct popular support, obtained through a referendum, for the measure. It almost certainly would have carried in 1987. If it had not, the outcome would have been no different than that which actually happened, but with much more bitterness, three long years of drama later.

Prime Minister Mulroney said prophetically, in the final days before the June 30, 1990, ratification expiry date, "Those for whom Meech Lake today is too much, will one day look back and beg for only the Meech Lake Accord."

After June of 1990, the constitutional dilemma arising from the failure of the Meech Lake Accord to be ratified appeared to have significantly reduced Prime Minister Brian Mulroney's options. There was also a strong new surge in the country for participation in the process, and resentment at being excluded. At issue, above all, was the question of fundamental political importance to all Canadian prime ministers and especially to Mulroney since his political career had been largely based upon it: national reconciliation and the place of Quebec in Confederation.

A Fresh Look at Potentials of a Democratic Society

Operating within this more limited political space, facing new constitutional initiatives blooming in several provinces (particularly Quebec), and boxed in by the proven impracticality of the three-year-and-unanimity amending formula bequeathed to Canada by the previous round of constitutional amendments under the Trudeau government, Mulroney seemed cautiously open to the promise of new approaches. Before long, he sketched for Progressive Conservative MPs and Senators a scenario that would begin with broad public consultation about Canada's future through new and inclusive methods. This would be paralleled by a narrower review of the actual constitution-making procedures that had caused frustration and failure over the Meech Lake Accord, and would be followed by the government distilling the main recommendations and bringing them before Parliament. The recommendations would then be discussed and refined into a new set of constitutional proposals, and then the whole package would be submitted to the people in a referendum.

The initiatives that the prime minister announced next began the implementation of this plan and marked fresh forward movement on the journey toward greater democratic participation. First, in October 1990, Mulroney unveiled a sort of halfway house on the road to full public involvement. The Citizens' Forum on Canada's Future, chaired by the *Ottawa Citizen* newspaper publisher Keith Spicer, would seek the views of "ordinary Canadians."

Citizens Respond to Opportunity for Participation

The Citizens' Forum was a move in the right direction, perhaps. It represented a fairly novel approach, although Canada had had citizens' community committees through the Depression and war years of the 1930s and 1940s which performed a similar grassroots function on an ongoing basis at virtually no cost. These earlier citizens' community committees, organized across the country, met regularly and funnelled observations, criticisms, and positive suggestions to Ottawa for consideration.

The 1990 Citizens' Forum, an exercise that consumed $26,000,000 in just eight months, was intended to generate ideas for the government's future constitutional plans and other reforms, to help defuse some of the public resentment at not having had a role in the Meech Lake process, and to buy time. It is not clear that it served any of these three goals particularly well, but, as a way-station on the road to direct democracy, it should not be judged by criteria that measure only the government's satisfaction with the results, nor should we have unrealistic expectations about what such an exercise could accomplish given its broad mandate and the short time allotment.

Rather than viewing the Spicer Commission from a top-down perspective, as a government might, its value can be seen by looking at the process from the ground-level perspective of the individuals and community groups who participated. From this angle—which I saw not only in televised town-hall meetings and read in the submissions and the final commission report, but also experienced personally as an MP attending such gatherings in the constituency I represented—the commission was a success. Its central message was that people wanted to be better informed about public issues and to participate more effectively in public affairs. The Spicer commission was, for all its cost and superficial recommendations, a special phenomenon, a glimpse of democracy and the town-hall meeting in late twentieth-century Canada.

Reluctant Parliamentarians Consider People Power

The second tentative step by the Mulroney government came in December 1990, when the prime minister announced the formation of a Special Joint Committee of the Senate and the House of Commons on the Process for Amending the Constitution of Canada. Cochaired by Senator Gérald Beaudoin and MP Jim Edwards, the committee's mandate was to answer four questions. Does Canada's current process involving agreements among the federal government and provinces, followed by votes in Parliament and provincial legislatures, work effectively? Does the current process allow sufficient participation by the public? Would the current process be improved by holding constitutional referendums, constituent assemblies, or by other reforms? Should changes be made to the amending procedure, which shapes the overall amendment process and is set out in Part V of the Constitution Act of 1982?

Mulroney had specifically included, within the committee's terms of reference, not only the clear inference that the existing amending procedure was "flawed" because it did not adequately involve public participation, but most significantly, the possibility of a referendum as part of the amending procedure in the future.

Like the Citizens' Forum, the Beaudoin-Edwards Committee was expected to do its work in short order. The committee's report, tabled in the Commons six months later on June 20, 1991, included a recommendation that future constitutional amendments be ratified by a referendum, although the committee was not prepared to suggest that the referendum ratification requirement be embedded in the Constitution itself; it was simply to be an option.

This recommendation was of little use to a prime minister increasingly looking for help in persuading his cabinet and caucus of the need to move to a referendum. The committee, having first failed to take seriously its study of the potential for direct democracy in this situation, and then failing to rise to the occasion that the prime minister had created to mark an historic point of departure, did nothing. Although the committee's report did discuss referendums—it had to because that was its mandate—it ended by merely observing that a referendum was an "option." Since this had always been the case, however, it meant the lacklustre committee was doing no more than pushing an empty wheelbarrow.

"Participation in Constitutional Change" Official Government Policy

The third indication that the Mulroney government was advancing towards direct democracy—in spite of the failure of the committee and its leadership to read all the clues—came in the throne speech of May 13, 1991. "You will be asked," Parliament was informed, "to approve enabling legislation to provide for greater participation of Canadian men and women in constitutional change."

The minister responsible for constitutional affairs, Joe Clark, indicated that referendum legislation confined to constitutional questions would be brought before Parliament, but then delayed it for a year. In the spring, Clark said the legislation would come in the fall. In early autumn, he said it would be by October. By November, after a meeting with Quebec Progressive Conservative caucus members, he unilaterally appeared to reverse the Mulroney government's stated policy by declaring to journalists that a referendum was "no longer an option."

That morning, after hearing Clark on the 7:00 A.M. CBC radio news, I decided to resign from caucus. By noon, after talking it through with my wife, Corinne, I reasoned it would be better to stay and fight within caucus, press the issue, and challenge the foot-dragging Joe Clark. It was awkward, given that I was also Clark's parliamentary secretary at External Affairs. In retrospect, it might have been better to leave on principle over the issue, but I thought that a one-day headline was not a trade-off equal to actually getting a referendum.

In the course of these months of oscillation and delay, Joe Clark spoke alternately about a referendum or a plebiscite. Although he now seemed reluctant to embrace direct voting, a decade earlier, when leader of the official Opposition, he had proposed that the BNA Act be patriated but that a Charter not be included in the Constitution until it had been referred to the people through a referendum. This truly commendable idea had been born in discussions of the Conservative party's constitutional policy committee headed by MP Jake Epp and Senator Arthur Tremblay, who, with other Progressive Conservative members, had proposed the ratification by referendum approach as part of a policy developed in the summer of 1980.[13] It had then been announced by party leader Clark at a press conference in Toronto at the Royal York Hotel.

Meanwhile, I had re-introduced my private member's bill, the Canada Referendum and Plebiscite Act (Bill C-287) into the House of Commons, as part of my ongoing effort to keep the legislation before Parliament in the belief that it (or some government version of the same bill) would eventually have to be enacted. Since 1988, I had continually kept this bill before Parliament, re-introducing it whenever a new session began, by this point some five times, and while it had been debated, the bill had not yet come to a vote. When I first introduced this Bill, on July 21, 1988, Eugene Forsey, scholar on Canadian constitutional affairs, came to my press conference and told reporters: "I am here to express my support for this bill. . . . Plebiscites would allow voters to have their say when all three parties take the same stand on a major issue."

Clark continued to delay, and even by April 1992 had not produced the enabling legislation for parliamentary consideration. I had become openly critical, and newspaper stories chronicled this conflict. By this time I had been moved to National Defence as parliamentary secretary, and Clark's portfolio was constitutional affairs, so we at least could spar without trying to work together simultaneously, the normal paradoxical pattern of public office holders.

From Policy to Statute—Constitutional Referendums

Finally, on May 15, 1992, almost a year after the throne speech, Government House Leader Harvie Andre tabled the legislation that would enable the Mulroney government to hold a direct popular vote on constitutional reform. Andre had been selected by a prime minister increasingly anxious for movement on the preparations for a national vote. In explaining the purpose of Bill C-81, "An Act to Provide for Referendums on the Constitution of Canada" (the Referendum Act), Andre emphasized that no decision to actually hold a referendum had yet been made, reflecting the cautious tone still favoured by many in the Mulroney cabinet. The bill was necessary, he noted, because no legislation existed to permit the federal government to hold a referendum. "It is a case of being prepared for any possibility," the minister said, cooling out the opponents while in fact proceeding to get the legislation moved forward through the Commons.

In its broad features, the 1992 Referendum Act provided that the Canada Elections Act would set the basic framework for holding a referendum; the wording of any ballot question would be approved by Parliament; groups and individuals who intended to spend more than $5,000 would have to register and disclose all expenses and contributions, including the names of contributors giving more than $250; free broadcasting time would be provided in equal amounts to those representing both sides of the question; and equal opportunity would be provided for all sides of the ballot questions to be presented through paid advertising.

By enacting this statute, the Mulroney government lived up to its throne speech pledge and succeeded where the Trudeau government had twice failed, when it brought in similar legislation for a national direct vote on the Constitution but never got it passed. As a result, Canada today is in the rare position of having legislation to enable the holding of a direct vote on the national statute books—a major milestone in our long journey towards public participation. Its first use came, as expected, and as authorized by Parliament, in the constitutional referendum of October 26, 1992.

"People Have Proprietary Rights in the Constitution"

It was during that campaign that Prime Minister Mulroney, in Toronto and speaking with *Globe and Mail* editors,[14] candidly talked about his transformed view of direct democracy. "I always thought, quite frankly, that under the British parliamentary system that a referendum was a kind of abdication of responsibility. I've changed my mind over the years," he confessed. "I've come to recognize that in a modern, pluralistic society like ours, people do indeed require a much greater degree of participation than a kick at the can every four years. And they have proprietary rights in respect of the constitution document," declared a prime minister who surely carried the scars to prove it. "Indeed there should be public consultation," said Mulroney, "and the ultimate in that is a referendum."

His government's legacy is that such a constitutional referendum law is now on the statute books of Canada, that no significant constitutional amendment will ever again be attempted in Canada without a ratification referendum, and that the antidemocratic inheritance from Sir John A. Macdonald, who in so many respects Brian Mulroney resembled, has happily and at long last been disavowed.

The correct answer now is: "The people's!"

FURTHER READING

Boyer, Patrick. *The People's Mandate: Referendums and a More Democratic Canada.* Toronto: Dundurn, 1992.

Boyer, Patrick. *Direct Democracy in Canada: The History and Future of Referendums.* Toronto: Dundurn, 1992.

Boyer, Patrick. *Hands-On Democracy.* Toronto: Stoddart, 1993.

Boyer, Patrick. *Law-Making by the People.* Toronto: Butterworths, 1982.

NOTES

1. Daniel Johnson, *Egalité ou indépendance* (Montréal: Les éditions renaissance, 1965).

2. "Scrapbook Debates," *Montreal Herald*, October 31, 1866 (Ottawa: Library of Parliament).

3. R. McGregor Dawson, *The Government of Canada*, 4th ed. (Toronto: University of Toronto Press, 1966), 41.

4. Sir Joseph Pope, ed., *Correspondence of Sir John A. Macdonald* (Toronto, 1921), 23.

5. Hon. John A. Macdonald to John Beattie, quoted in Joseph Pope, *Confederation: Being a Series of Hitherto Unpublished Documents Bearing on the British North America Act* (Toronto: Carswell, 1895), 21.

6. Dawson, *The Government of Canada*, 41.

7. *The Canadian Encyclopedia*, 1 (Edmonton: Hurtig Publishers, 1988), 489; see also, P. B. Waite, *Arduous Destiny: Canada 1874–1896* (Toronto: McClelland & Stewart, 1971).

8. Ibid., 185–86.

9. House of Commons, *Debates*, October 20, 1977, 53.

10. Stephen Clarkson and Christina McCall, "Trudeau's Great Paper Chase," the *Globe and Mail*, October 27, 1990, D1, D5.

11. Ibid.

12. Alan Cairns, "The Process of Constitution-Making" (Paper presented at the conference "The Canadian Mosaic: Democracy and the Constitution," University of Ottawa, April 28–29, 1990), 1.

13. Robert Sheppard and Michael Valpy, *The National Deal* (Toronto: Fleet Books, 1982), 94.

14. The *Globe and Mail*, October 23, 1992, A8.

THE CHARLOTTETOWN ACCORD: A Retrospective Overview

Martin Westmacott

INTRODUCTION

The discussion surrounding the ratification of the Charlottetown Accord was one of a series of constitutional debates that preoccupied the attention of Canadian political leaders from 1960 to the present. A review of these debates reveals a number of common issues: the appropriate constitutional relationship between Quebec and English Canada; the degree of consensus required to patriate the Canadian Constitution; the appropriate distribution of constitutional authority between Ottawa and the provinces; and, the implications and consequences of entrenching a bill of rights. At the core of the most recent debate was an attempt to formulate a constitutional amendment that would reflect the duality of Canadian society, accommodate legitimate regional constitutional demands within English Canada, and provide recognition to other communities of Canadians such as the aboriginal peoples.

The Charlottetown Accord of 1992 represented one of the largest packages of proposals for constitutional reform in the history of Canada.[1] It was unanimously endorsed by the Government of Canada, by all 10 provincial premiers and the political leadership of the Yukon and the Northwest Territories, and by four aboriginal groups.[2] This degree of elite unanimity was striking in itself, but a special added feature was that the public would be consulted via a referendum. The specific question posed to Canadians on October 26, 1992, was "Do you agree that the Constitution of Canada should be renewed on the basis of the agreement reached on August 28, 1992?"[3] Hidden within this question, however, were a number of competing constitutional visions which have dominated constitutional politics since 1867.[4]

There are several books and numerous articles that document in detail the events surrounding the negotiation of the Charlottetown Accord, that describe, evaluate and assess the specific provisions of the Accord, and that recount the details of the referendum campaign in the autumn of 1992.[5] The objective of this article is not to replicate these works; rather, the focus is to provide an overview and summary assessment of the major provisions of the Charlottetown Accord. The article is intended to serve as a "primer" for students to work on a more detailed analysis and evaluation of the subject.

ESTABLISHING THE CONTEXT—QUEBEC, OTTAWA, AND NINE PROVINCES

On June 23, 1990, the Meech Lake Accord died when it was not ratified by the legislatures of Manitoba and Newfoundland. The ratification process had been initiated on June 23, 1987, when the Accord was endorsed by the Quebec National Assembly. The time period for ratification was three years and formal ratification required the unanimous consent of all 10 provincial legislatures and the Parliament of Canada. As the ratification debate unfolded, it became increasingly apparent that while the Meech Lake Accord had significant popular support within Quebec, it was not enthusiastically endorsed by English Canada.[6]

Within Quebec, there was an intense and emotional response to the demise of the Meech Lake Accord.[7] Support for Quebec sovereignty increased dramatically in the immediate post–Meech Lake period and there was a widespread belief that Quebec's minimum and fundamental constitutional priorities had been rejected by English Canada. English Canada, as Lucien Bouchard reminded the Quebec electorate during the referendum debate in October 1995, had said No to Quebec in 1990.

Reaction within English Canada to the defeat of the Meech Lake Accord was dramatically different from that within Quebec. Campbell and Pal note that Ottawa had concluded that "Canadians were constitution weary"[8] and there appeared to be within English Canada, in particular, no desire to engage in constitutional discussions in the immediate aftermath.[9] The Mulroney government had focussed virtually all its attention on the final negotiations surrounding the Meech Lake Accord and had failed to develop a strategy that could be employed if the Accord was not ratified. All federal planning had proceeded on the assumption that the Meech Lake Accord would be ratified.

The defeat of the Meech Lake Accord left Ottawa scrambling for an appropriate constitutional response to the sense of anger and disillusionment within Quebec, and to the very strong desire for a "pause" in constitutional discussions within English Canada. In attempting to devise a new strategy, Ottawa concluded that any future constitutional initiative must be more comprehensive and more inclusive than the provisions found in the Meech Lake Accord. The "closed-door" process employed during the negotiations of the Meech Lake Accord was felt to have deprived many important interest groups of an opportunity to participate in the constitutional debate. Post–Meech Lake constitutional strategy now demanded a process that was perceived to be both "open" and "consultative." During the period leading up to the negotiation of the Charlottetown Accord, the federal government followed a constitutional strategy that often appeared to lack a central focus and direction. The Mulroney government recognized that if future constitutional initiatives were to acquire legitimacy there must be extensive consultation and debate prior to ratification. Yet, there is also evidence to indicate that during this period Ottawa continued to employ the traditional processes of elite accommodation in searching for a new constitutional accord.[10] Furthermore while Ottawa recognized that future reforms must be more inclusive and address the concerns of all Canadians, the federal government appeared at times to be unduly influenced by Quebec's constitutional demands and by the deadline that had been set by Quebec for the conclusion of the post–Meech Lake round of constitutional discussions.[11]

In response to the defeat of the Meech Lake Accord, the government of Quebec announced that it would only participate in bilateral discussions with Ottawa and would not negotiate as one of 10 provinces with Ottawa on the issues of constitutional reform. It is evident that the strategies employed by Ottawa and Quebec in the post–Meech Lake period, as well as the multilateral negotiations between Ottawa, nine provinces, and the aboriginal groups, influenced the content of the Charlottetown Accord. It was not by accident that the Charlottetown Accord contained proposals that were designed to accommodate multiple and competing interests. Critics of the Accord argued that it lacked a coherent philosophy and a focussed vision of Canada. Many of the proposals were ill-defined and lacked the degree of specificity demanded by particular provincial governments or by specific single-issue interest groups. The Mulroney government attempted to broker a compromise that would balance the demands of Quebec for a radically decentralized federal state, based on the principle of duality and the recognition of Quebec as a distinct society, with a conception of Canada that envisaged a federation of 10 equal provinces in which decisions were made on the basis of majority rule.

In 1990, the Quebec Liberal Party created a committee chaired by a longtime member of the party, Jean Allaire, to develop a post–Meech Lake constitutional platform and strategy. As opposition to the Meech Lake Accord continued to strengthen outside Quebec, the committee focussed its attention on developing a constitutional strategy for Quebec that envisaged a radically decentralized federal system. The Allaire Report was adopted as policy by the Quebec Liberal Party at a convention in March 1991. Within Quebec, the Charlottetown Accord was evaluated in terms of the accommodations provided by the Meech Lake Accord and by the recommendations of the Allaire Report.

In contrast, the proposals for renewing the federal state were assessed in English Canada against both contemporary as well as traditional aspirations such as institutional reform (Triple-E Senate), the inherent right to self-government for aboriginal peoples, and the maintenance of national standards. While the Charlottetown Accord represented a compromise that accommodated federalist elite opinion and the demands of the leadership of the aboriginal community, it failed to satisfy grassroots concerns in many local communities. The lack of clarity and precision in several key provisions of the Accord left many controversial issues unresolved.

THE CHARLOTTETOWN ACCORD

As noted earlier, the Charlottetown Accord represented a complex package of proposals for constitutional reform. Peter Hogg has observed that the legal text of the Charlottetown Accord resembled an amendment to complex taxation legislation rather than an amendment to a nation's constitution.[12] In fact, the Canadian electorate was being asked to express an opinion on sixty constitutional proposals. Rather than discussing these proposals individually here, the Accord will be divided into four broad categories for purposes of analysis: the Canada clause; institutional reform; distribution of legislative authority between Ottawa and the provinces; and the inherent right to self-government for aboriginal peoples.

One of the most important and contentious provisions in the Charlottetown Accord was the proposed addition of a so-called Canada clause that would outline the distinguishing elements of the Canadian political community. The clause was included in the Accord in response to demands within English Canada for an expression of national unity and a pan-Canadian identity. Specifically, the amendment would be an addition to the Constitution Act, 1867, providing guidelines for the Supreme Court to interpret the written part of the Constitution of Canada, including the Charter of Rights and Freedoms. While the insertion of the clause would not confer legislative authority on either the Parliament of Canada or provincial legislatures, or confer special rights on particular individuals, the Canada clause would help define the context in which the Supreme Court would interpret the Constitution. The notion of a Canada clause prompted a very emotional and divisive debate during the referendum campaign in the fall of 1992. At the core of the controversy was a debate about the fundamental principles that define the Canadian nation going back to the Meech Lake Accord discussions of Quebec's presumed distinctiveness.

The Meech Lake Accord had included an interpretative clause that came to be known as the distinct society clause. This provision stipulated that the entire Constitution of Canada should be interpreted in a manner that was consistent with the duality of Canadian society. Specifically, the clause recognized that two linguistic communities, English- and French-speaking Canadians, "constitute[d] a fundamental characteristic of Canada."[13] Quebec was recognized as a "distinct society" within Canada and the Legislature of Quebec as well as the Government of Quebec were mandated "to preserve and promote the distinct identity of Quebec".[14]

Supporters of the Meech Lake Accord argued that the distinct society clause reflected a fundamental reality of Canadian society and accommodated one of Quebec's long-standing demands. Critics attacked the clause on the grounds that it described only one of the features of Canadian society and failed to include other important characteristics and values that define the Canadian political community—the multicultural nature of Canadian society as well as the existence of other communities such as the aboriginal peoples. The failure to delineate clearly the characteristics and qualities that define Quebec as a distinct society was of particular concern to former prime minister Pierre Trudeau and the former premier of Newfoundland, Clyde Wells. Finally, there was a public perception in English Canada that the inclusion of an interpretive clause had the potential to undermine the legislative authority of Ottawa, expand the legislative jurisdiction of the provinces (Quebec in particular), and undermine the protection of individual rights guaranteed by the Charter of Rights and Freedoms. Recognizing Quebec as a distinct society would provide the Quebec National Assembly with a standing and stature unlike any other province in the federation.

Given the emotional and divisive debate surrounding the attempt at ratifying the Meech Lake Accord, the Mulroney government concluded that if an interpretive clause was to be included in the Constitution Act, 1867, it must be more inclusive and specifically refer to principles other than dualism that define Canadian society. In addition, the recognition of Quebec as a distinct society required a more precise definition.

The Canada clause contained in the Charlottetown Accord attempted to define a vision of Canada that would reflect the multiple and conflicting visions of Canada and that would be more inclusive than the distinct society clause found in the Meech Lake Accord. Quebec would be recognized as a distinct society within Canada and the Quebec National Assembly and the Government of Quebec would continue to be mandated "to preserve and to promote" Quebec's distinctiveness. However, an important addition to the Charlottetown

Accord was a phrase that defined the characteristics that constituted Quebec's distinctiveness: "a French-speaking majority, a unique culture and a civil law tradition."[15] In addition, the Canada clause instructed that the Constitution of Canada be interpreted in accordance with a series of principles and values that were central to the Canadian political community—"democracy, the rule of law, a parliamentary and federal system, the aboriginal peoples of Canada and their enhanced rights, official language minorities, cultural and racial diversity, individual and collective rights, gender equality, and the equality and diversity of the provinces."[16]

Supporters of the Accord, including the ten provincial premiers, the leaders of three of the federal parties, the heads of major aboriginal groups, and leading business and social figures argued that the Canada clause addressed many of the concerns expressed by the critics of the Meech Lake Accord and provided more specific direction to the Supreme Court. In contrast, sovereigntists in Quebec argued that the guarantees found in Meech Lake had been weakened by the inclusion of a lengthy list of principles defining the nature of Canadian society. The Supreme Court would thus be required to balance multiple and, in some instances, competing values when interpreting the Constitution of Canada. Critics of the Accord implied that the supremacy of the Charter of Rights and Freedoms could be undermined and that a "hierarchy of rights" could result in future constitutional entitlements for particular communities based on language or ethnicity. The debate surrounding the proposed entrenchment of "the Canada clause" reinforced awareness of the competing notions of Canadian society. It involved the inability of Canadians to define collectively the basic values and principles that reflect the nature of their political community.

Both the Meech Lake Accord and the Charlottetown Accord contained proposals for reform of Canada's national political institutions, the Supreme Court of Canada and the Parliament of Canada (the House of Commons and the Senate). The provisions in the Charlottetown Accord with regard to the Supreme Court are virtually identical to the provisions found in the Meech Lake Accord. Both Accords would have entrenched the Supreme Court of Canada in the Constitution of Canada. The Supreme Court was created by the Parliament of Canada in 1875; however, the proposal in the Meech Lake Accord would, in Peter Hogg's judgment, ensure "that the existence and principal characteristics of the Court are entrenched in the Constitution beyond the reach of the unilateral legislative power of the federal Parliament."[17] The Charlottetown Accord proposed that the Supreme Court of Canada be recognized as "the general court of appeal for Canada"[18] and be comprised of nine judges.[19] Quebec would be guaranteed a minimum of three judges on the Supreme Court.[20] Finally, all of the provinces would be guaranteed a role in the nomination of candidates for a vacancy on the Supreme Court.[21] In particular, when an appointment was made to the Supreme Court to fill a vacancy from Quebec, the Government of Quebec would have the opportunity to nominate candidates.[22] However, appointments to the bench would continue to be made by the governor general on the recommendation of the prime minister of Canada.

The Charlottetown Accord contained significant reforms to the Parliament of Canada (the House of Commons and the Senate). The intent of the proposed reforms was to moderate the dominance of the largest and most populous provinces (Ontario and Quebec) in the governance of the nation and guarantee the smaller and less populous provinces more effective representation in Ottawa.

One of the most contentious proposals included in the Charlottetown Accord was the proposal to create a Triple-E Senate—equal, effective and elected. The issue of Senate reform in general, and a Triple-E Senate in particular, had been a central feature of the proposals for constitutional renewal developed by Alberta and Newfoundland. Proponents of a Triple-E Senate envisaged an Upper House comprised of an equal number of senators elected from each province and empowered with sufficient constitutional authority to block legislation that had been approved by the House of Commons. However, not all provinces endorsed the principle of a Triple-E Senate. Two provinces in particular were hesitant to endorse a proposal that would substantially reduce their influence as the two most populous provinces in the governance of the nation. Senate reform was a key issue dominating the discussions (August 1992) leading up to the final negotiation of the Charlottetown Accord.[23] In order to reach an agreement, both the proponents and the opponents of a Triple-E Senate were forced to compromise. The provisions of the Charlottetown Accord envisaged a Senate elected either directly by the electorate of each province or indirectly by the provincial or territorial assemblies.[24] The option of indirect election was included at the insistence of Quebec. Each province would elect six senators with one senator elected from each of the territories (for a total of 62). In return for supporting the principle of equal representation, Quebec was guaranteed 25 percent of the seats in the House of Commons in perpetuity. Senate elections would be held at the same time as elections to the House of Commons. Senators could not be members of the cabinet.

Two other divisive issues were: the legal relationship between the House of Commons and the Senate, and the veto power of the Senate over legislation that had been approved by the House of Commons. The Senate would not be a "confidence chamber." Therefore, if legislation was defeated in the Senate, there was to be no requirement by law or by convention that the prime minister tender his or her resignation to the governor general or request a dissolution of the House of Commons. The maintenance of this convention of parliamentary government ensured a dominant role for the House of Commons.

With regard to the legislative power of the Senate, the Accord provided for a variety of provisions that could be employed by the Upper House. For example, the Senate could only delay "money bills"—legislation pertaining to the granting of "supply" or the raising of revenue—for a maximum of thirty days.[25] However, legislation that affects the French language and culture to a significant degree required the consent of the House of Commons and the Senate, including the agreement of a majority of English- and French-speaking senators. The Senate had an absolute veto power with regard to legislation that involved "fundamental tax policy changes that are directly related to natural resources or electrical energy."[26] The Senate could block the will of the House of Commons in this area and there was no provision for a legislative override. Finally, legislation that did not fall within any of the specialized categories could be temporarily blocked by a simple majority vote in the Senate. However, a legislative impasse would be resolved by a simple majority vote in a joint sitting of the House of Commons and the Senate.

The Charlottetown Accord provided for an increase in the size of the House of Commons from 295 to 337 members to reflect more accurately the principle of "representation by population." Specifically, Ontario and Quebec would each gain 18 additional seats in the House of Commons, while British Columbia and Alberta would gain four seats and two seats respectively. In one of the most controversial provisions, Quebec would have been guaranteed 25 percent of the seats in the House of Commons in perpetuity, notwithstanding the size of the population of Quebec. This provision was specifically included to alleviate concern in the province that the numerical size of Quebec's representation in the House of Commons would decline in the future. Perhaps more than any other, this provision, coupled with reference to Quebec's "alleged" distinctiveness, undermined support for the Accord in Western Canada. In particular, many residents of British Columbia believed that the guarantee given to Quebec could deny their own province the increased representation in the House of Commons that would be directly proportional to future increases in the provincial population.

In summary, the Charlottetown Accord envisaged a number of significant reforms to Canada's national political institutions. In particular, the proposal for a Triple-E Senate was designed to enhance the influence of the smaller, less populous provinces in the governance of the nation. For those federal and provincial politicians who negotiated the Accord, the provisions reflected a reasonable compromise between the divergent and competing interests of the provinces. However, David Elton has observed that critics of the Accord continue to believe that the proposals "were seen as a creative way to perpetuate the status quo rather than a fundamental restructuring of Canada's national institutions."[27] In essence, the Accord failed to satisfy those advocates of a Triple-E Senate who wanted an American-styled Upper House. While the Canadian Senate would be elected, it would not have the degree of independence from the executive branch of government (the cabinet) that the American Senate had from its executive branch of government (the president). On a wide range of issues the Canadian Senate could not use its legislative authority to permanently veto legislative initiatives that had been approved by the House of Commons. Furthermore, the redistribution of seats proposed for the House of Commons, designed to significantly enhance representation from Ontario and Quebec and which guaranteed Quebec a minimum of 25 percent of the seats in the House of Commons, undermined the original rationale for institutional reform that had been at the centre of the debate, namely restraint of the population concentrated in Ontario and Quebec.

One of the issues central to the debate surrounding constitutional renewal has been the appropriate distribution of legislative authority between Ottawa and the provinces. Since 1960, Quebec, in particular, has consistently defined as one of its most pressing constitutional priorities, transfer of legislative authority to ensure that the Quebec National Assembly has the constitutional authority necessary to enhance the province's distinct identity. A related issue was the expenditure of funds by the Parliament of Canada (the federal spending power) in areas of provincial jurisdiction. Quebec had pressed for a constitutional limitation on the use of the federal spending power in areas of provincial jurisdiction, and now demanded that Ottawa respect the distribution of powers outlined in the Constitution Act, 1867, by withdrawing from areas of provincial jurisdiction such as health, welfare, and social security.

Any discussion of the appropriate distribution of legislative authority between Ottawa and the provinces divides the provinces into at least two groups. For example, Alberta, British Columbia, Ontario, and Quebec have argued for a decentralization of powers and a reduction in Ottawa's presence in areas of provincial jurisdiction. These provinces continue to believe that provincial governments are capable of delivering services to provincial populations more effectively and efficiently in areas such as health, welfare, social security, culture, and labour market development and training. In contrast, the less populous and less affluent provinces have resisted (with a few notable exceptions such as the fishery) a decline in federal government intervention or a significant reduction in federal funding. These provinces have come to rely heavily on federal transfers to provide services in key areas of public policy.

A second issue related to the distribution of legislative power is whether a particular province, or group of provinces, should be granted constitutional authority that would not necessarily be allocated to other provinces. Since 1960, every premier of Quebec has argued for a special status for Quebec; that is, that legislative authority be allocated to Quebec but not necessarily to all of the other provinces. The notion of a special status based on perceived needs (economic, linguistic, or cultural) implies an asymmetrical relationship between Ottawa and some of the provinces. The concept of asymmetrical federalism has been advanced by Quebec as a mechanism to accommodate both Quebec's demand for a more decentralized federal state and the desire within English Canada for a stronger federal presence.[28] To date, proposals for an asymmetric distribution of powers have been strongly resisted by both Ottawa and the less affluent provinces in English Canada.

Both the Meech Lake Accord and the Charlottetown Accord contained provisions that would have changed the distribution of legislative authority between Ottawa and the provinces. The proposed amendments would have resulted in a larger role for provincial initiatives in fields such as immigration and a reduced federal presence in several areas of provincial jurisdiction.

Under the terms of the Charlottetown Accord, Ottawa agreed to negotiate intergovernmental agreements (at the request of a province) to withdraw from six provincial areas of jurisdiction—forestry, mining, tourism, housing, recreation, and municipal affairs.[29] Those provinces that accepted the federal offer would receive fiscal compensation. In addition, these intergovernmental agreements could be constitutionalized to ensure a greater degree of permanence and avoid unilateral action by Ottawa or the provinces.

Under the provisions of the Charlottetown Accord, culture and labour market training were to be recognized as areas of provincial jurisdiction. Ottawa would continue to retain a cultural role by exercising jurisdiction over national institutions such as the CBC and the Canada Council. With regard to labour market development and training, Ottawa would continue to set "national policy objectives for the national aspects of labor market development."[30]

With regard to the federal spending power, both the Charlottetown Accord and the Meech Lake Accord called for a constitutional limitation on the authority of the Parliament of Canada to spend money in areas of provincial jurisdiction. In particular, a province could "opt out" of new federally funded programs within an area of provincial jurisdiction and receive fiscal compensation from Ottawa, "if that province carries on a program or initiative that is compatible with the national objectives."[31] In addition, the Charlottetown Accord contained a provision that obligated Ottawa and the provinces to develop a framework for future expenditure of money by Ottawa in areas of provincial jurisdiction.[32]

The inclusion of provisions to limit the use of the federal spending power in areas of provincial jurisdiction prompted a major debate about the role of the national government in establishing and maintaining minimum standards of service for all Canadians in areas such as health, welfare, and social security. Critics of the Meech Lake Accord argued that its provisions could undermine Ottawa's ability to maintain national programs with national standards in critical public services. For example, Canadians were reminded that, if the provisions of the Meech Lake Accord had been in place in the 1950s and 1960s, many of the initiatives undertaken by Ottawa would have been negated by provinces opting out of national programs and receiving fiscal compensation from Ottawa.[33] Supporters of the Charlottetown Accord believed that the provisions would not reduce Ottawa's constitutional authority but would provide an important element of flexibility, thus enabling the provinces to better meet the needs of local communities.[34]

As with many of the other provisions of the Charlottetown Accord, the proposals for changes in the distribution of powers reflected a compromise among multiple and competing views. Within Quebec, the provisions of the Accord were evaluated against the contents of the Allaire Report and judged unacceptable. The degree of decentralization envisaged in the Accord failed to satisfy Quebec's historic demand for a radically decentralized federal state. Within English Canada, concerns were expressed that the provisions of the Charlottetown Accord would result in a significant reduction in the constitutional authority of Ottawa. Finally, for advocates of asymmetrical federalism, the Charlottetown Accord represented a lost opportunity to present a viable federalist alternative to sovereignty.[35]

One of the most significant inclusions to the Charlottetown Accord was the recognition of the inherent right to self-government for the aboriginal peoples of Canada.[36] Between June 1990 and August 1992, the leadership of the four national aboriginal communities (the Assembly of First Nations, the Native Council of Canada, the Inuit Tapirisat of Canada, and the Métis National Council) were extremely successful in influencing both the process employed to negotiate the Accord and its specific content. As noted earlier, Ottawa had concluded that if a new package of proposals for constitutional reform was to acquire legitimacy, the process must be perceived to be "more open" and "more inclusive." In March 1992, the minister of Constitutional Affairs, Joe Clark, agreed to a multilateral process of negotiations that involved aboriginal representation and participation at virtually every meeting leading to the final negotiation of the Charlottetown Accord.[37]

The most significant resulting provision was the recognition that "the Aboriginal peoples of Canada have the inherent right of self-government within Canada"[38] and that aboriginal governments constitute "one of three orders of government in Canada."[39] The term *inherent* was significant because it implied that the right to self-government was a right that existed prior to its proposed inclusion in the Charlottetown Accord;[40] prior, in fact, to the very existence of Canada.

While there was support for the insertion of this principle in the Constitution, concern was expressed by several provinces (Quebec, Alberta, and Newfoundland) that the concept of self-government required qualification. As a consequence, "a contextual statement" was included in the Accord which defined the context in which "the inherent right to self-government" would be exercised.[41] In the words of Mary Ellen Turpel, "it was to be 'within Canada,' subject to federal and provincial laws in the interest of peace, order, and good government, and subject to a provision that no new land rights would be created by implication."[42]

With regard to aboriginal representation in national political institutions, the Accord recommended aboriginal representation in the Senate and urged that the issue of aboriginal representation on the Supreme Court and in the House of Commons be examined. Finally, the Accord stipulated that a mechanism be developed to ensure "Aboriginal consent to future constitutional amendments that directly refer to the Aboriginal peoples."[43]

The Accord outlined a detailed process for negotiating aboriginal self-government involving Ottawa, the provinces, and representatives of the aboriginal communities across Canada.[44] If, after a five-year period, negotiations were unsuccessful, the Accord stipulated that the aboriginal people would have access to the courts to litigate the right to self-government. Federal and provincial statutes would continue to be enforced until they were replaced by aboriginal laws. Once enacted, aboriginal laws would be subject to the Charter of Rights and Freedoms; however, aboriginal governments could also use the notwithstanding clause to exempt aboriginal laws from Charter application (Sect. 2, Sections 7-15).

CONCLUSION

The Charlottetown Accord was decisively rejected by the Canadian electorate on October 26, 1992. The Charlottetown Accord was a lengthy, highly complex document that, in the final analysis, failed to satisfy the constitutional demands of many regional and provincial political communities. In addition, it failed to meet the rigid requirements of a constitutional amending formula that demanded unanimous agreement of Ottawa and all ten provincial legislatures before the Accord could be ratified. As a consequence, Canadians continue to search for a constitutional consensus that will accommodate the diverse interests that currently divide the Canadian political community.

In accordance with the provisions of the 1982 amending formula, ratifying the Accord required the consent of ten provincial legislatures plus the Parliament of Canada. The Accord was defeated by a national majority (54.2 percent) and was decisively rejected by provincial electorates in the four Western Provinces and in Quebec.[45] It is important to note that the electorate in four of the provinces and in one of the territories supported the Accord. Voters in three of the Maritime Provinces (New Brunswick, Newfoundland, and Prince Edward Island) strongly endorsed it. Residents of Ontario narrowly endorsed the Accord (49.8 percent in favour, 49.6 percent opposed) while in Nova Scotia the Accord was narrowly defeated (51.1 percent to 48.5 percent). In the Northwest Territories, the Accord was endorsed (60.2 percent) while in the Yukon, the Accord was decisively rejected (56.1 percent).[46]

Is it difficult to speculate on the future direction of constitutional reform in Canada given the defeat of the Meech Lake Accord in 1990 and the Charlottetown Accord in 1992. At the present time, constitutional reform is not an immediate priority on the political agenda of Ottawa or any of the provincial governments (including Quebec). The strategy of building a comprehensive package of constitutional proposals comparable to the Charlottetown Accord has been rejected by Ottawa and all of the provinces. Rather than formal constitutional amendment, intergovernmental administrative arrangements are now seen by many provinces (excluding Quebec) as a more effective means of facilitating change within the federal system. Even though it is unlikely that there will be another referendum before 1999, Ottawa and Quebec will continue to manoeuvre for a strategic advantage in the period leading up to the next referendum in Quebec.

NOTES

1. Peter Russell notes that the federal proposals of September 1991 were "large and diffuse." In his view, the only proposals that were more comprehensive were the proposals put forward by former prime minister Trudeau in 1978. See Peter Russell, *Constitutional Odyssey: Can Canadians Become a Sovereign People?* 2nd ed. (Toronto: University of Toronto Press, 1993), 171.

2. Robert M. Campbell and Leslie A. Pal, "The Rise and Fall of the Charlottetown Accord" in Robert M. Campbell and Leslie A. Pal, *The Real Worlds of Canadian Politics: Cases in Process and Policy,* 3rd ed. (Peterborough: Broadview Press, 1994), 176. Peter Russell notes that the four

aboriginal groups who negotiated the Charlottetown Accord were the Assembly of First Nations, the Native Council of Canada, the Inuit Tapirisat of Canada, and the Métis National Council. See Russell, *Constitutional Odyssey*, 192.

3. Robert M. Campbell and Leslie A. Pal, "The Rise and Fall of the Charlottetown Accord" in Campbell and Pal, *The Real Worlds of Canadian Politics*, 176.

4. These competing constitutional visions are referred to in Russell, *Constitutional Odyssey*.

5. For example, see Russell, *Constitutional Odyssey*, Kenneth McRoberts and Patrick Monahan, eds., *The Charlottetown Accord, the Referendum, and the Future of Canada* (Toronto: University of Toronto Press, 1993) and Robert M. Campbell and Leslie A. Pal, "The Rise and Fall of the Charlottetown Accord" in Campbell and Pal, *The Real Worlds of Canadian Politics*, 142–210.

6. Campbell and Pal, *The Real Worlds of Canadian Politics*, pp. 149–150.

7. Ibid., 150.

8. Ibid., 150.

9. Ibid., 149–150.

10. Ibid., 157–59.

11. Ibid., 157.

12. Peter W. Hogg, "Division of Powers in the Charlottetown Accord" in McRoberts and Monahan, eds., *The Charlottetown Accord*, 92.

13. See Rand Dyck, *Canadian Politics: Critical Approaches*, 2nd ed. (Toronto: Nelson, 1996), Appendix C, 648–53 for the provisions of the Meech Lake Accord. In particular see section 2(1)(A) of the Meech Lake Accord in Dyck, *Canadian Politics*, 648.

14. Section 2(3) of the Meech Lake Accord in Dyck, *Canadian Politics*, 648.

15. See Dyck, *Canadian Politics*, 654 for the Canada clause in the Charlottetown Accord. In particular see section 2(1)(C).

16. Dyck, *Canadian Politics*, 60.

17. Peter W. Hogg, *Meech Lake Constitutional Accord Annotated* (Toronto: Carswell, 1988), 31.

18. For details of the Draft Legal Text of the Charlottetown Accord, see McRoberts and Monahan, eds., *The Charlottetown Accord*, 315–61. In particular see section 101A(1), 337.

19. See Draft Legal Text section 101A(2) in McRoberts and Monahan, eds., *The Charlottetown Accord*, 338.

20. See Draft Legal Text Section 101B(2) in McRoberts and Monahan, eds., *The Charlottetown Accord*, 338.

21. See Draft Legal Text section 101C in McRoberts and Monahan, eds., *The Charlottetown Accord*, 338.

22. See Draft Legal Text section 101C(3) in McRoberts and Monahan, eds., *The Charlottetown Accord*, 338.

23. Russell, *Constitutional Odyssey*, 213.

24. For details of the proposals for Senate reform contained in the Charlottetown Accord, see Russell, *Constitutional Odyssey*, 213–15. See also Consensus Report on the Constitution, Charlottetown, August 28, 1992, in Russell, 243–46.

25. For details of the veto powers of the Senate, see Russell, *Constitutional Odyssey*, 214–15. See also Consensus Report on the Constitution, Charlottetown, August 28, 1992, in Russell, 243–46.

26. See Draft Legal Text section 34(1) in McRoberts and Monahan, eds., *The Charlottetown Accord*, 324.

27. David Elton, "The Charlottetown Accord Senate: Effective or Emasculated?" in McRoberts and Monahan, eds., *The Charlottetown Accord*, 55.

28. For a discussion of the concept of asymmetrical federalism see Reg Whitaker, "The Dog That Never Barked: Who Killed Asymmetrical Federalism?" in McRoberts and Monahan, eds., *The Charlottetown Accord*, 107–14.

29. For details of the provisions regarding the distribution of legislative authority contained in the Charlottetown Accord see Consensus Report on the Constitution, Charlottetown, August 28, 1992, in Russell, *Constitutional Odyssey*, 249–54.

30. Ibid., 251.

31. Ibid., 249.

32. Ibid., 249.

33. For example, see Deborah Coyne, "The Meech Lake Accord and the Spending Power Proposals: Fundamentally Flawed" in Michael D. Behiels, ed. *The Meech Lake Primer: Conflicting Views of the 1987 Constitutional Accord* (Ottawa: University of Ottawa Press, 1989), 245–71.

34. See, for example, Stephan Dupré, "Section 106A and Federal-Provincial Fiscal Relations" in Behiels, ed. *The Meech Lake Primer*, 272–81.

35. Reg Whitaker, "The Dog That Never Barked: Who Killed Asymmetrical Federalism?" in McRoberts and Monahan, eds., *The Charlottetown Accord*, 114.

36. For details of the Charlottetown Accord pertaining to aboriginal peoples see Consensus Report on the Constitution, Charlottetown, August 28, 1992 in Russell, *Constitutional Odyssey*, 254–61.

37. Mary Ellen Turpel, "The Charlottetown Discord and Aboriginal Peoples' Struggle for Fundamental Political Change" in McRoberts and Monahan, eds., *The Charlottetown Accord*, 121–22.

38. Consensus Report on the Constitution, Charlottetown, August 28, 1992 in Russell, *Constitutional Odyssey*, 255.

39. Ibid., 255.

40. See Mary Ellen Turpel, "The Charlottetown Discord and Aboriginal Peoples' Struggle for Fundamental Political Change" in McRoberts and Monahan, eds., *The Charlottetown Accord*, 125.

41. Consensus Report on the Constitution, Charlottetown, August 28, 1992, Russell, *Constitutional Odyssey*, 255.

42. Mary Ellen Turpel, "The Charlottetown Discord and Aboriginal Peoples' Struggle for Fundamental Political Change" in McRoberts and Monahan, eds., *The Charlottetown Accord*, 126.

43. Consensus Report on the Constitution, Charlottetown, August 28, 1992, Russell, *Constitutional Odyssey*, 262.

44. Ibid., 256–58.

45. Russell, *Constitutional Odyssey*, 227.

46. Ibid., 227.

QUEBEC SECESSION AND
THE 1995 REFERENDUM

Robert Young

INTRODUCTION

On Monday October 30, 1995, the people of Quebec voted No in a referendum to the proposition that their province would become a sovereign country. The margin of the No victory was terribly thin: 50.6 percent to 49.4 percent. If fewer than 30,000 people had switched to the Yes side, Canada would have been thrown into the deepest political turmoil of its history. We should make no mistake about this. A Yes vote would have produced an unprecedented level of uncertainty about the future: right across the country, while the dollar's value plummeted and interest rates rose sharply, Canadians would not have known whether trade with Quebec would continue, whether the North American Free Trade Agreement (NAFTA) would still apply to Canada, what currency they would be using in twelve months, or even whether Canada would continue to exist.

Unquestionably, the Quebec sovereignty movement poses the greatest current challenge to Canadian federalism. It is essential to have some understanding of the political dynamics of separatism, and that is the purpose of this article. After a brief discussion of the history of the movement, we will turn to the recent referendum, and then to an analysis of support for sovereignty; then we will see how separation can be understood as a strategic game of threat and counterthreat, and also how this logic played out during the referendum. A brief account of the postreferendum strategies of the federalists and the sovereigntists will conclude this very short treatment of a complex, difficult, and vital issue.

THE HISTORICAL CONTEXT

If nationalism means a shared sense of collective identity, then it has existed among Quebecers for a very long time—at least two centuries. If nationalism refers to a "people" seeking sovereign self-government, then this is a relatively recent phenomenon, dating from the mid-1960s.[1] But of course a "people" doesn't seek self-government or anything else. One of the greatest errors made in analyzing collectivities is to refer to them as single entities, and to make statements like "Quebec wants more powers" or "Alberta favours free enterprise." This is a mistake because within these entities are millions of individuals holding a very wide range of opinions. Some Quebecers are centralists and some Albertans are socialists, for instance. So it is more accurate to speak of the Quebec separatist movement, a group of people committed to sovereignty, whose aim is to propagate the message that this goal is desirable. If enough individual Quebecers are so persuaded, then the objective of independence can be achieved.[2]

One of the key features of this movement is that it is spearheaded by a powerful, deeply entrenched political party, the Parti Québécois (PQ). While supported by majorities within the trade unions and other social organizations, and by older nationalist associations, the sovereigntist project is embodied in the PQ. With the old Union Nationale eliminated from the scene, partisan politics in Quebec now revolves around the confrontation between the sovereigntist PQ and the federalist Parti Libéral du Québec (PLQ), and this pattern appears to be stable. As a party that intermittently forms the government, the PQ gains the opportunity while in power to advance its policies, increase its legitimacy, and recruit new talent into the movement.

An important element of the nationalist project during the 1960s and 1970s was to redefine Quebec as a "global society"; that is, a fully articulated and modern society, one relatively nondependent on links with Canada (as was, conceptually, the old "Canada français"). Associated with this has been the doctrine of pluralism; that is, Quebecers are not defined homogenously by language, religion, or ethnicity, and so sovereignty is a civic project that can appeal to all elements of Quebec society. At the same time, however, a wellspring of sovereigntist support has always been a sense of shared history and common culture (based on the French language), and this shows part of the movement's dilemma. In order to achieve their goals, the sovereigntists have had to affirm the distinctiveness of the "nation" or the "people" against the "Other" (English Canada), "while at the same time denying in the name of a rejuvenated future what the nation has in large part actually been."[3] These tensions are never far beneath the surface in a party that includes people with world-views ranging from narrow ethnic nationalism to liberal cosmopolitanism to inclusive socialism.

During the 1980s, Quebec sovereigntists benefitted from the unfinished business left when the federal government led by Pierre Trudeau patriated the Constitution, with its Charter of Rights and Freedoms and amending formula, without the consent of Quebec's National Assembly. It is true that the Charter was popular among Quebecers, but many also believed that Quebec had an established right to a veto over constitutional change that would affect its vital interests; this flowed from the deeply rooted conception of Canada as a country created by two founding peoples or nations. As well, there was no explicit recognition in the Constitution that Quebec was a province unlike the others, because of its civil-law tradition and predominant use of French.[4]

The Meech Lake Accord was to rectify these perceived defects, but it failed to be ratified in 1989. Widely seen in Quebec as a refusal by the rest of Canada (ROC) to accept Quebecers' distinctiveness, this event caused an unprecedented rise in support for sovereignty. It also led Lucien Bouchard, who had quit the federal cabinet of Brian Mulroney over changes to Meech, to found the Bloc Québécois, a federal party, established to protect

Quebec's interests and fight for sovereignty in Ottawa. The surge of sovereigntist support also led to one more attempt at constitutional renewal. After long and complex negotiations among Ottawa, the provinces, and aboriginal organizations, Quebec premier Robert Bourassa finally signed on to a sweeping package of constitutional amendments that was known as the Charlottetown Accord. Submitted to plebiscites in Quebec and the rest of the country in 1992, the Accord was defeated. To the sovereigntists, who campaigned against the deal, the whole Charlottetown experience demonstrated that ROC was incapable of reaching an acceptable constitutional accommodation with Quebec. And indeed, many of the arguments against Charlottetown that were made in ROC, particularly by supporters of Preston Manning's Reform party, were directed towards elements of the accord—Quebec's veto, recognition of it as a "distinct society," and its guarantee of 25 percent of the House of Commons seats—that were popular among many Quebecers.

In any event, the federalist forces in Quebec were much weakened by these episodes. At the federal level, Progressive Conservative support in Quebec collapsed in the October 1993 federal election, and the Bloc took 54 of the province's 75 seats. Paradoxically, Mr. Bouchard became leader of Her Majesty's official Opposition. Then the PQ, led by Jacques Parizeau, defeated Daniel Johnson's PLQ to win the September 1994 provincial election. With support for their option hovering around 45 percent, the sovereigntists appeared to have a lot of momentum. Mr. Parizeau formed a highly centralized and disciplined government, and began to drive towards a referendum that was to be held in June 1995.

THE 1995 REFERENDUM

The sovereigntists' objective was to swing enough voters over to the Yes side to win a referendum. To this end, they had to concentrate on the "soft nationalists"; that is, voters in the middle of the spectrum who are committed neither to sovereignty nor to federalism. The government tabled a draft bill on sovereignty in the National Assembly, and initiated a major exercise in public consultation, with regional commissions holding hearings throughout the province and receiving briefs from various organizations. This carefully orchestrated exercise was designed to focus attention on sovereignty and to educate the public about its advantages. Then the National Assembly would pass the bill, an action that the referendum would ratify.

But the PQ drive stalled. The draft bill contained clauses about territory, citizenship, the currency, international treaties, economic association with Canada, and the apportionment of assets and debts, and even though the PLQ formally boycotted the public hearings, the commissions heard a great many queries about these and other matters. As the sovereigntist option became more concrete, questions and doubts multiplied. Many citizens demanded more information about what future sovereignty would bring. In particular, they wanted to know about future relations with Canada, because they suspected that economic and political disruption could be costly to them.

By the spring, with support for sovereignty sagging into the low forties, the sovereigntists were in some disarray. Into this breach stepped Mr. Bouchard. At the Bloc convention in Montreal, he made a major *virage* ("change of direction"), by suggesting that sovereignty should be accompanied by a "Partnership" with Canada. This would be an economic arrangement, but it also could involve joint political institutions to manage the common economic space. The *virage* caused an enormous shock within the sovereigntist movement, because it appeared to make sovereignty conditional, at least in part, on the maintenance of economic and political relations with Canada, which was anathema to hard-line sovereigntists.[5] But at the insistence of the popular Mr. Bouchard, who declared he would not campaign in a losing cause, a sovereigntist coalition was put together around the partnership proposal: this was enshrined in a formal, interparty agreement signed on June 12, 1995.[6]

So, in September 1995, the referendum process that was finally unveiled was based on both sovereignty and partnership. A bill introduced into the National Assembly laid out provisions for negotiating a partnership, as well as principles about a new Quebec constitution, territory, citizenship, the currency, treaties, continuity of laws, and provisions for federal employees. But it also declared that "The National Assembly is authorized, within the scope of this Act, to proclaim the sovereignty of Québec."[7] The actual referendum question was "Do you agree that Québec should become sovereign, after having made a formal offer to Canada for a new Economic and Political Partnership, within the scope of the Bill respecting the future of Québec and of the agreement signed on June 12, 1995?"

The federalist side derided the ambiguity of the question and attacked the legitimacy of the whole process. As Prime Minister Jean Chrétien was quoted as saying about the June agreement, "They are not changing the substance of the problem. They still want to separate but they don't have the guts to say so."[8] Similarly, throughout the campaign, the federalists denounced the duplicity of the sovereigntists' tactics, argued that a Yes vote was really a vote for "separation," and pointed both to the economic loss that would follow a Yes vote and also to the emotional attachments to Canada that would be ruptured. But despite the confidence that reigned in the federalist camp, the sovereigntist side made steady gains throughout the referendum campaign, gains that were solidified after Mr. Parizeau declared that Lucien Bouchard would be the chief negotiator of the partnership, and the latter took the effective lead of the Yes side. When polls in the last week of the campaign showed the Yes forces leading, near-panic swept the No side, and Mr. Chrétien was led on October 24th to promise that a No vote would produce constitutional change in Canada—recognition of Quebec as a distinct society, restoration of its conventional veto over constitutional change, and substantial devolution of federal jurisdiction to the provinces. This desperate offer may have turned the tide.[9]

ANALYZING SOVEREIGNTY'S APPEAL

The Quebec sovereignty movement has been studied very thoroughly indeed. Some analyses are basically structural, focussing on Quebecers' inferior position within the Canadian economy and society, or on the rise of a francophone middle class, or on the role of the Quebec state in enabling a Québécois business class to emerge. Regardless of structural factors that may be evolving in ways more or less conducive to the strengthening of the movement, however, support for sovereignty at any time is a matter of individual choice, particularly when that choice is to be registered at the ballot box. Perhaps surprisingly, analysts are in substantial agreement about the considerations which determine that choice.

In a very general theoretical schema, Hudson Meadwell has argued that support for sovereignty is a function of counterhegemony, which involves the formation—or strengthening—of a collective identity distinct from that of the larger society, along with "a set of institutions that are an alternative to those of the central state."[10] Levels of support are increased by socialization into a Québécois identity and by the mobilization efforts of activists. But the constraint upon the movement's growth is that people are risk-averse: their support for sovereignty is limited by their fear of economic loss, especially in the period of transition to independence.

Stéphane Dion has produced a somewhat similar account.[11] But the key element of collective identity for him is linguistic. The fear of assimilation—of the weakening of the French language through immigration, adverse federal court rulings, and the decline of francophone communities outside Quebec—is a strong motivator of support for sovereignty. Throughout the 1970s and 1980s, "francophone Quebecers increasingly perceived the Quebec government as the collective protector for French speakers and the federal government as a kind of intruder state. This positive perception of the provincial government and negative perception of the federal government extended from the linguistic issue to cultural, social and even economic areas."[12]

Dion also identified another underlying factor in support for sovereignty—confidence. This has to do with increasing francophone control of the Quebec economy and state, and also with the view that a sovereign Quebec could perform at least as well in the global economy as it does when inserted into an inefficient, complicated and debt-ridden federation that is slow to adapt to international forces. The combination of fear and confidence drove sovereigntist support to record levels in the early 1990s, when it was supplemented by a third important factor—a sense of rejection. This swept Quebec when the Meech Lake agreement was not ratified in ROC.[13]

This general emphasis on language, identity, and economic expectations is supplemented by solid empirical research. One recent study found that the sense that French is threatened was a significant predictor of support for sovereignty.[14] In fact, the belief that French would be strengthened in a sovereign Quebec was associated as much with Yes support as was the belief that the economy would become stronger after independence. On the economic front, many studies show that fear of material loss is indeed a restraint on support for sovereignty, and a factor more powerful than anticipated economic gains, except among the young, who, perhaps, feel they have less to lose.[15]

Finally, a comprehensive analysis of opinion among francophone Quebecers investigated three main factors underpinning their choice: the sense of identification with Canada and Quebec, evaluations of the federal system, and expectations about the standard of living in a sovereign Quebec.[16] The second factor—rational assessments of the operation of the federal system and of its costs and benefits—counted very little in predicting support for sovereignty (although optimism that an agreement could be reached on decentralizing powers within the federation did reduce the inclination to vote Yes). The first factor—identification—was by far the most important: "the great majority of francophone Quebeckers define themselves as Quebeckers first, and this pushes them toward the sovereignty option. Many, however, feel some attachment to Canada, and this pushes them toward the decentralized federalism option."[17] And economic expectations were also highly significant. Among those who expected the standard of living to worsen after sovereignty, support for the option was almost 20 percent lower than it otherwise would have been. The combination of attachment to Canada and fear of economic loss cut heavily into the Yes vote among francophone Quebecers.

So the appeal of sovereignty is complex and multifaceted. At base is the primordial sense of collective identification among francophone Quebecers. Over time, this has been increasing while attachment to Canada has decreased.[18] A large part of this identification is rooted in the common language, the position of which might well be more secure in a sovereign Quebec than in Canada. Support for sovereignty can also be increased when the collectivity can be portrayed as rejected or humiliated by Canadians in the rest of the country (or, more compellingly, by the "Rest of Canada" *en bloc*), as in the Meech episode. Perceptions that the federal system cannot be reformed also fuel sovereigntist sympathies. And last is the notion that Quebecers might be better off in a sovereign country. This could occur if a small, flexible, adaptable, consensual society might fare better within the contemporary global economy—with its many regimes that guarantee access to markets—than it does within a rather ponderous and inflexible federal system.[19] Less reasonably, it could also occur if the economy worsened to the point that people came to believe that they couldn't be worse off.

But people are also led to reject separation, again for many reasons, which tend to mirror those above. One is their emotional attachment to Canada, their sense of identification with the country as a whole. Another is the perception that the federation is not threatening, but flexible and accommodating. Last is the fear that sovereignty would bring economic loss, either in the long term or over the period of transition to independence. In the referendum debate, the economic arguments became the critical fighting ground between the Yes and the No sides.

SECESSION GAMES AND THE ECONOMICS OF QUEBEC SEPARATION

In international relations theory, the interactions between states are often studied as strategic games. These are not lighthearted games, but rather contests in which two parties can either co-operate (as in setting up a trade regime or signing nuclear-missile control treaties) or defect (when one refuses to co-operate because this serves its self-defined interests). Similarly, constitutional negotiations between Quebec and the rest of Canada (ROC) can be analyzed in game-theoretic terms.[20] Of course this approach is somewhat misleading. It tends to reinforce the perception that the two "sides" are both different and homogeneous (as when one describes "Quebec's goals" or "ROC's preferences," for example, neglecting the real diversity of opinion among the people within each unit). It also obscures the fact that the two entities may not really be distinct: ROC does not exist as a political entity, because Quebec remains embedded in Canada and Quebecers are represented in the federal government.

Nevertheless, it is possible for analytic purposes to conceive of two sides, each with some ordering of constitutional preferences. In Quebec, for example, the preferences might be: (1) a reformed, decentralized federation, (2) sovereignty-association, (3) the status quo, and (4) full-scale sovereignty, involving a rupture of relations with Canada. In ROC, the preferences might be: (1) the status quo, (2) a decentralized federation, (3) a rupture of relations, and (4) sovereignty-association. Obviously, there are a great many possible constitutional outcomes of such strategic games, depending on what the orderings of preferences really are, what the starting point is, and which side moves first.

But game theory shows the importance of strategic moves and of threat and bluff. For example, by not passing the Meech Lake Accord (decentralized federalism), ROC risked that Quebecers would vote for sovereignty, because they might really prefer this outcome over the status quo. Similarly, were Quebecers to vote Yes in a referendum on sovereignty-association, they would run the risk that ROC's preferences would be as listed above, so that it would not negotiate a partnership arrangement but would settle for a minimal level of economic and political integration—a real rupture of relations—even though it would be costly. Obviously it might be in ROC's interest to portray its preferences as being like this, in order to deter Quebecers from voting Yes.

All this shows the fine line walked by the federalist side in the 1995 referendum campaign. On the one hand, the federalists had to dispel the view that separation would be costless. While the sovereigntists argued that the political institutions and economic agreements of their proposed partnership would protect Quebecers from economic disruption and loss, the federalists had to show that such structures were unrealistic and that a Yes vote would entail heavy costs. On the other hand, the federalists had to appeal to the genuine sense of attachment to Canada felt by many Quebecers, and so their predictions about economic costs could not appear as threatening, dismissive, or insulting.

A final lesson of game theory for separation concerns the importance of solidarity. When countries or collectivities are the "actors," their preferences are really the politically weighted sum of what all the individuals in the population prefer. Under the pressure of events, people's preferences can change, sometimes very quickly indeed. So in a strategic interaction between ROC and Quebec, the initial preference orderings of the actors could shift. After a Yes vote especially, the eventual outcome could depend significantly on the collective determination of one side or the other to achieve its objectives, that is, on public solidarity and support for the positions taken by leaders.

All these themes have permeated analyses of the consequences of separation. What a Yes result would produce is a question of vital importance to all Canadians and especially to voters in Quebec who had to make a choice at the polls in 1995 based largely on their estimation of these consequences. Into this debate, drawn by the stakes involved, have plunged a great many scholars and commentators, joining the politicians whose task it has been to make predictions about the future, and especially about what would happen after a Yes vote.

There have been a great many studies of Quebec separation.[21] They can be categorized as legal, economic, and political. While the legalities of Quebec secession are a matter of much current interest, they are murky indeed. Sovereigntists try to argue that Quebecers are a people, that they therefore have a right of self-determination, and that this right extends to lawful secession. Others argue that separation can only occur according to Canadian law, and that this would involve a constitutional amendment to remove Quebec from the purview of the Constitution Acts. The issue is made more complex by the presence of minorities within Quebec that have, arguably, rights as Canadian citizens, and especially by aboriginal claims to large parts of the province, and to protection by the government of Canada.[22] In the end, the legal arguments founder on a lack of precedent. A separating Quebec could possibly issue a unilateral declaration of independence (UDI), and attempt to exert control over its territory. This would produce enormous uncertainty: people would not even know which law applied in Quebec. Then the stance of Canada would be crucial, since it would be the main contender to resist such control. ROC might resist a UDI; on the other hand, were Canada to recognize Quebec's sovereignty then the matter, effectively, would be settled. So the legalities dissolve into politics.

In economic studies, most analysts distinguish between long-term costs and benefits and transition costs. There is general agreement that Quebec would be a viable economic unit in the long term, particularly were it to remain in the World Trade Organization and NAFTA, (which are, once more, political questions). But short-term transition costs could be severe. These would consist of transaction costs—the losses caused by having to negotiate new arrangements, transfer public servants, set up new administrative systems, and so on. Another component would be fiscal costs—the burden imposed on Quebec's finances as federal transfers and expenditures in the province ended, and as the new state took on some portion of Ottawa's debt. The greatest transition cost, however, would be caused by uncertainty. Simply enough, as the future suddenly became less predictable, economic actors would change their existing behaviour. In the wake of a Yes vote, uncertainty would affect trade flows, levels of investment, employment, and tax revenues. As well, interest rates would rise because of the greater perceived risk of default on loans, and since the risk of holding Canadian dollars would be greater, the value of the currency would decline as investors liquidated both real and financial holdings.[23]

Three aspects of this economic analysis are important. First, short-term transition costs could be severe enough to produce large long-run burdens. Second, many of these transition effects would be felt throughout Canada, not just in Quebec. Third, the transition costs are highly variable: apart from some irreducible minimum of transaction and uncertainty costs, the size of the damage would depend straightforwardly on the politics of separation. Were negotiations to be delayed, or the parties to refuse to co-operate about matters such as the transfer of programs and responsibilities, costs would mount, and were negotiations to break down entirely—in confusion and perhaps hostility—then the short-term costs would rise astronomically.

About these political scenarios, analysts have been divided. Before the 1995 referendum, some predicted that a Yes vote would produce a political meltdown. There would be no authority competent to represent ROC and capable of conducting negotiations, the claims of aboriginals and Quebec federalists could not be denied, negotiations over the debt would break down, the PQ government might resort to a UDI, this would be resisted, and so on: the result would be a terribly costly mess with no predictable outcome. Others argued that a Yes would produce a crisis and a response from ROC to accept the result in principle, that negotiations, although very difficult, would result in substantive agreements under the pressure of the mounting costs; that Canada would manage to reconstitute itself as a going concern, without Quebec; and that two separate entities would emerge after a short, painful transition period.[24] The former scenario has characterized many attempts at separation; the latter has been found in all those cases where secession has been peaceful.[25]

Debate about all these issues continues today, though, as will be discussed, it has been affected by the results of the 1995 referendum. But before that historic event, it is safe to say that on the major questions about separation the analysts were as divided as the politicians. And in the referendum campaign all these arguments surfaced, within the strategic framework of the deadly serious game between the federalist and sovereigntist forces.

THE REFERENDUM DEBATE

Over the course of the 1995 referendum campaign, a great many arguments about separation were made by politicians supporting the Yes and the No sides. One dimension of the debate was the Constitution. At the outset of the campaign, with a comfortable lead in the polls, the federalist side stuck to its basic position about constitutional change: there would be none. The No forces consistently argued that the existing framework was adequate, and flexible enough to accommodate the real needs of all Canadians. Until the last week of the campaign, the federalists insisted that the onus was on the sovereigntists to prove why their option—"separation"—was necessary for Quebecers.

The Yes side argued that constitutional reform had proven impossible in the past, and that a No vote would subject Quebecers to the centralizing tendencies of Ottawa, as well as to the rising view in ROC that all provinces are fundamentally equal. The Yes alternative was full constitutional sovereignty for Quebecers as a "people," along with a partnership that would not only maintain the economic union but also provide a framework within which Quebecers would negotiate with Canada on a new basis—*Égal-à-Égal* ("equal to equal"). The partnership proposal seems to have dominated on this dimension, as the credibility of the notion increased among the electorate between April and October 1995.[26]

Another dimension was national identification. The No side stressed that Canada is a wonderful country, in which Quebecers had a proud and honourable history, and in which they have a great deal of influence. At the end of the campaign, when some polls showed the Yes forces with a slight lead, Mr. Chrétien powerfully stressed this theme in a major televised address to the country: "Have you found one reason," he asked, "one good reason, to destroy Canada?"[27] But this dimension offered much scope to the sovereigntists, and especially to the charismatic Mr. Bouchard. In emotionally charged discourse, the separatists recited the long series of oppressions and humiliations that Quebecers had suffered. They argued that a Yes would mark the historic moment when Quebecers declared themselves, finally, to be an autonomous people, with francophones becoming a majority within their own country rather than a minority within an anglophone state.[28]

In the view of some, these strong nationalist strains of discourse explain the rise in Yes support, as many Quebecers were led to vote on the basis of their ethnic identity. But this does not seem to be the case. According to a recent analysis of poll results, between June and October 1995 intentions to vote Yes increased among francophones from 52 percent to 62 percent.[29] But a stronger sense of identity, or the greater relevance of identity, added only about 1 percent to the Yes vote. More important were economic expectations: over this period, voters became much less pessimistic about the economic ramifications of sovereignty. This change seems to have added about 6 percent to the Yes vote. So the economic arguments were critical in the contest.

On the economic dimension, one sovereigntist position was that secession would be beneficial in the long run (as wasteful duplication would end, and policies could be custom-tailored to the Quebec economy). But the central message was that there would be no losses in the transition period. Here, the guarantor was the partnership: Quebec-Canada negotiations would ensure that disruption would be minimal. For example, Bill 1 stated that the Canadian dollar would be retained, that Quebec would accede to NAFTA, that unemployment insurance and pensions would continue to be paid by Quebec, and that an agreement would be made about the "equitable apportionment of the assets and liabilities of the Government of Canada." Such reassurances were hammered home day after day in the course of the campaign.

It was very awkward for the federalists to counter these arguments. Their essential position was that a Yes vote would represent a leap into the unknown, with no guarantees about anything. Sovereignty meant "separation," and an unpredictable and uncertain future. At times the federalist side was more precise about a Yes vote's consequences. The federal minister of Finance stated that if NAFTA failed to apply to Quebec, a million jobs could be in peril, Daniel Johnson argued that the PQ's plan to use the Canadian dollar would not work, and business leaders warned of economic damage.[30] Commentators and some provincial premiers disparaged the sovereigntists' proposed partnership as unrealistic and not in ROC's interests.[31] And, towards the end of the campaign, even Mr. Chrétien stated that separation would create a Quebec where people "would no longer enjoy the rights and privileges associated with Canadian citizenship. Where Quebeckers would no longer share a Canadian passport or a Canadian dollar—no matter what the advocates of separatism may claim."[32] For the most part, however, the federalists simply dismissed these matters as "hypothetical", and emphasized the terrible uncertainty that a Yes would create.[33] The prime minister was quoted as saying near the end of the campaign, "The mechanisms after a Yes vote are very nebulous. All I know is that with a No vote, you don't have to worry about such hypothetical questions. We all remain Canadians."[34]

But the sovereigntists had a tremendous advantage on the economic dimension. They could, and did, dismiss all dire predictions. They simply depicted all warnings of economic loss as threats and bluffs, as part of a transparent strategy. Of course, they argued, the Yes side wanted to avoid Quebec sovereignty. So, *before* Quebecers have made their choice, it makes sense that the No side would emphasize the costs of independence, and it is similarly rational that they would inflate the apparent costs by making threats about nonco-operation in the wake of a Yes vote. But if Quebecers actually did vote Yes, the federalist strategy would have failed. And *after* this became clear, ROC would immediately have to change its course, and co-operate with Quebec, in order to minimize its own losses. It would have to opt for a tranquil management of the transition to sovereignty, for joint arrangements to diminish uncertainty, and for an economic association that would avoid the costs to its own citizens of disrupting the economy. In terms of game theory, ROC would back off from a "rupture of relations" and settle for sovereignty-association, out of its own self-interest.[35] This analysis dissolved all dire predictions into threats that were understandable as bluffs. So they were not credible. It was safe to vote Yes. As Mr. Bouchard put it, sovereignty "is a powerful springboard to go and get a partnership which will impose itself after an assessment of each other's interests."[36] Again, Mr. Bouchard, late in the campaign: "My worries are about the fact that Quebecers have too often been impressed by the attempts to raise a scare in their minds. But I trust, as we have been seeing in this campaign, that fear has been overcome by confidence. I'm happy to see Quebecers no longer take scare tactics seriously."[37]

This was a difficult argument for the federalists to counter. The only rebuttal would be to lay out, definitively, what would happen after a Yes vote. But it was not obvious who in the No camp had the authority to lay out the terms of a separation, with respect to the currency, trade arrangements, agricultural policy, the division of the debt, citizenship, and other dossiers. Few people had even thought about these matters. Moreover, these positions could have been portrayed by the sovereigntists as an opening position in bargaining, rather than a credible bottom line. And, were the terms harsh, this would have contradicted the federalist position on the national-identification dimension, one that appealed to a sense of community, shared citizenship, and affection. Finally, setting the conditions of separation would have meant accepting the rules of the game, and especially that a narrow Yes victory would bring sovereignty. This the No side was not prepared to concede. And so, as the federalists were lagging at the end of the campaign, the only alternative open was to promise constitutional reform.

SECESSION'S FUTURE

Some essential features of the separation issue have remained unchanged in the wake of the 1995 referendum. Among francophone Quebecers, the basic factors determining support for sovereignty—identification, economic apprehensions, and the ever-present possibility of rejection—continue to operate. But much else has changed. There has been a rapid turnover in political leadership, in both the federal cabinet and the provincial capitals. The economic situation has evolved. Most significant, however, has been a fundamental change in people's expectations. This is because of the narrow referendum result. Canadians everywhere have been forced to see that separation is possible, whereas few took the possibility seriously before October 1995. This has led to new militancy among the anglophone and aboriginal minorities in Quebec, with an insistence on their "right" to remain part of Canada should Quebec secede. More generally, Canadians have been led to think about what would happen if Quebecers voted Yes. "Where do my interests lie?" they have asked. And more importantly, they think: "What *should* my governments do?" This profound re-evaluation has not yet manifested itself in new political movements or organizations in ROC, but it means that any new move towards secession will be played out within a very different context of public opinion.

On the federalist side, it has been left to Ottawa, largely, to deal with the aftermath of the referendum. The federal government has adopted a "two-track" strategy. Track One (or Plan A, as it is sometimes called) involves accommodating Quebecers' evident desire for change. So, in late 1995, a resolution passed by the House of Commons recognized Quebec as a distinct society, and stipulated that this fact should be taken into account throughout government.[38] In early 1996, an act was passed stating that the federal government would support no constitutional amendment that had not been agreed to by Quebec, Ontario, British Columbia, and majorities in the Atlantic and Prairie provinces.[39] This restored the Quebec veto, though not constitutionally. As well, Ottawa moved to devolve authority over some important functions to the provinces; most noteworthy here was employment training, control over which had long been demanded by Quebec governments.

In parallel, Track Two (or Plan B) involves measures that recognize the possibility of separation. Ottawa was determined not to allow the PQ government to control the ground-rules governing this eventuality. This strategy was designed to throw up roadblocks to secession, and to demonstrate to Quebecers that the event would be a difficult and costly one. So, federal ministers encouraged Quebec minorities to believe they should be able to secede from a separating province, and they argued that a majority greater than 50 percent of the population should be required to legitimize any decision as great as secession. Further, Ottawa referred three questions about the legalities of secession to the Supreme Court of Canada: these were framed, essentially, to show that separation had to be accomplished by a constitutional amendment in order to be legal. Quebec could not undertake a unilateral declaration of independence.

Overall, Ottawa continues to walk a fine line between accommodating Quebecers' traditional demands and raising their fears about separation. It is unlikely to pursue any more radical restructuring of the federation, one that could prove difficult for the soft nationalists to reject.[40]

As for the sovereigntists, they were thrown into disarray after their narrow referendum loss. Mr. Parizeau resigned, and Mr. Bouchard moved to lead the PQ and to become premier of Quebec. Navigating carefully between the demands of governing the province and the hard-liners within the party, Mr. Bouchard has declared that there will be another referendum, but only after another election in Quebec. In the meantime, his priorities appear to be getting the provincial deficit under control and stimulating economic growth, especially in the depressed Montreal region. This, of course, could increase Quebecers' confidence and reduce their fears of secession. At the same time, the premier decries any changes in the federation as merely cosmetic, and continues to extol the virtues of an eventual Quebec-Canada partnership.

So the future of separation is not easy to predict. The same basic tug of sentiments continues in Quebec. The salience of the issue in the Rest of Canada has increased enormously, while people's opinions have become more divided. The strategic game about the costs and benefits of secession has, if anything, been rendered sharper and harder. And the debate about Quebec secession—an apparently perennial challenge to Canadian federalism—continues.

NOTES

1. For basic background references, see David Cameron, *Nationalism, Self-Determination and the Quebec Question.* (Toronto: Macmillan of Canada, 1974); William Coleman, *The Independence Movement in Quebec* (Toronto: University of Toronto Press, 1984); Kenneth McRoberts, *Quebec: Social Change and Political Crisis.* 3rd ed. (Toronto: McClelland & Stewart, 1988; and Alain-G. Gagnon, ed., *Québec: State and Society*, 2nd ed. (Scarborough: Nelson Canada, 1993).

2. Some clarification of terms is desirable. I use *sovereignty* in its relatively neutral, international-law sense to refer to a state possessing the formal ability to exercise a monopoly of legitimate force over a given territory. As the Quebec sovereigntists often put it, this means the power to make all laws, collect all taxes, and sign all treaties applying to the citizenry. *Independence* is a much looser term that implies national autonomy; in reality, however, all sovereign states are more or less constrained by other states and by actors such as firms and nongovernmental organizations. *Separation* can sometimes refer rather neutrally to the process through which one state disengages from another, but in the Quebec debate its unpleasant connotations of disruption and isolation make it a preferred term of the federalist side (hence the basic federalist slogan in October 1995 was "NON à la Séparation"). *Secession* is a more neutral term than separation: it means that one part of a sovereign state withdraws from that jurisdiction and itself becomes sovereign.

3. Charles Taylor, "Nationalism and the Political Intelligentsia: A Case Study." *Queen's Quarterly* 72 (1965): 153.

4. See Guy Laforest, *Trudeau and the End of a Canadian Dream*, trans. Paul Leduc Browne and Michelle Weinroth (Montreal and Kingston: McGill-Queen's University Press, 1995).

5. The new position harkened back to that of René Lévesque, the principal founder of the PQ, who consistently advocated "sovereignty-association." A referendum asking for popular approval to negotiate such an arrangement was conducted by the first PQ government in 1980 and was defeated. When Lévesque departed the political scene, the hard-liners under Mr. Parizeau eventually gained the upper hand within the party.

6. The June 12th agreement was made between Mr. Bouchard, Mr. Parizeau, and Mario Dumont, leader of l'Action démocratique du Québec. (The last was a new party, composed mainly of disaffected Liberals, with a constitutional position vaguely in favour of sovereignty but also favouring an association with Canada. It had taken about 10 percent of the vote in those ridings it contested in the 1994 provincial election.) The June 12th agreement provided that a Yes referendum

vote would authorize (1) negotiations with the rest of Canada about an economic and political partnership, and (2) a declaration of sovereignty within a year whether or not the negotiations produced such an agreement. The agreement is found in Quebec, National Assembly, 1st Session, 35th Legislature, Bill 1: An Act Respecting the Future of Québec (Québec: Québec Official Publisher, 1995), Schedule.

7. Ibid.

8. Rhéal Séguin, "Leaders Sign Referendum Agreement," the *Globe and Mail*, June 13, 1995, A4.

9. Another possible cause of a shift towards the No—if, indeed, there was one—was the large pro-Canada rally organized in Montreal on the Friday before the referendum. While this demonstrated the affection felt for Quebecers by many people in the rest of Canada, and while it may have energized the No campaigners, it could also be seen by the "soft nationalists" as unwelcome outside interference in a matter to be decided by Quebecers themselves, and there was also an element of clinging affection to the event that may have alienated some voters, especially women. At least as noteworthy as the rally is the fact that the weather across Quebec on the day before the referendum was terribly autumnal, with dark skies and steady, cold rain. Had this not been a Sunday, and one so conducive to sombre reflection, the Yes might have carried.

10. Hudson Meadwell, "The Politics of Nationalism in Quebec," *World Politics* 45 (1993): 215.

11. Given that Professor Dion became the federal minister of Intergovernmental Affairs in the wake of the 1995 referendum, his analysis is of more than usual interest.

12. Stéphane Dion, "Explaining Quebec Nationalism," in R. Kent Weaver, ed., *The Collapse of Canada?* (Washington: The Brookings Institution, 1992): 96. It is important to note that linguistic concerns in Quebec are not mere matters of nostalgia or emotion; language is a public good whose maintenance benefits all its speakers. There are real costs (reflected in salary levels) when one has to work, less efficiently, in another language.

13. See Maurice Pinard, "The Dramatic Reemergence of the Quebec Independence Movement," *Journal of International Affairs* 45 (1992): 471–97; and, for a reading more sympathetic to the sovereigntists, see Édouard Cloutier, Jean H. Guay, and Daniel Latouche, *Le Virage: l'évolution de l'opinion publique au Québec depuis 1960* (Montréal: Québec/Amérique, 1992).

14. Richard Nadeau and Christopher J. Fleury, "Gains linguistiques anticipés et appui à la souveraineté du Québec," *Canadian Journal of Political Science* 28 (1995): 35–50.

15. Pierre Martin, "Générations politiques, rationalité économique et appui à la souveraineté au Québec," *Canadian Journal of Political Science* 27 (1994): 345–59.

16. André Blais and Richard Nadeau, "To Be or Not to Be Sovereignist: Quebeckers' Perennial Dilemma,"*Canadian Public Policy* 18 (1992): 89–103.

17. Ibid., 97.

18. Richard Simeon and Mary Janigan, eds., *Toolkits and Building Blocks: Constructing a New Canada* (Toronto: C.D. Howe Institute, 1991), 11–14.

19. See Pierre Fortin, "How Economics Is Shaping the Constitutional Debate in Quebec," in Robert Young, ed., *Confederation in Crisis* (Toronto: James Lorimer, 1991), 35–44; and Daniel Latouche, "Le Québec est bien petit et le monde, bien grand," in Alain-G. Gagnon and François Rocher, eds., *Répliques aux détracteurs de la souveraineté du Québec* (Montréal: vlb éditeur, 1992), 345–72.

20. Louis M. Imbeau, "Le compromis est-il encore possible? La négociation constitutionnelle de l'après-Meech à la lumière de la théorie des jeux," in Louis Balthazar, Guy Laforest, and Vincent Lemieux, *Le Québec et la Restructuration du Canada 1980–1992* (Sillery: Septentrion, 1991), 281–309; Robert A. Young, "The Political Economy of Secession: The Case of Quebec," *Constitutional Political Economy* 5 (1994), 221–45.

21. For a comprehensive review of them, up until 1995, see Robert A. Young, *The Secession of Quebec and the Future of Canada* (Montreal: McGill-Queen's University Press and the Institute of Intergovernmental Relations, 1995), 93–126.

22. See Canada, Royal Commission on Aboriginal Peoples, *Canada's Fiduciary Obligation to Aboriginal Peoples in the Context of Accession to Sovereignty by Quebec*, 2 vols. (Ottawa: Minister of Supply and Services Canada, 1995).

23. For a very dispassionate analysis of these issues, see Canada, Economic Council of Canada, *A Joint Venture—The Economics of Constitutional Options*, Twenty-Eighth Annual Review (Ottawa: Minister of Supply and Services Canada, 1991), 77–93.

24. For an analysis of works in these two schools—which are not quite so distinct as depicted—see Stéphane Dion, "The Dynamics of Secessions: Scenarios after a Pro-Separatist Vote in a Quebec Referendum," *Canadian Journal of Political Science*, 28 (1995): 533–51.

25. See Robert A. Young, "How Do Peaceful Secessions Happen?," *Canadian Journal of Political Science* 27 (1994): 773–92.

26. Guy Lachapelle, "La Souveraineté Partenariat: Donnée Essentielle du Résultat Référendaire et de l'Avenir des Relations Québec-Canada," in John E. Trent, Robert Young, and Guy Lachapelle, eds., *Québec-Canada: What Is the Path Ahead?* (Ottawa: University of Ottawa Press, 1996), 41–63.

27. The *Globe and Mail*, October 26, 1995.

28. See, for example, Jeffrey Simpson, "Bouchard electrifies Yes voters, fulfilling an old and powerful dream," the *Globe and Mail*, October 12, 1995; Jeffrey Simpson, "The most powerful voice for secession utters an appealing message," the *Globe and Mail*, October 13, 1995; and Michel Venne, "L'incroyable remontée du OUI," *Le Devoir*, October 28–29, 1995.

29. André Blais, Richard Nadeau, and Pierre Martin, "Pourquoi le Oui a-t-il Fait des Gains pendant la Campagne Référendaire?" in Trent, Young and Lachapelle, eds., *Québec-Canada*, 72–80.

30. Alan Freeman, "Million Quebec Jobs in Peril," the *Globe and Mail*, October 18, 1995; Elizabeth Thompson, "Quebec's Dollar Would Be Worth 63 Cents: Johnson," the Montreal *Gazette*, October 20, 1995; and Ann Gibbon, "Bombardier CEO Attacks Yes Side Again," the *Globe and Mail*, October 4, 1995.

31. Jeffrey Simpson, "Quebec's Yes Side is Wallowing in Dreams and Delusions About the Future," the *Globe and Mail*, October 6, 1995; Scott Feschuk, "No Ties if Yes, Quebec Warned," the *Globe and Mail*, July 24, 1995.

32. The *Globe and Mail*, October 26, 1995.

33. As one journalist put it, in the federalist discourse, "Separation is not so much an evil as a non sequitur." Paul Wells, "Be vewy, vewy quiet," *Saturday Night*, September 1995, 17.

34. André Picard, "Beware Canada's Mood, PM Warns," the *Globe and Mail*, October 27, 1995.

35. This analysis was no doubt aided because it was compatible with the stereotypical view of English Canadians as calm, rational, and economically motivated.

36. Rhéal Séguin, "Sovereignty timetable unclear," the *Globe and Mail*, October 20, 1995.

37. Hubert Bauch, "Verdict Will Be Accepted Whatever It Is: Bouchard," the Montreal *Gazette*, October 27, 1995. Similarly, and typically, Mr. Parizeau responded to anxieties that Quebec's industrial milk quota would not be maintained under sovereignty: "When people start talking about boycotts, we have to say calm yourselves a little bit. If they hurt Quebec farms, they hurt their own, too. That's why the argument on the milk quota is false. It doesn't stand up." (Philip Authier, "Yes Voters Have Nothing to Fear, Parizeau Says," the Montreal *Gazette*, October 29, 1995.) For an analysis making this argument, see Parti Québécois, *La Souveraineté: Pourquoi? Comment?* (Montreal: Parti Québécois, 1990), 35: "As a strategy, federal politicians might be tempted to

say now that they will not negotiate, in order to dissuade Quebecers from supporting sovereignty. But when the event occurs they will change their attitude, because of political and economic realities." See also Rodrique Tremblay, "Constitutional Political Economy and Trade Policies Between Quebec and Canada," in Gordon Ritchie et al., eds., *Broken Links*, Canada Round Series No. 4, (Toronto: C. D. Howe Institute, 1991), 70–81. For an analysis of why the argument is false, see Robert Young, "The Political Economy of Secession: The Case of Quebec," *Constitutional Political Economy* 5 (1994), 221–45.

38. For the resolution and Mr. Chrétien's arguments in favour of it, see Canada, House of Commons, *Debates*, 1st Session, 35th Parliament, November 29, 1995, 16971–74.

39. Canada, *Statutes of Canada*, 42-43-44 Elizabeth II, ch.1, An Act Respecting Constitutional Amendments. (This had been introduced in late 1995 as Bill C-110.)

40. David Cameron, "Does Ottawa Know It Is Part of the Problem?," in Trent, Young, and Lachapelle, eds., *Québec-Canada*, 293–98.

FEDERALISM AND PUBLIC POLICY

Public policy relates to the outputs of governments and to courses of action (or inaction) adopted to address issues of concern. Implementation of policy involves application of assorted instruments (expenditure, regulation, etc.) according to legislative mandates and jurisdictional guidelines. These mandates and guidelines involve respect for the division of governing power and the political necessity of reconciling diverse political communities. Federalism involves not only institutional and legal arrangements, it is also concerned with policy strategies and design. Federalism encourages governments to be attentive to constitutional realities in crafting policy responses. Governments acting beyond their jurisdictional authority will be restrained by some combination of intergovernmental pressure, legal challenge, and public outcry. It is thus important that the interaction of federalism and public policy be explored and assessed.

The three essays that follow offer examinations of several key policy fields—broadcasting and communications, social policy expenditures, and taxation. Each of these fields has unique issues of interest. Collectively they share the common challenge of government strategies being shaped and constrained by the character of Canada's federal system. Comparing the debates and events arising in the various fields should offer useful insights into (a) the complexities of policy-making, (b) the interconnection of policy and flows of government funding, and (c) how federalism defines which communities may act in response to particular issues.

Jonathan Rose explores the battles over governing authority in the field of broadcasting and communications. Both federal and provincial governments have grappled over jurisdiction and policy direction. This has led to intense intergovernmental conflict and legal confrontations. Paul Barker explores the evolution of social policy debates and the complicated issue of balancing jurisdiction with expenditure capability. The federal government has often intervened in matters of provincial responsibility through use of its fiscal capability, the so-called federal spending power. Federal governments have argued that they serve a national interest in the maintenance of country-wide programs meeting critical social needs. Currently, debt reduction efforts have dampened federal government enthusiasm for major financial commitments and have led provincial governments to chart independent courses of action. Hugh Mellon, meanwhile, surveys the Goods and Services Tax in light of the Chrétien government's efforts to harmonize it with provincial sales taxes. Retail sales taxes are a significant source of government revenues in Canada. Control over these revenues and their collection is guarded by governments. However, the prolonged unpopularity of the GST and the ill-considered nature of party rhetoric in the 1993 election campaign have produced a search for federal-provincial harmonization. The political fallout has been heated and problematic for the Chrétien cabinet.

In analyzing these chapters students should consider several fundamental points. First, who has governing authority? How is this authority exercised and what restraints, if any, have arisen due to intergovernmental pressure, government finances, court actions, or other relevant constraints? Second, what are the respective interests at stake for the differing levels of government? Remember that communities or groups may be affected by issues without necessarily having authority over them. Third, how do finances come into play? Finally, there is the issue of whether federalism complicates policy unduly or whether it matches issues with the appropriate political community.

DISCUSSION QUESTIONS

1. Why is authority over broadcasting and communications so controversial? What is at issue?

2. Should provinces have separate educational broadcasting channels? Might it be better to have only one national broadcasting educational system?

3. Why might Quebec governments argue for a greater measure of authority over broadcasting? What about your own provincial government?

4. What objectives do you think governments are trying to achieve by legislating broadcasting regulations? Should any government attempt to encourage particular types of viewing habits or programming? Why or why not?

5. Should our major social programs be in the hands of national or provincial governments? Why or why not?

6. Have Canadian social programs operated due to, or in spite of, the formal division of powers? Why or why not?

7. Should we as a country have common social programs or should they vary in accordance with local or provincial cultures?

8. Can, or should, the federal government be able to influence national social policy if it is reducing its spending on the programs involved? Why or why not?

9. How did provinces gain the ability to levy sales taxes? Should both levels of government charge sales taxes? Why or why not?

10. What is involved with the issue of tax harmonization? Should this be a guiding principle in our tax policy? Why or why not?

11. Assess the nature of the agreement arrived at by Ottawa and three of the Atlantic provinces. What is its political significance? Were the provinces "bought off"?

12. How should taxing authority be divided up in a federation? Why?

FEDERALISM, BROADCASTING, AND THE SEARCH FOR COMMUNITY

Jonathan Rose[1]

Karl Deutsch has said that the strength of a nation can be measured by the durability of its communication links. In Deutsch's words, "the wider this range [of communications], the more broadly integrated ... is the community, or the 'body politic'."[2] This view sees the political system not so much as a set of institutional arrangements but rather as an elaborate communication network. Cohesive communities are those that share information on a variety of subjects across a wide number of communication channels. Others have echoed the same thought in different ways. Claus Mueller has written that "language can be understood as a cultural and political guidance system. ... It provides the group or individual the means to identify with a given culture or political entity".[3] Murray Edelman argues that language constructs people and that community is a result of a shared vocabulary.[4]

Studying federalism cannot be divorced from an examination of community. The outcome of recent political events such as the slim federalist victory in the 1995 Québec referendum suggests that creating a cohesive political community may be at the heart of our recent political problems. Whether solutions to contemporary problems involve increased centralization, decentralization, or greater cost sharing, it must be remembered that all of these modes of federalism are really discussions about the calibre and locus of community. Indeed, debates about which jurisdiction ought to have control over a policy area cannot be conducted without first recognizing the ramifications that various policy positions have on the development and creation of community.

In our mass media saturated world, much of what we learn about ourselves as a nation comes from television. In a variety of ways, television can be said to foster important values about who we are and how we understand politics. While the literature over the precise effects of television on these things is not definitive, there are few who deny television's power to shape and transform a polity.[5] To give but a few statistics to support this: the average Canadian spends almost 23 hours in front of the television per week[6] and sees television as more informative than magazines, radio, or newspapers.[7] Some studies have shown that children aged three to five watch an average of nineteen to twenty hours of television a week, making it one of the most important activities in terms of time for a young child.[8] In 1993, Statistics Canada reported that adolescents spent over seventeen hours a week in front of the tube.[9] James Curran has gone so far as to say that "The mass media have now assumed the role of the Church, in a more secular age, of interpreting and making sense of the world to the mass public."[10] There can be little doubt that the mass media play a crucial role in defining our world and helping us understand who we are as Canadians. Indeed, broadcasting has been one of the ways in which the federal government has developed a national community.

This essay has two purposes. First, it discusses the judicial evolution of broadcasting as a jurisdictional issue in federalism. As we shall see below, both the Judicial Committee of the Privy Council (JCPC) and the Supreme Court have been supportive of federal control in this area. The effect of this is to encourage a particular kind of community. The second purpose of this essay is to use broadcasting as a case study to examine some larger issues of federalism. In particular, the examination of broadcasting raises several inherent tensions within federalism and provides a backdrop to explore the relevance of a geographically based arrangement of power in an age where distance matters less. To borrow Harold Laski's phrase uttered in the 1930s, are we witnessing the "obsolescence of federalism"?[11]

Broadcasting, which, of course, did not exist at the time of Confederation, is not mentioned in the original British North America Act (now called the Constitution Act, 1867). Judicial interpretation has seen it as a federal power falling under the peace, order, and good government clause. Authors such as David Smith have written that while broadcasting might appear at first blush to fall within federal jurisdiction, there are good reasons to argue that provincial and regional concerns ought to be paramount.[12] In Quebec, for example, strong provincial control has been the rallying cry for governments of all political stripes. Successive governments there have argued that provincial control is an important way of meeting the francophone majority's cultural aspirations. Saskatchewan, Manitoba, and Alberta have also argued for greater provincial control, not for linguistic imperatives, but as a way of "creating and reinforcing regional identities"[13] according to John Jackson. Rowland Lorimer and Jean McNulty add that "while it would be incorrect to say that the Prairie provinces are not interested in the cultural arguments advanced by Québec, historically they placed a higher value on arguments concerning their historical rights to own and control telecommunication carriers and systems in their territory."[14] There has, thus, always been a tension between regional demands for greater autonomy in order to have diversity in broadcasting programming on the one hand, and federal government control in order to have uniformity across provinces on the other.

JURISDICTIONAL ISSUES—ROUND I: THE RADIO REFERENCE, 1932

In federal states, jurisdictional issues are rarely solved by merely referring to a constitution. Ambiguity and impression seem to be the hallmarks of a constitution, whereas claims made by either level of government about controlling certain policy areas are usually quite specific. Disputes are resolved by courts that weigh and assess the competing claims of both governments. This is the case with broadcasting in Canada. This section of the essay looks at several important Supreme Court cases. The purpose of this is to demonstrate the level of ambiguity in the Constitution, to show the very different ways federal and provincial governments see the federation and to discuss the far-ranging implications of judicial decisions.

The first time that the regulation of airwaves was discussed by the courts was in 1931 by the Supreme Court of Canada. At that time, the Supreme Court was not the highest judicial authority in Canada. The decision of the Court was "referred" to the JCPC by the Governor General in Council, that is, the federal cabinet. (A reference is a procedure whereby the federal government asks the Supreme Court to render an opinion on the validity of actions it is contemplating). While the central issue in this reference case concerned the capacity of the federal government to enter into international agreements, the Radio case was significant because it established a precedent about which level of government would have control over radio and by extension, broadcasting.

Specifically, the JCPC was to answer two questions, "(1) has the Parliament of Canada jurisdiction to regulate and control radio communication? (2) If not, in what particulars is the jurisdiction limited?"[15] To the first question, the Court answered in the affirmative, by a margin of three to two, that indeed Parliament had the jurisdiction to control radio. To the second question, they answered that jurisdiction was not limited. The Court's foresight in recognizing radio as an important federal power is evident in their statement that "radio communication is a matter of national interest and importance, and is a class of subject which affects the body politic of the Dominion; it is moreover a matter as to which there must be a single legislative authority throughout Canada".[16] Since the transmission of broadcasting was more clearly a federal head of power as provincial governments were excluded from jurisdiction over telegraphs in section 92(10)(a), the Court found that broadcasting seemed to be a reasonable extension of that federal head of power.

Not surprisingly, counsel for the provinces saw things in a different way. They argued that the sphere of broadcasting ought to be divided into receivers and transmitters, with the provinces having control over the receivers and the federal government having control over the transmitters. The provincial claim was that broadcasting—or at least the receiving part of it—ought to fall either under property and civil rights (section 92(13) of the Constitution Act, 1867) or section 92(16), matters of a merely local or private nature in the province. The provincial argument was that some receivers, such as beacons, buoys, and lighthouses, are clearly federal matters (falling under section 91(10)), but those that are not clear ought to fall to the provinces under the residual power of property and civil rights.

The federal claim was similar to the conclusions reached by the Aird Commission of 1929, that because of its enormous power, broadcasting was an instrument of education for the national interest. Moreover, the federal government was successful in persuading the court that radio was best seen as an undivided sphere of jurisdiction. The Court decided that "broadcasting as a system cannot exist without both a transmitter and receiver ... the system cannot be divided into two parts independent of the other."[17] In their conclusion the judgment read that "a divided control could only lead to confusion and inefficiency."[18] Though the Court was divided, the radio case was one of the early victories for the federal government in the rulings of the JCPC and clearly established the federal government as the dominant power in the field of broadcasting.

The federal government wasted no time legislating in this area. Based on the Court decision, the Conservative federal government in 1932 under R. B. Bennett created the Canadian Radio Broadcasting Commission (CRBC), whose far-ranging mandate gave it the ability to control virtually all aspects of broadcasting in Canada from regulation of frequencies to the establishment of new stations. Prime Minister Bennett's words in the House of Commons suggested that the federal government would give its newfound responsibilities high priority:

> ... this country must be assured of complete Canadian control of broadcasting from Canadian sources. ... Without such control, broadcasting can never be ... the agency by which national consciousness may be fostered and sustained and national unity still further strengthened.

> ... no other scheme than that of public ownership can ensure to the people of this country, without regard to class or place, equal enjoyment of the benefits and pleasures of radio broadcasting.[19]

Unfortunately this noble sentiment was not equalled by federal action. The establishment of the CRBC would portend a future pattern for the federal government: lofty rhetoric for the virtues of a Canadian-controlled broadcasting system, but far less support for actions that would ensure this. While the CRBC had enormous potential power, it was inadequately financed and encountered administrative and political problems.[20] As a vehicle to promote public radio it was unsuccessful. The first Broadcasting Act marked an inauspicious way for the federal government to begin its foray into the communications field.

Four years later the newly elected Liberal government of Mackenzie King created the Canadian Broadcasting Corporation (CBC) in 1936. This marked the first of four times the Broadcasting Act would be amended to include new changes in the communications environment. The CBC was created as a crown corporation in order to reflect the important distinction that it would be a public and not a state broadcaster. By this time there was a clear message about the character and assumptions of broadcasting in Canada. They were first, that the airwaves are public and administered by the government in trust; second, the broadcasting system should be Canadian-owned; third, access ought to be universal; fourth, the system should be a blend of private and public; and finally, quality, not country of origin, should be the main criterion for broadcasting programs.[21] If the CRBC was ineffective in regulating services, the CBC seemed more than eager to assume the responsibilities left in the wake of the CRBC. The Broadcasting Act would not change after 1936 until 1958 when television dramatically challenged the ability of the federal government to control broadcasting.

JURISDICTIONAL ISSUES, ROUND II: THE CASE OF CABLE—CAPITAL CITIES AND DIONNE, 1977–78

The next time the scope of federal power in broadcasting was tested was in 1977 and again the following year in 1978. The two cases were noteworthy as they were the first time the Court ruled on the federal government's ability to legislate television. In both *Capital Cities Communications Inc. et. al., v. CRTC*[22] and *The Public Service Board v. Dionne*[23] the Supreme Court heard whether the Canadian Radio Television Commission had the jurisdiction through Parliament to control all aspects of cable television. (The CRTC is the federal agency, which, *inter alia*, regulates private and public broadcasting). In the first case, what was being contested was the practice of the CRTC to allow cable operators to substitute Canadian commercials for American advertisements on American television stations near the Canadian border. In the second, the issue was whether the Québec Public Service Board was able to authorize François Dionne to operate a cable distribution enterprise in specific areas of Québec.

In the *Capital Cities* case, the appellants, led by operators of television broadcasting stations in Buffalo, New York, and supported by five provinces, (Québec, Ontario, Saskatchewan, Alberta, and British Columbia), argued the same kinds of claims made 45 years earlier in the *Radio* case. In an excessively narrow reading of federal control of broadcasting, the provinces conceded that there is exclusive federal jurisdiction "so far as concerns the reception of foreign or domestic television signals at the antennae of the cablevision companies,"[24] but argued that federal power was exhausted once those cable signals were disseminated to residential subscribers. The provinces argued that they should have power over television content from the point of distribution at the cable company to the reception at the subscriber's home.

As with *Radio Reference*, the existence of exclusive federal authority for broadcasting was upheld. The Supreme Court was not willing to sever jurisdiction of broadcasting into channel and content, where the provinces controlled the former and Ottawa the latter. Moreover, the Court argued that the cable system was "no more than a conduit for signals from the telecast"[25] and that cable should be considered a single undertaking under federal authority regardless of whether signals are received from the air or coaxial cable.

The year after the *Capital Cities* case, the *Dionne* case again tested the legislative competence of the federal government with respect to television broadcasting. In keeping with previous decisions, the Supreme Court found that exclusive legislative authority resides with the federal government, including all methods of distribution (cable, radio). In making this decision, the Supreme Court was not concerned with the area in which signals were transmitted (i.e., whether or not they were exclusively intraprovincial), but rather with what the service consisted of. Bora Laskin, writing for the majority, said, "...where television broadcasting and receiving is concerned there can no more be a separation for constitutional purposes between the carrier system, the physical apparatus, and the signals that are received and carried over the system than there can be between railway tracks and the transportation service provided over them...."[26]

The Court was split six to three, with the three dissenting judges from Québec who argued that exclusive federal jurisdiction extended to "the radio communication aspect," not the cable distribution aspect."[27] Justice Pigeon took exception to Laskin's reasoning that federal jurisdiction in one area necessarily means that any undertaking related to such activities should automatically come under federal jurisdiction, citing the telephone industry as an example of divided jurisdiction within the communications industry. Essentially Pigeon's argument was that telephone lines are often under provincial control, so why can't coaxial cables, which serve a similar function, be under provincial control? The problem with this reasoning is that telephones and broadcasting do not serve the same purposes. Telephones have no political function, the mass media do.

In both cases, if we strip away the veneer of the legal arguments made by both sides, the essential claims being made are clear and significant. The cable company and the provinces that were represented argued that because cable has a local character (i.e., its signals may be received intraprovincially and may be distributed to those in a small geographic area, such as part of a city) it ought to be under provincial control. The federal government argued successfully that "single undertakings" such as cable have an important national dimension that goes beyond the desire for provinces to articulate a regional identity. What is at stake here is not just the ability of the CRTC to regulate the commercials of border stations. Rather, these cases raised questions about the capacity of governments to foster a Canadian culture in an era of growing North American interdependence.

On one level, the actions of the provincial governments are a way to obtain greater control over television content. Several provinces, Québec in particular, had and still have a vibrant and culturally rich public broadcaster on television and radio. Had the efforts of the provincial governments been successful, they would have opened the door to greater provincial autonomy and control of content.

On another level, these cases are significant because they highlight recurring problems of federalism. First, is community better fostered by local control that encourages diversity in public policy or is community created by developing national standards established by the strong presence of a federal government? The Court held that an attempt to foster national community was more important than the sectoral interests of the provinces. Second, how can a service such as broadcasting, which transcends geography, be regulated under a system (federalism) whose primary purpose is to divide power based on spatial demarcation? The provinces creatively tried to fit a square peg into a round hole by contending that dissemination of cable signals was local in nature and therefore should be subject to provincial control. On this, as we have seen, the Court (with the notable exception of the Québec judges) was not persuaded. We will return to both of these themes later.

JURISDICTIONAL ISSUES, ROUND III: KELLOGG'S, 1978

The federal government's victory would be short lived. Three months after the *Capital Cities* and *Dionne* cases, the Court was somewhat more circumspect about which level of government has competence in the arena of broadcasting. What was at issue in *A.-G. Québec v. Kellogg's of Canada*[28] was whether a provincial statute, which forbade the use of cartoons in children's advertising on television, was *ultra vires* (or beyond the scope of) provincial power. In essence, did provincial legislation that gave Québec some control over content of television (children's advertising) contravene the principle of exclusive federal competence in broadcasting?

Unlike the other cases, in this one, the Court sided with the provincial government. It said that the power to regulate and control broadcasting was not at issue but that what was at stake was the right of a provincial government to regulate property and civil rights in a province (section 92(16) of the Constitution Act, 1867).[29] In keeping with his strong federalist inclinations, Chief Justice Bora Laskin wrote a dissenting opinion stating that "we are concerned with the right to a particular medium which is within exclusive federal competence, and the generality of the challenged provincial legislation does not aid the province."[30] More pointedly Laskin argued that he wanted to

> expose the assertion of the appellant herein for what it is, namely, an attempt to control the content of television programmes. I do not think that a rational distinction can be drawn between television programmes which originate with the television station or come in from outside the Province and those which are bought for and paid for by a commercial advertiser.[31]

Laskin's comments remind us that radically different views of the role of the federal government in the economy can prevail and that the power of the provincial authority over "property and civil rights" can be a powerful receptacle for the courts to place government powers. This case challenged the up-to-then sacrosanct idea that broadcasting was one of the few exclusively federal powers.

With the exception of *Kellogg's*, the judiciary from the JCPC to the Supreme Court has been remarkably consistent over the years about the roles of the federal and provincial governments in the field of broadcasting. These cases clearly demonstrate how judicial reasoning has a clear normative element that has explicitly acknowledged the federal government as the dominant actor in this field. This normative element sees broadcasting as important to nation-building and that this task should be carried out by the central government.

Understanding the basis for assigning jurisdiction to a government for broadcasting can only be rooted in practical as well as philosophical grounds. As such, the cases discussed above provide a good way in which to grasp a central dynamic of federalism: the need to balance administrative considerations with philosophical reasons. The administrative criteria include things such as accountability, simplicity, and avoiding externalities (powers of provinces should not affect those outside of the province). The philosophical criteria are things such as policy preferences of the public and a concern for the identity of subnational communities, both of which are subject to great differences of opinion.

WANING FEDERAL SUPPORT FOR BROADCASTING?

Beginning in 1976 the federal government began to reconsider its historic obligation for broadcasting. This was a result of several conjunctural events, not the least of which were the Supreme Court cases discussed above, but also including the increasing role of the provinces in educational broadcasting, the fiscal crisis of the federal government, and the election of the Parti Québécois government in Québec. The federal Liberal government's retreat was surprising because it meant turning its back on influential reports such as the Massey Commission of 1951 and the Fowler Commission of 1957, which argued that the burden of national unity is borne by broadcasting, and that the responsibility would be best carried out by a strong federal presence in this field. Significantly, these two reports blamed private stations for the increased American presence on television.

By retreating from this field, was the federal government also distancing itself from its traditional role as public broadcaster? The answer to this question is not clear because the behaviour of the federal government is not clear. For example, a year after the *Capital Cities* and *Kellogg's* cases, the federal government moved to *strengthen* its control of broadcasting through Bill C-16, which attempted to apply the federal powers of broadcasting to the whole field of telecommunications. The Canadian Radio Television Commission became the Canadian Radio Television-telecommunications Commission. Section 3(a) of the new act to amend the CRTC said:

> Efficient telecommunications systems are essential to the sovereignty and integrity of Canada, and telecommunications services and production resources should be developed and administered so as to safeguard, enrich and strengthen the cultural, political, social and economic fabric of Canada.[32]

While the federal government was on the one hand strengthening its rhetorical commitment to broadcasting it was, on the other, sending some clear messages to the provinces that it no longer wanted a jurisdictional monopoly on broadcasting. The federal government may have had sound political reasons to do so, however. Perhaps the writing was on the wall and Ottawa was merely responding to the political climate of the time. As Peter Russell says about the *Capital Cities* and *Dionne* cases, "in federal-provincial relations it is nice to have goodies on the shelf that you can afford to give away if it becomes politically necessary to make concessions."[33] It must be remembered that this was a time when federalism was under attack from several quarters. In Québec, the Parti Québécois government's battle over sovereignty often took place on the bloody grounds of broadcasting policy. The strongest federal voice in Québec was Liberal Leader Robert Bourassa, who argued for "cultural sovereignty," a policy that in some quarters of Québec might seem federalist, but anywhere else would certainly be viewed as strongly decentralist. Federal presence in broadcasting was also under attack in other provinces, where it was argued that the increasing availability of satellite technology and cable rendered a federal monopoly in this area difficult to enforce.

It was also around this time that Ottawa was re-examining the role of a national broadcaster. By reducing its financial commitment to the CBC, its major commitment to broadcasting, the federal government was willing to support its words of federal retrenchment with actions. As a result, the CBC was forced to rely more on advertising than its parliamentary appropriation. The ratio of parliamentary appropriation to advertising steadily increased from the mid-1960s to 1977 when advertising represented only 17 percent of the CBC's revenue and Parliament was responsible for the remaining 83 percent. Advertising has grown in importance to the CBC's financing, climbing from 17 percent in 1977 to 33 percent in 1996.[34] While funding for the CBC rose by 18 percent in real dollars from 1984 to 1994, federal government spending increased 38 percent over the same period.[35] A recent committee reviewing the CBC mandate said:

> The CBC's increasing dependence on advertising revenue (in part to offset the reductions in Parliamentary funding) has caused its television services to become more commercial and competitive, and has compromised their [*sic*] ability to deliver a distinctive, high quality program service;[36]

While this was written in 1986, it appears that the mid-1970s marked a turning point in the CBC's ability to "deliver a distinctive, high quality program service." Specifically, it was around 1976 that the government began rethinking its commitment to the CBC. That was the year Ottawa said that it was ready to modify its monopoly position in communications. At a meeting of premiers, the provinces agreed in principle to a constitutional proposal that would have given them increased authority over intraprovincial communications systems.[37] Two years later, in 1978, at a first ministers' conference, Prime Minister Trudeau made his government's intentions clear when he said:

> The present constitution, as interpreted by our highest courts over the years, seems to assign almost the entire field to the Parliament of Canada. We believe, however, that today's reality and the future, as we can best foresee it, requires a more varied approach.[38]

The "varied approach" that Trudeau was talking about was a result of Saskatchewan and Nova Scotia urging that cable distribution systems and provincial telecommunications systems be exclusively provincial. While Ottawa was willing to concede some jurisdictional room, it was not willing to capitulate to the provincial demands. Instead it argued for concurrency in the field of cable distribution with provincial paramountcy in some areas. The specific policy areas were a topic of some disagreement: the provinces wanted federal paramountcy in largely technical matters only; the federal government countered with paramountcy in "Canadian content, Canadian broadcast programs and services, and technical standards."[39] As befits the stereotype of first ministers' conferences, in the end nothing was changed and the meeting got bogged down with what Roy Romanow et al. later called "exchanges of technical detail and industry jargon incomprehensible to ministers and other 'on-expert' officials."[40]

Two years later at the 1980 first ministers' conference, the topic of control over communications was again on the agenda. Again, Ottawa was willing to concede considerable room to the provinces with respect to controlling intraprovincial communications with the notable exceptions of the CBC, defence and emergency communications and frequency spectrum allocation, where the federal government would maintain paramountcy.[41] The provinces balked at the federal offer, arguing that it did not address the key areas of programming and broadcasting.

Throughout this period, the federal government's strong rhetorical commitment to the CBC but weak financial one can be traced to a central dynamic of federalism. A. V. Dicey, in an often quoted passage, said one of the necessary preconditions for federalism is that citizens "must desire union, and must not desire unity."[42] In many ways, Dicey's statement summarizes much of what went wrong in the field of broadcasting.

It might be useful to explore in greater detail what precisely this simple but important principle means. Federalism is, in large part, a tenuous balancing act between allowing autonomy of regions and respect and encouragement of regional distinctiveness on the one hand, and the encouragement of central institutions and common practices to promote national unity on the other. This is what K. C. Wheare meant when he uttered his famous maxim that federalism allows "a method of dividing powers so that the general and regional governments are each, within a sphere, co-ordinate and independent."[43] As such, federalism requires the appropriate mixture of centrifugal (decentralizing) and centripetal (centralizing) forces. It also requires a tension that many students who lived through the Meech Lake and Charlottetown rounds of constitutional negotiations will recognize: equal treatment of provinces in theory, but special (distinct?) treatment of them in reality. This is what is meant by the terms symmetrical and asymmetrical federalism. This balancing act is well summarized by David Cameron, who has described federalism as "a device designed to cope with the problem of how distinct communities can live a common life together without ceasing to be distinct communities."[44]

In many instances, the federal government in Canada has responded to the unique demands of particular regions. It has created "union without unity." One need only be reminded of the Québec Pension Plan or 16(2) of the Charter of Rights and Freedoms, which makes French an official language having equal status to the use of English in New Brunswick but not in other provinces, to see examples of asymmetry in action. The rationale for diverse public policy-making in these cases, as always in a federation, is to respond to the demands of a pluralistic society. Linguistic, religious, and cultural practices vary across the country and federalism allows for an institutional mechanism to accommodate these societal cleavages.

In the field of broadcasting, the federal government's policies suggested that it believed "union equals unity."

As early as the 1920s the Canadian government saw that the most serious threat to Canada's cultural sovereignty was foreign domination of our radio airwaves. In response to this, the federal government began developing a homogeneous view of broadcasting that paid no heed to regional or linguistic differences. It believed that the threat of the United States was severe enough to warrant such a blanket policy. Perhaps the die was cast when, in 1932, Graham Spry, one of the founders of the nationalist lobby group called the Canadian Radio League, uttered his famous Mannichean line, "the question is the state or the United States."[45] Such a sentiment cast the state in the role of protector against American cultural imperialism and fit well with the prevailing elite view of democracy and concomitant notions of citizen competence.

The reality was that a homogeneous and united policy approach ignored the situation in French Canada.[46] While the mandate of the CBC was to provide service in both French and English, the task of providing comparable levels of service to both language groups became too great, and the state was left to provide a national service that aided Canadian identity. A study written for the Massey Commission noted the differences in French and English services in 1949 when it said "the French radio network imported 6.7 percent of its programmes from foreign sources while the Trans-Canada (English) network imported 20.4 percent."[47] Recent audience survey data echo these important differences. In 1993, the last year for which data were available, 37 percent of Québec programming was from foreign sources, while in the rest of Canada foreign sources accounted for 74.5 percent.[48] The so-called problem of Americanization then was—and still is—largely confined to the English service. But this did not alter the policy of the federal government.

Canadian broadcasting has always been regarded as a "single system." If there was a bifurcation, it was the distinction between public and private broadcasters. Filion argues that the existence of single regulatory agencies such as the Board of Broadcast Governors and the CRTC "implied that all components were equally accountable for the pursuit of national objectives."[49] Such a single system did not encourage diversity, but rather saw federalism as the same treatment of provinces irrespective of their political culture or language. As Filion concludes, "ironically, by reinforcing the collective (national) identity of the québécois citizens, broadcasting turns the quest for one Canadian identity into a futile experience."[50]

In an area as sensitive as culture, the federal government's historical response has been to treat the country as a homogenous whole. Not only did this not do justice to the very profound and important differences in Québec, it ignored other sensitive regional particularities as well. One can almost hear the frustration of the Québec government at the 1979 first ministers' conference:

> Québec, the heartland of French Canada, feels justified in reasserting with insistence and conviction its will to assume the development and control over all communications in its territory. Communications are all the means or resources through which specific values of a community are transmitted, such as its language and culture, its attitudes and way of life; it seems meaningless to us to entrust to another majority the task of developing a communications policy for Quebeckers.[51]

In the quest to respond to the threat of Americanization, many observers of Canadian culture have called for a more unified approach to funding our national broadcaster. This, it is argued, is the best way to stave off American influence.[52] Not only does such an approach ignore the Québec situation, it also ignores the diversity that exists among provinces in broadcasting. This position assumes that the primary threat to broadcasting lies in the possibility of our culture being subsumed under the deluge of American television programming. But is this so? Perhaps the problem lies not with the application of the federal principle, but with the principle of federalism itself.

THE OBSOLESCENCE OF FEDERALISM?

Federalism is predicated on geographic divisions. More specifically, one of its primary assumptions is that the dominant cleavage in society is territorial. Territory is the *sine qua non* of any understanding of federalism. This must be so, because federalism is an arrangement of power based on *spatial differences*, not differences in language, culture, religion, etc.

These other cleavages are seen as something that federalism responds to, so that in federal states the boundaries of subnational units often are made along linguistic lines (Québec in Canada, cantons in Switzerland) or religious and ethnic lines (Malaysia, India). The justification for these subnational units is to preserve diverse ways of living within a single political entity.

In a discussion of how powers are distributed in a federation, scholars use geography as an important criterion. For example, R. L. Watts suggests that powers in a federation should be allocated such that they avoid externalities.[53] In other words, a subnational government should not have power over a subject matter that affects citizens living outside of its borders. The commonly used phrase of "watertight compartments" perhaps best encapsulates this idea of discrete sources of power. A variation of this is the desire to allocate powers in an effort to avoid spillovers. This means that the effect of a government's power should not "spill over" to another jurisdiction. For example, provinces that have control over egg-marketing schemes cannot use that power to limit the importation of eggs from another province, as this would spill over to the federal power over trade and commerce. (This was the outcome in the *Chicken and Egg Reference Case* of 1971). Powers can be allocated according to the interests and needs of a particular region. The "autonomous communities" of Spain allow the interests of the Basques or the Catalonians to be preserved, while special concessions were made to the Borneo states when they joined the Malaysian federation. In Canada, Québec's use of the Civil Code responds to its historical traditions.

If federalism "takes geography seriously" can it respond to these other cleavages that are nonterritorial in nature? The list of those who are saying that it is time to rethink the importance of federalism is diverse in terms of concern and approach. Alan Cairns has written widely about how the Charter of Rights and Freedoms is changing how we understand who we are as citizens. Cairns believes that the Charter is making us less citizens of provinces and more rights-holders. Cairns calls this new class of empowered Canadians "Charter Canadians." By this he means that one's identity shifts from the region or province to an abstract concept called rights. Cairns also notes that the transformation that has taken place in urban areas and among Canadians traditionally excluded from politics poses a further challenge to federalism:

> The ethnicity of the new non-aboriginal, multicultural, and multiracial Canada largely concentrated in metropolitan centres cannot be "managed" by federalism. ... Canadians are becoming a new people for whom the past of Wolfe and Montcalm is truly another country and for whom federalism has declined in instrumental value.[54]

Others, such as John Porter in *Vertical Mosaic* and Charles Taylor in *The Pattern of Politics,* have seen federalism as a way of blocking "creative politics." Federalism reinforces traditional cleavages of region and language and prevents a dialogue about genuine problems such as class. Feminists, such as Jill Vickers, have argued that federalism is inhospitable to the interests of women because the "demands of women's movements do 'not fit neatly into jurisdictional boxes' in the current Canadian federal system."[55] Vickers argues that the concerns of women involve all three levels of government, and thus, federalism is a structural barrier that disperses the efforts of women among all three levels.

These concerns may reflect an inability on the part of federalism to respond to policy concerns or the demands of citizens, and thus federalism, if seen as an analytical tool, may be less relevant in dealing with traditional tasks of government such as communications. This is one field of endeavour where borders matter very little. New technologies such as the so-called death star, which would allow direct-to-home satellite transmission, do not pay any heed to divisions of power. According to Robert Pike, their arrival here will result in "hundreds of U.S. signals featuring pay-per-view movies, existing cable fare and conventional TV."[56] Not only will its arrival make a hornet's nest out of the CRTC's ability to regulate, it will strip away the capacity of *any* government to control content — Canadian or otherwise.

Universal addressability further makes a mockery out of developing national unity through broadcasting. This technological innovation, whereby cable companies can address programs to individual homes based on the recipients' class, occupation, hobby, religion, gender, or sexual orientation to name a few, seriously challenges the capacity of government to respond to public policy goals. The replacement of telephone wire and coaxial cable with fibre-optics will further expedite this innovation because its virtually limitless bandwidth will encourage individuals to choose among a vastly increased range of programming. Indeed, the fragmentation of audiences, interests, and identity through new technology makes questions about divisions of power seem almost quaint.

We do not need to look into the future to see the erosion of the capacity of governments to act in the area of communications. The Internet provides us with a powerful example. Over 3.5 million Canadians use the Internet to view images of paintings in the Louvre, read on-line stock quotations, peruse some of the world's great newspapers, learn about how to make beer, play chess with people they've never met in other countries, and follow their favourite sports teams. The things that one could follow on the Net are limited only by one's imagination. More than providing new sources of information, the Internet stands as an ideal metaphor for the futility of federalism.

In a recent federal government study of the "challenge" of the information highway, the traditional kinds of questions visited by every government commission and task force studying culture re-appear. The report notes the importance of Canadian content, restates the desire to encourage artistic and creative expression, and waxes eloquently about the importance of disseminating Canadian content abroad. But what is different about this report is an underlying theme that recognizes the growing inability of governments to act in matters technological. The Information Highway Advisory Council argued that governments should play a limited role in the new technologies and that this role should be about establishing "a favourable economic, investment, legislative and regulatory environment that addresses the concerns of all stakeholders."[57] One does not need to be a technological determinist to see that the prism of federalism—which in the past allowed us to view power divided between levels of government and exhausted between them—may be less useful in examining contemporary challenges faced by government.

CONCLUSION

Does this mean that federalism is not a useful analytical tool to examine broadcasting? On the contrary, the case study of broadcasting tells us several important things. First, it tells us about the territorial logic of federalism and that far from being a mere institutional arrangement, federalism has a certain kind of bias that can be used to foster certain values, such as the responsiveness of provinces to the unique demands of their citizenry. Second, that communications, and broadcasting in particular, is intrinsic to creating a vibrant body politic. And third, that in a world that is on the one hand being fragmented into smaller and more specialized market shares, and on the other, converging through the forces of globalization, federalism may offer us a tantalizing way to accommodate both of these dual pressures. Finally, federalism is a good analytical tool to examine broadcasting for what it reveals about the strengths and weaknesses of both the tool (federalism) and the object of study (broadcasting).

This essay questions the ability of federalism as an institutional structure to respond to some contemporary problems. By examining how broadcasting has been understood by the JCPC and later the Supreme Court, we are able to see that debates about jurisdictional issues are really debates about community. The essay has attempted to demonstrate what reasons the Court has given in its support of federal government dominance in broadcasting. While the Court often frames questions about community in the form of "which level of government should have jurisdiction," new broadcasting technologies will force governments to rethink their ability to undertake the tasks asked of them in liberal democracies. Such a problem is an appropriate one to ponder in a book entitled *Challenges to Canadian Federalism*.

NOTES

1. I would like to thank the editors for their comments and Mike Krywy for his assistance in preparing this chapter.

2. Karl Deutsch, *The Nerves of Government* (London: Free Press, 1963), 150.

3. Claus Mueller, *The Politics of Communication* (New York: Oxford University Press, 1973), 18.

4. Murray Edelman, *Constructing the Political Spectacle* (Chicago: University of Chicago Press, 1989).

5. See Tannis MacBeth Williams, ed., *The Impact of Television: A Natural Experiment in Three Communities* (New York: Academic Press, 1986).

6. Statistics Canada, *Television Viewing, 1993*, Catalogue No. 87-208, 7.

7. See Figure A.7, "Ranking television against other media" and Figure A.8, in Helen Holmes and David Taras, *Seeing Ourselves: Media Power and Policy in Canada,* 2nd ed., (Toronto: Harcourt Brace Jovanovich, 1996, 330.

8. Aletha Huston and John Wright, "Television and Socialization of Young Children" in Tannis MacBeth, ed., *Tuning In to Young Viewers* (Sage: Thousand Oaks, CA, 1996), 40.

9. Statistics Canada, *Television Viewing, 199*, 21.

10. James Curran, "Communications, Power and Social Order" in Michael Gurevitch et al., editors, *Culture, Society and the Media* (London: Methuen, 1982), 227.

11. Harold Laski, "The Obsolescence of Federalism" in *The New Republic* 98 (1939).

12. David E. Smith, "Broadcasting in the Federation: National Power, Divided Purpose," in David Shugarman and Reg Whitaker, eds., *Federalism and Political Community: Essays in Honour of Donald Smiley* (Broadview: Peterborough, 1989).

13. John Jackson, "Broadcasting: Centralization, Regionalization, and Canadian Identity" in Benjamin Singer, ed., *Communication in Canadian Society,* 3rd ed., (Scarborough: Nelson, 1989), 190.

14. Rowland Lorimer and Jean McNulty, *Mass Communication in Canada*, 2nd ed., (Toronto: McClelland & Stewart, 1991), 161.

15. In "Re: Regulation and Control of Radio Communication in Canada," *The Law Reports of the Incorporated Council of Law Reporting*, House of Lords, JCPC, 1932, 305. This section draws on

Frederick Fletcher's "Federalism and Communication Policy: Communications and Confederation Revisited" in Shugarman and Whitaker, eds., *Federalism and Political Community*, 385–405.

16. Ibid., 308.

17. Ibid., 315.

18. Ibid., 317.

19. House of Commons, *Debates*, May 18, 1932, 3035–36.

20. Arthur Siegel, *Politics and the Media in Canada*, 2nd ed., (Toronto: McGraw-Hill, 1996), 106.

21. These are taken from the Task Force on Broadcasting Policy, *Report* (Ottawa: Minister of Supply and Services Canada, 1986), 9.

22. *Capital Cities Communication Inc. et al., v. CRTC*, [1977] 81 D.L.R. (3d), 609.

23. *The Public Service Board v. Dionne*, [1978] 83 D.L.R. (3d), 181.

24. *Capital Cities Communications et al., v. CRTC*, [1977] 81 D.L.R. (3d), 617.

25. Ibid., 621.

26. *Public Service Board v. Dionne,* [1978] 83 D.L.R. (3d), 181.

27. Ibid., 183.

28. *A.-G. Québec v. Kellogg's of Canada*, [1978] 83 D.L.R. (3d) 314.

29. Ibid., 320.

30. Ibid., 316.

31. Ibid., 317.

32. House of Commons, *Debates*, Bill C-16, November 9, 1978.

33. Peter Russell, "The Supreme Court and Federal-Provincial Relations: The Political Use of Legal Resources" in R. D. Olling and M. W. Westmacott, eds., *Perspectives on Canadian Federalism* (Scarborough: Prentice Hall, 1988), 95.

34. CBC Annual Reports, 1977 to 1996.

35. Department of Canadian Heritage, *Making Our Voices Heard: Canadian Broadcasting and Film for the 21st Century* (Canada: Supply and Services, 1996), 129. This figure represents a decrease of 23 percent of purchasing power in constant dollars.

36. Ibid., 128.

37. Ronald Keast, *The Role of Provinces in Public Broadcasting* (Study prepared for the Task Force on Broadcasting Policy, 1986), 19.

38. Quoted in Roy Romanow, John Whyte, and Howard Leeson, *Canada: Notwithstanding* (Toronto: Carswell, 1984), 30.

39. Ibid., 31.

40. Ibid., 32.

41. Ibid., 78.

42. A. V. Dicey, *Introduction to the Study of the Law of the Constitution*, 8th ed. (London: Macmillan, 1915), 137.

43. Kenneth C. Wheare, *Federal Government*, 4th ed. (Toronto: Oxford, 1963), 10.

44. David Cameron, *Nationalism, Self-Determination and the Québec Question* (Toronto: Macmillan, 1974), 107.

45. See Canada, *Special Committee of Radio Broadcasting: Minutes of Proceedings and Evidence.* (Ottawa: King's Printer, 1932), 564.

46. This section draws from the arguments made by Michel Filion, "Broadcasting and Cultural Identity: The Canadian Experience" in *Media, Culture and Society v.* 18 (1996).

47. Quoted in Ibid., 455.

48. See Tables 2B and 11A, "Percentage Distribution of Television Viewing Time, by Origin (Fall 1993)" in Statistics Canada, *Television Viewing, 1993*, 22, 32.

49. Filion, "Broadcasting and Cultural Identity" in *Media, Culture and Society*, 459.

50. Ibid., 464.

51. Quoted in Romanow, Whyte and Leeson, *Canada: Notwithstanding*, 78.

52. See for example, John Meisel "Escaping Extinction: Cultural Defence of an Undefended Border" in D. H. Flaherty and W. R. McKercher, *Southern Exposure: Canadian Perspectives on the United States* (Toronto: McGraw Hill Ryerson, 1986) and Robert Pike, "Canadian Broadcasting: Its Past and Possible Future" in Singer, *Communication in Canadian Society*, 4th ed.

53. R. L. Watts, *Administration in Federal Systems* (London: Hutchinson, 1970), 66.

54. Alan Cairns, *Charter versus Federalism: The Dilemmas of Constitutional Reform* (Kingston: McGill-Queen's University Press, 1992), 112.

55. Jill Vickers, "Why Should Women Care about Federalism?" in D. Brown and J. Hiebert, eds., *Canada: The State of the Federation, 1995* (Kingston: Institute of Intergovernmental Relations, 1995), 138. Vickers credits the phrase "do not fit neatly into jurisdictional boxes" to Linda Trimble, "Federalism, the Feminization of Poverty and the Constitution," in *Conversations Among Friends: Entre Amis: Proceedings of an Interdisciplinary Conference on Women and Constitutional Reform*, ed., David Schneiderman (Edmonton: Centre for Constitutional Studies, University of Alberta, 1991), 87.

56. Pike, "Canadian Broadcasting" in Singer, ed., *Communication in Canadian Society*, 62.

57. Information Highway Advisory Council, *Connection Community Content: The Challenge of the Information Highway* (Ottawa: Ministry of Supply and Services Canada, 1995), 109.

DISENTANGLING THE FEDERATION: Social Policy and Fiscal Federalism

Paul Barker

Social policy in Canada is inextricably linked to federalism. Major programs in the areas of health, social assistance, and postsecondary education are the product of relations between federal and provincial governments, with the programs assuming the form of complex fiscal arrangements through which the federal government offers financial assistance to the provinces. Though both federal and provincial governments have their own exclusive social programs, the welfare state in Canada has been in large part a creation of the interplay of public authorities at the federal and provincial levels.

In the past decade, some important developments have taken place that affect federal-provincial arrangements for social policy. Limits were placed on the availability of federal funding to the provinces, and the two levels of government together proposed changes in the constitutional rules underlying future arrangements. The federal government also attempted to insert itself more directly into the arrangements, but failed in this effort. The most recent development, and most significant, has involved an actual reduction in the level of federal contributions and greater autonomy for the provinces in the operation of social programs.

The intent of this essay is to examine these developments and their implications. Such a task requires an appreciation of both the rationale and history of the fiscal arrangements, but the greater part of the discussion naturally focusses on the current changes. The essay suggests that the most accepted interpretation of recent developments is that they constitute a major step towards the disentanglement of the two levels of governments. The federal role will be reduced substantially, and social programs will diverge quite dramatically across the provinces with the dissipation of a national presence. Another interpretation, though, is possible. The provinces might indeed acquire more leeway, yet this need not erode the basic similarity of social policies in the provinces. Moreover, the federal government may eventually re-emerge as an integral component in the making of social policy. The future of fiscal federalism is not as clear as it might first seem.

PRELIMINARY CONSIDERATIONS

A beginning point for understanding the importance of federalism to social policy in Canada is the Constitution. The Constitution Act, 1867, equips the federal government with a large capacity to generate revenues for spending, but places a great deal of the legislative authority for social programs with the provinces. At Confederation this had little effect because government involvement in health, education, and welfare was minimal. But with the growth in the importance of social programs, this allocation of revenues and responsibilities has proved unworkable, and various fiscal arrangements involving the transfer of financial assistance from the federal government to the provinces have become necessary. Key to the arrangements has been a further element of the Constitution, namely the federal spending power. This authority permits the federal government to spend in areas of provincial jurisdiction.

Historically, the fiscal arrangements for social policy have served various purposes, all of which can be related back to the handling of social policy in the Constitution. At times, the purpose has been to bridge the vertical "fiscal gap" caused by the constitutional allocation or mismatch of revenues and expenditures, while at other times the desire has been to assist the poorer provinces in such a way that all parts of the country are able to offer comparable levels of public services.[1] Sometimes the intent is to convince provinces to establish programs that might otherwise not have been developed sufficiently or even introduced. The concern here is not so much the absence of revenue, but rather provincial reluctance to commit themselves to particular programs in the public interest. Lastly, national unity has been the object of the arrangements. In this form, the arrangements amount to "bonds of nationhood," forged out of a sense among Canadians that they share common services with one another.[2]

The fiscal arrangements for social policy rely on an assortment of grants that are used in various combinations. There are conditional grants that require the provinces to comply with conditions relating to the operation of programs and unconditional grants that can be spent in any way the provinces wish. Another fiscal device is the cost-matching or shared-cost grant, which reimburses the provinces for a percentage of their expenditures—an enticing incentive for provinces to spend in areas for which reimbursement is available. On some occasions, the desire is simply to transfer a set sum of money that is unrelated to provincial spending, and this is called a block fund. Finally, an arrangement may involve the transfer of either cash or tax points or both. A tax point transfer entails the federal government decreasing its level of taxation so that the provinces may increase theirs by a similar amount. The overall level of taxation remains the same, but the distribution of taxing power changes in favour of the provinces.

It is these grants and their use in federal-provincial arrangements that help to give this area of federalism "an air of grotesque unreality, untrammelled by logic and the ordinary restrictions and meaning of words...."[3] But some degree of comprehension can be gained if it is realized that the arrangements reflect the interests of the respective levels of government and the forces that shape the underlying nature of Canadian federalism. In other words, the character of the arrangements for social policy at any one time represent a barometer of relations between the federal government and the provinces. The relations might suggest a *decentralized* federal state, in which the effect of ambitious political elites and the allocation of powers allows provincial interests to come to the forefront. Alternatively, a *centralized* type of federalism that places the national government in a dominant position may surface as a result of larger societal forces. What has to be appreciated is that the fiscal arrangements are also political arrangements.

PAST TO THE PRESENT

Federal-provincial fiscal arrangements for social policy have always been a part of Canadian federalism. The primary arrangements, however, began to emerge shortly after World War II. In 1948, the federal government established a series of cost-matching and block grants for various activities in health care. Three years later, in 1951, it began transferring per capita grants directly to universities. In the next couple of years, four new arrangements were set up in order to provide social assistance to seniors, the disabled, the blind, and the chronically unemployed. The funding in these new arrangements involved the use of cost-matching, conditional grants that required the provinces to spend in order to receive federal funding and to comply with federal program conditions.

Each of these arrangements represented a first step towards setting up major arrangements in the areas of health, welfare, and postsecondary education. Eventually, they would be eclipsed by more encompassing agreements, but they had established the necessary groundwork. Also, their character revealed that Ottawa, in the immediate postwar period, held the upper hand. Education was a provincial responsibility, yet the federal government had entered into this area with its per capita grants, arguing that "it was 'in the national interest to take immediate action to assist universities ...'."[4] The use of cost-matching and conditional grants, too, showed the influence of the federal government, for they allowed Ottawa to shape provincial financing and administration of social programs.

In 1957, two major fiscal arrangements appeared. One was the Equalization program which entailed the federal government making unconditional grants to the poorer provinces. Though complicated in structure, Equalization had a simple aim, and that was to help the less well-off provinces in the financing of public services. The other arrangement, which was essential to the eventual emergence of a national health care system, dealt with hospital care. It employed cost-matching grants to provide provinces with an incentive to establish insurance plans for hospital care. The federal government would pay for roughly one-half of provincial costs in this area, a bargain that few provinces could ignore. But there were conditions, ones that would act to make the hospital plans similar. Individual agreements had to be signed governing the operation of hospitals and committing the provinces to the provision of in-patient and out-patient services for all residents.

The next decade witnessed the emergence of additional arrangements. It also saw a change in relations between the two orders of government. Up to now, the federal government was the senior party in federal-provincial fiscal arrangements, the natural "aftermath" of the success of Ottawa in dealing with the Depression and the war effort.[5] But in the 1960s the provinces—especially Quebec—challenged the federal government, relying on their constitutional authority over important areas of policy and a greater competence in the forming and administering of programs. Changed relations became evident in the new arrangements. In 1960, the federal government agreed to a tax point transfer for the financing of universities in Quebec. The province of Quebec, which was now undergoing a profound social transformation, rejected federal cash grants paid directly to institutions of higher learning, but tax points were less intrusive and hence more acceptable. A few years later the federal government, again responding to provincial pressures, offered tax points in place of existing grants for social assistance, hospital insurance, and other areas of social policy. Only Quebec accepted because the other provinces were uncertain of the value of the tax points. Nevertheless, the very offer revealed the strengthening of provincial influence in fiscal relations.

In 1966, a significant new arrangement, the Canada Assistance Plan (CAP), was established. It collapsed previously established welfare arrangements into one and hinged on an equal sharing of the costs between the two levels of government. It also took note of "provincial demands for flexibility," establishing only a few conditions relating to eligibility and administration.[6] In the same year, federal legislation authorized the federal government to pay for approximately one-half of the cost of provincial medical care plans. It also stipulated that the plans comply with conditions of universality, comprehensiveness, portability, accessibility, and public administration. Though the imposition of the conditions seemed a return to federal dominance, in reality they amounted to general principles and were less confining than those for hospital insurance.[7] A year later, in 1967, the final element in the set of major federal-provincial fiscal arrangements came into view. Under this new relation, which dealt with postsecondary education, the federal government transferred to the provinces a combination of tax points and cash grants equal to one-half of the operating expenditures of universities and colleges. The arrangement would replace the old per capita payments and effectively extend the tax point transfer for Quebec to the other provinces. Unlike the recently established arrangements for health care and welfare, there would be no program conditions.

The two levels of government acting together had made provision in the respective provinces for comparable social programs. This was an important accomplishment, yet neither level was content. For the provinces, the conditions limited their ability to make social programs more effective, and the lure of federal bargains—cost-matching grants—distorted their spending preferences. Also, the very presence of the federal government in areas of provincial jurisdiction proved irksome, especially to Quebec, which felt that Ottawa was skirting the Constitution through the use of fiscal arrangements. As for the federal government, what increasingly became important was the cost of their participation in the fiscal arrangements and the fact that large chunks of federal spending were dependent on the decisions of provincial governments.

Presently, in 1977, a partial solution was offered. A new arrangement called Established Programs Financing (EPF) was set up for health and postsecondary education. It provided for a block grant composed equally of tax points and cash grants, with the cash transfer increasing annually by growth in the economy and population. The replacement of the cost-matching grants with block grants pleased the federal government and some of the provinces, the former because its spending on social programs was no longer a product of provincial spending and the latter because the rigidities and the distorting effects would be gone. EPF soon, however, turned out to have some weaknesses in the eyes of the federal government. Annual increases in the transfers remained unacceptably high. Also, the federal government believed that the provinces were failing to keep up their spending on health care and postsecondary education, and the conditions affecting health care—which had been maintained under EPF—were being violated with the emergence of direct patient charges. As a result of these perceived shortcomings, Ottawa placed temporary limits on increases in the grant for higher education and threatened to establish program conditions for universities and colleges. Most controversially, it passed the Canada Health Act, which had the effect of banning direct patient charges.

From the end of World War II to the middle of the 1980s, the federal government and the provinces had combined their efforts to provide Canadians with major social programs. As the conflict over EPF suggested, relations had not always been cordial, but the two levels together had made a substantial commitment to social life in Canada. The Equalization program channelled large, unconditional grants to the less well-off provinces so that no province would be without basic public services. The Canada Assistance Plan (CAP) helped the provinces finance expensive social welfare programs, and federal-provincial agreements ensured reasonable access for all Canadians to higher education and health care. By 1985, these arrangements together made possible the transfer of nearly $23 billion, which in some provinces meant that close to one-half of total revenues took the form of federal contributions.

RECENT DEVELOPMENTS

In the past decade, some important developments have emerged that influence fiscal arrangements for social policy. The ones that came to fruition involved a diminution of the federal presence and pushed the arrangements in a "decentralist direction."[8] Even some of those that miscarried sought to move federalism in Canada towards a more decentralized form. But other failed endeavours saw the federal government struggling to maintain a role, a reminder that any effort at disentanglement has to confront forces that cause governments to come together in a federal state.

Factors behind these developments included those that had always affected the fiscal arrangements. But there were some new ones as well. Arguably the most important of the new ones was the "deteriorating financial position of the federal government."[9] Since the mid-1970s, the federal government had been experiencing sizeable budget deficits, but in the early 1980s the problem assumed much larger dimensions. The effect was to limit the ability of the federal government to contribute to fiscal arrangements. A second force was globalization and the internationalization of economic activity. To remain competitive in this new environment, Canada had to restructure its social programs.

LIMITS

In 1985, the federal government announced new limits on its contributions for postsecondary education and health. Under EPF, annual increases reflected changes in GNP, but commencing in the fiscal year 1986–87 the formula for increases would be growth in GNP less two percentage points. The announcement initiated a series of limits on federal contributions for EPF, CAP, and Equalization. In 1989, the federal government once again changed the EPF formula, this time to GNP less three percentage points. A year later, it superseded this change with a freeze on annual increases aside from those that followed from gains in population. Beginning in the fiscal year 1988–89, and occurring as well in 1989–90, 1990–91, and 1993–94, the ceiling on Equalization grants, set in the early 1980s, came into effect. As for CAP, the federal government deemed that starting in 1990–91, annual increases in funding made under this arrangement would be limited to 5 percent for the well-off provinces of Ontario, Alberta, and British Columbia.

The limits on transfers stemmed largely from "the persistent and alarming increases in the federal deficit and debt...."[10] Without gaining some control over its deficit, the federal government believed that its reputation and that of Canada would suffer in the new global economy. As well, the need to finance the debt that emerged from the annual deficits increasingly ate into federal spending. Given that the transfers represented a substantial portion of federal spending, it was inevitable that they would become part of the deficit-reduction exercise.

The provinces reacted angrily to the federal limits on contributions. They accused the federal government of transferring its deficit problem to them, a charge with some foundation. During the period 1989–92, cumulative provincial deficits rose from $1.5 billion to $22.8 billion. The unilateral nature of the changes—the fact that the federal government made the decisions on its own—also bothered the provinces. British Columbia was so angered by the limit on CAP that it challenged the legality of the action. The province lost its case in the Supreme Court of Canada, but the court action demonstrated the degree of animosity felt towards the federal government.

The nature of relations between the two orders of government was not the only concern. The effect of the funding limits on the affected programs also attracted a great deal of attention. With respect to welfare assistance, there was the fear that federal limits would translate into lower levels of benefits and services in the affected provinces. As for post-secondary education, concerns revolved around the emergence of larger classes, higher tuition fees, and a general decline in the quality of education. As it turned out, some of these fears were realized in relation to education. Class sizes grew, provincial funding for postsecondary institutions declined, and university tuition fees rose.

Though there were clearly concerns about welfare and postsecondary education, the major worry was over health care. As in the other areas, an expressed fear was the impact on the overall quality of services. A more specific concern related to the size of the cash grant. In 1986–87, the cash grant was 55 percent of the total EPF transfer, but by 1994–95 it had fallen to 46 percent; and projections suggested that the cash grant would disappear by the turn of the century. The cash grant was calculated as the difference between the yield of the tax points and the total EPF entitlement. The fact that the value of the points was growing and the overall entitlement was frozen meant that the difference between the two—the grant— was decreasing in size. What unsettled many about the looming demise of the cash grant was that the federal government would be without the means to enforce health care conditions. Tax point transfers could not be withheld, but cash grants could, and this latter possibility ensured that provincial health plans would continue to offer comprehensive care to all residents at no direct charge. Now this leverage, the threat to deny provinces federal funding, was to disappear. Moreover, provincial governments, faced with decreased financial support and sensing the end of the federal presence, would begin immediately to make changes that violated conditions stipulated under the Canada Health Act. This would spell the end of the country's national health care system.

To some extent, these concerns, like those in other areas, had some validity. In some provinces direct patient charges became evident, which constituted a direct violation of the federal health legislation. A more subtle change related to the de-insuring of previously covered health services. Provincial plans were now becoming less comprehensive. There were also indications that provinces would be less willing to fully insure residents who received care in other locales. This would limit the portability of provincial health plans. A final reform undertaken by nearly all provinces concerned the regionalization of provincial health plans, a development that led the provinces "down divergent paths" and challenged "the concept of a 'national system'."[11]

Underlying all the specific concerns about the individual programs was a more general one. A major purpose of federal-provincial arrangements was to ensure for reasons of fairness and efficiency that the provinces were able to offer a comparable set of services. Equalization had been specifically designed for this purpose, but the other arrangements also had an equalizing effect through provisions in their formulae and the enforcement of conditions. But now the latter were weakening and the prospect of greater provincial differentiation and disparity became visible. Equalization would have to compensate for this, yet the sense of a "sharing community" that underpinned Equalization might dissipate in the absence of truly national programs for health care, postsecondary education, and welfare.[12] The very thing that now made Equalization essential—the perceived decay in national programs—also weakened its foundations.

CONSTITUTIONAL CHANGES

In 1987, two years after the initial announcement of limits on federal transfers, the prime minister and the premiers agreed to a package of constitutional amendments known as the Meech Lake Accord. The impetus for the Accord had been the need to respond to Quebec's demands for changes in the Constitution. One element of the package dealt with the federal spending power, the main basis of federal participation in areas of provincial jurisdiction. Typically, fiscal arrangements had been the preferred way of adjusting the Constitution to meet the social needs of the nation, but occasionally the constitutional rules themselves had been amended. In relation to the federal spending power, the Meech Lake Accord obliged the federal government to compensate provinces who decided to set up their own alternatives to new national shared-cost programs. The only requirement was that the alternative had to be "compatible with the national objectives."

In many minds, the provision amounted to a well-founded attempt to place limits on the use of the federal spending power. For past and present governments of Quebec, the power "was a device for illegitimate federal incursions into areas of provincial jurisdiction." Some of the other provinces, too, felt a degree of animosity towards the power, believing it symbolized "federal dominance, federal determination of provincial priorities, and provincial dependence on federal largesse which could be altered at federal whim."[13] Now this would be changed. The provinces could opt out of new national shared-cost programs and receive federal financial assistance by simply ensuring that their programs reflected "national objectives," a term that was widely interpreted to give provincial governments great latitude.

As the Accord and its provisions were being deliberated, an example of how the new spending power might work emerged. In 1988, the federal government proposed a federal-provincial arrangement for child care. At the time, assistance for child care was available under CAP, which meant that only those in need were eligible. The proposed arrangement imposed no conditions with respect to eligibility, and the federal government also refrained from stipulating standards relating to the quality of child care services. This was to be the future of fiscal federalism. To avoid provincial opting out of new programs, the federal government would attach few, if any, conditions to its transfers, leaving the provinces with much flexibility. More generally, the spirit of Meech Lake—the need to accommodate Quebec and other provinces—would pervade fiscal arrangements between the two levels of government.

Neither the constitutional limit on the spending power nor the child care arrangement survived. The child care proposal succumbed to the deficit-fighting battle at the federal level, and the restrictions on the spending power disappeared when the Accord failed to gain the necessary approval of all ten provinces. In 1992, a further attempt was made to amend the constitutional rules. The Charlottetown Accord was a comprehensive set of constitutional proposals that included the spending power provision found in the Meech Lake Accord. However, the Charlottetown Accord, like its immediate predecessor, failed to gain acceptance. This, though, was not the end of the spending power provision. It would appear later, albeit not in the form of a constitutional amendment.

FEDERAL INITIATIVES

During the period in which the limits on federal transfers had been initiated and the constitutional amendments had been proposed, a Progressive Conservative government, led by Brian Mulroney, had been in office at the federal level. In 1993, the Liberal party, under the leadership of Jean Chrétien, took power and shortly thereafter, in 1994, announced two initiatives affecting federal-provincial arrangements for social policy. One involved a full-scale review of social security programs in Canada; the other entailed a four-year study of health care. What united the two was the fact that both added up to a unilateral attempt on the part of the federal government to take a more prominent role in the operation of social programs under federal-provincial arrangements. With its limits on contributions to the provinces, the federal government had influenced the financing of the social programs, but now it wanted to become more involved in the actual structuring of these programs.

The Social Security Review entailed an examination of federal social programs, post-secondary education, and CAP. It determined that the effects of globalization had made these programs "out of date and in need of reform."[14] If Canada was to take its place in the new global economy, the social security system had to be restructured. For postsecondary education, the review proposed that the cash component allotted to higher education under EPF be eliminated in favour of a new federal student loan program. With respect to CAP, two basic proposals were forwarded, one that suggested weakening the conditions to better facilitate the transition from welfare to work and the other the redirection of CAP funds to federal income support plans. The proposals represented major—even "radical"—adjustments to the fiscal arrangements, especially those that recommended the substitution of federal programs for transfers to the provinces.[15]

The Social Security Review soon fizzled out. The provinces wanted no part of the proposals. Those affected by the limits on CAP were still greatly upset with the federal government, and the election of a separatist government in Quebec in 1994 did nothing to make matters easier for the review. Most important was the determination of the federal government to deal with its fiscal situation, even with a new party in power. As the Social Security Review began its work, the federal government announced that major cuts to social security would be forthcoming, placing the review in a "fiscal straightjacket" and undermining any notion of federal leadership in social policy.[16]

The other federal initiative dealt with health care. The National Forum on Health, chaired by the prime minister himself, would undertake a four-year review of medicare. Like the Social Security Review, the Forum was driven in part by forces of globalization and a desire to contribute "to the development of a new vision of health for the 21st century."[17] But the Forum stumbled over provincial opposition. For the provinces, the federal government was at the same time reducing transfers and trying to define the future of provincial health plans—a case of trying to call the tune *without* paying the piper. Though the Forum engaged some Canadians in debate, it operated in relative obscurity and its four-year mandate was cut in half.

THE CANADA HEALTH AND SOCIAL TRANSFER

The latest development affecting fiscal arrangements and social policy is also the most significant. In 1995, the federal government announced that CAP and EPF would be combined to produce a new arrangement named the Canada Health and Social Transfer (CHST). The conditions for health care would remain under the CHST, but those for CAP would be reduced to the sole requirement that no residency requirements be established. Also, funding for health, welfare and postsecondary education under the CHST would be reduced from $29.7 billion in 1995–96 to $26.9 billion in 1996–97 and then to $25.1 billion in 1997–98. The core cause of the CHST was the now familiar desire of the federal government to deal with its serious fiscal situation.

In one respect, the new arrangement was a continuation of the federal policy of placing limits on federal transfers. But in another it represented a qualitatively different policy stance.[18] The CHST went further than merely limiting transfers—it actually reduced them. The structural changes to CAP, too, made the CHST different. It imposed a federal offer: fewer conditions for fewer dollars. Also, the federal pronouncements revealed a willingness to allow the provinces to be in the driver's seat when it came to major social policy areas. Until this time, the federal government had insisted that its role had been little influenced by changes in transfers, but the nature of the CHST effected a change in this disposition.

Reaction to the new arrangement was negative. Many of the criticisms echoed those made earlier in the face of federal limits, except they were made more angrily and vociferously. It was contended that the CHST hastened the end of the cash grant, a development that not only made it difficult to enforce national standards but also amounted to a surreptitious repeal of the popular Canada Health Act.[19] As the CHST was announced, the federal government and Alberta were engaged in a dispute over patient charges. Eventually, the federal government would prevail, but only through the threat of withholding federal funding—an action that would soon be impossible to undertake with the end of the cash grant. A further line of attack centred on welfare and social services. Without the condition that funds be spent on all persons in need, provinces were "free to provide financial assistance to whichever 'deserving' applicants they choose," and the replacement of the matching grant with a block fund would weaken the incentive to spend in this area.[20] Particularly worrisome was that the pooling of CAP and EPF funds in the new CHST arrangement would allow for a redistribution of financing away from welfare to the more popular health and postsecondary education plans.

Supporters of strong social policies also levelled a more general accusation against the CHST: it would destroy the national social system that had been so carefully structured over the years. The fiscal arrangements had allowed the provinces the flexibility to mold social plans to meet their specific needs while at the same time ensuring adherence to some basic principles. The blanket of social programs that had served and united Canadians would turn into a patchwork quilt, and one that would become increasingly threadbare in the less well-off provinces. Ottawa had surrendered its role as guarantor of national social programs, a role that was "rightfully the responsibility of the federal government."[21] Only interprovincial co-ordination could now ensure a national quality to social programs, and this was considered a highly complicated and dubious means of achieving this end.[22]

The provinces shared in some of these criticisms. But some, the well-off ones, were more accepting of reduced federal funding if accompanied by less federal intrusion. Especially important here was the elimination of most of the conditions under CAP, for they had obstructed creative policy-making in the area of social assistance. Eventually, an interprovincial council of social policy ministers (excluding Quebec) proposed that a clear line be drawn between federal and provincial responsibilities. Ottawa would have control over welfare payments and unemployment insurance, and responsibility for social services, health, and postsecondary education would lie with the provinces. The provinces had seen the CHST as a chance to solidify control over areas they considered essential. Some of the provinces also made it clear that they were more than capable of establishing comparable provincial plans through interprovincial co-operation. *National* standards did not have to be *federal* standards.

The federal government felt the sting of the criticisms and reformed the CHST in the following year. Payments under the new arrangement would be frozen at 1997–98 levels until 1999–2000. But after this time there would be increases in the payments, though admittedly they would be moderate. Perhaps more important, the cash grant would not be permitted to fall below $11 billion during the period 1998–99 to 2002–03.

The federal government believed that this met the major provincial and public concerns over the new arrangement. Federal funding would eventually rise, providing the CHST with "secure, stable and growing long-term funding."[23] Also, the cash grant, the central concern of many, would be preserved. But the federal record of broken promises and unkept commitments made claims about a reformed CHST ring hollow. Moreover, accompanying developments served to indicate that little had changed, that the social policy system would undergo a clear decentralization of authority. A new federal-provincial arrangement for child care, announced in late 1995, fell victim to provincial reticence and federal budget priorities. In early 1996, the federal government unilaterally limited the range of its spending power, indicating that it would not establish new national shared-cost programs without the agreement of the majority of the provinces and that provinces could opt out of any new programs with compensation if they set up similar plans. The re-emergence of limits on the spending power was in large measure a response to the close vote in the Quebec referendum. This same factor also precipitated a further development: federal participation in labour market training would be severely curtailed, and the provinces would now have primary responsibility for this important area of public policy. Finally, the federal government and the provinces were to come together to set new principles and enforcement mechanisms for social programs operating under federal-provincial fiscal arrangements. It was believed that this would result in greater provincial control.

THE FUTURE

A safe prediction for the future of social policy and fiscal arrangements is strong provincial governments and increasing differentiation in provincial plans for health, welfare, and postsecondary education. The CHST and other actions in the past decade pointed the country in this direction. Reduced overall federal funding, weakened enforcement mechanisms, elimination of standards, restrictions on the federal spending power, abdication of traditional federal responsibilities point toward a disentangled, decentralized, and differentiated federation in the area of social policy. A recent decision of British Columbia to establish residency requirements for welfare and violate a condition under the CHST seemingly foreshadows what is to come. Yet, while easy to argue, this future is not a certainty. Some evidence suggests that the absence of a prominent central government does not necessarily mean the end of national programs. Since 1977, provinces have maintained fairly similar health plans in the face of continued federal cutbacks,[24] and a " 'national' " system for postsecondary education has emerged over the years in the absence of any federal standards.[25] Also, developments outside the arrangements are telling. For instance, the provinces have developed comparable primary and secondary education systems "without policy intervention and harmonization by the federal government."[26]

If this evidence is unconvincing, then perhaps the effects of globalization may be more compelling. Globalization, or the internationalization of economic life, demands that social policy play a much more important role in ensuring the competitiveness of a nation. Social polices must be both less expensive and more effective, and the impact of this has been to create a certain uniformity in social policy initiatives across the world. In health policy, for example, the movement towards community-based services and the adoption of "managed care" arrangements pervade many western democracies. In the new global economy, the national government may give way to international forces in the moulding of national standards.

Admittedly, a large question mark hangs over this line of reasoning, and that relates to the ability of the Equalization program to compensate for any widening provincial disparities that might emerge with greater provincial control. There is a fear that the legitimacy of Equalization might erode with the decline of the federal presence. However, recent events suggest that this fear may be exaggerated. While social programs have been cut under the CHST, payments under Equalization have actually grown. It appears that the Canadian population remains committed to this program.

The safe prediction also foresees a weakened federal government. It is a victim of the globalization phenomenon, the pressures of the provinces—especially Quebec—and most immediately of its own fiscal situation. Yet, again, a different outcome is possible. Globalization does indeed weaken the traditional roles of nation-states, but the challenges of globalization call out for a new federal role in equipping Canada in the new global order.[27] As for the fiscal situation, projections show that the federal government should be experiencing budget surpluses by the early part of the next century.[28] This fact, along with projected deficits at the provincial level, may once again make federal financial participation possible and necessary in areas of provincial jurisdiction. Quebec is arguably the most difficult challenge for the national government, but an old solution - different arrangements for Quebec— could solve this particular problem. In other words, "asymmetrical federalism" or the differentiated treatment of provinces ,could ensure a role for the federal government.

In the very short term, the fiscal arrangements for social policy are headed in a decentralist direction. The federal government will be weaker and provinces may be tempted to use their new freedom to diverge from one another. But after this initial phase a different situation may emerge, one that manages to preserve the national element of provincial social plans and that eventually offers greater room for a national government.

NOTES

1. Richard M. Bird, "Federal-Provincial Fiscal Arrangements: Is There an Agenda for the 1990s?," in Ronald L. Watts and Douglas M. Brown, eds., *Canada: The State of the Federation, 1990* (Kingston: Institute for Intergovernmental Relations, 1991), 112.

2. A. W. Johnson, "The Meech Lake Accord and the Bonds of Nationhood," in Katherine E. Swinton and Carol J. Rogerson, eds., *Competing Constitutional Visions: The Meech Lake Accord* (Toronto: Carswell, 1988), 146.

3. R. MacGregor Dawson quoted in D. V. Smiley, *Canada in Question: Federalism in the Eighties*, 3rd ed. (Toronto: McGraw-Hill Ryerson, 1980), 165.

4. George E. Carter, "Financing Post-Secondary Education Under the Federal-Provincial Fiscal Arrangements Act: An Appraisal," *Canadian Tax Journal* 29, no. 5 (September–October 1976): 505.

5. Edwin R. Black and Alan C. Cairns, "A Different Perspective on Canadian Federalism," in Peter J. Meekison, ed., *Canadian Federalism: Myth or Reality?* 3rd ed. (Toronto: Methuen, 1977), 39.

6. Rand Dyck, "The Canada Assistance Plan: The Ultimate in Cooperative Federalism," *Canadian Public Administration* 19, no. 4 (Winter 1976): 592.

7. Malcolm G. Taylor, *Health Insurance and Canadian Public Policy: The Seven Decisions That Created the Canadian Health Insurance System and Their Outcomes*, 2nd ed. (Montreal and Kingston: McGill-Queen's University Press, 1987), 362.

8. Thomas J. Courchene, *Celebrating Flexibility: An Interpretative Essay on the Evolution of Canadian Federalism* (Toronto: C. D. Howe Institute, 1995), 1.

9. Peter M. Leslie, "The Fiscal Crisis of Canadian Federalism," in Peter M. Leslie, Kenneth Norrie, and Irene K. Ip, eds., *A Partnership in Trouble: Renegotiating Fiscal Federalism* (Toronto: C. D. Howe Institute, 1993), 1.

10. George E. Carter, "Federal Restraints on the Growth of Transfer Payments to the Provinces Since 1986–87: An Assessment," *Canadian Tax Journal* 42, no. 6 (1994): 1506.

11. Jeremiah Hurley, Jonathan Lomas, and Vandna Bhatia, "When Tinkering is Not Enough: Provincial Reform to Manage Health Care Resources," *Canadian Public Administration* 37, no. 3 (Fall 1994): 514.

12. Leslie, "The Fiscal Crisis of Canadian Federalism," 5.

13. Richard Simeon, "Meech Lake and Shifting Conceptions of Canadian Federalism," *Canadian Public Policy-Analyze de Politiques* 14 Supplement (September 1988): S17.

14. Human Resources Development Canada, *Improving Social Security in Canada: A Discussion Paper* (Ottawa: Minister of Supply and Services Canada, 1994), 21.

15. David M. Cameron, "Shifting the Burden: Liberal Policy for Post-Secondary Education," in Susan Phillips, ed., *How Ottawa Spends 1995–96: Mid-Life Crises* (Ottawa: Carleton University Press, 1995), 165.

16. Ken Battle and Sherri Torjman, "Green Light, Red Flag: Caledon Statement on the Social Security Review," in *Critical Commentaries on the Social Security Review* (Ottawa: Caledon Institute of Social Policy, 1995), 222.

17. Canada, Office of the Prime Minister, *Opening Remarks by Prime Minister Jean Chrétien to the National Forum on Health*, October 20, 1994, 2.

18. Courchene, *Celebrating Flexibility*, 39–40.

19. Keith G. Banting, "Who 'R' Us," in Thomas J. Courchene and Thomas A. Wilson, eds., *The 1995 Federal Budget: Retrospect and Prospect* (Kingston: John Deutsch Institute for the Study of Economic Policy, 1995), 180.

20. Ken Battle and Sherri Torjman, "How Finance Re-Formed Social Policy," in Daniel Drache and Andrew Ranachon, eds., *Warm Heart, Cold Country: Fiscal and Social Policy Reform in Canada* (Ottawa and Toronto: Caledon Institute for Social Policy/Robarts Centre for Canadian Studies), 425.

21. Robin Boadway, "The Implications of the Budget for Fiscal Federalism," in Thomas J. Courchene and Thomas A. Wilson, eds., *The 1995 Federal Budget,* 105.

22. Roger Gibbins, "Decentralization and National Standards: 'This Dog Won't Hunt'," *Policy Options* 17, no. 5 (June 1996): 7–10.

23. Canada, Department of Finance, *Budget Plan* (Ottawa: Her Majesty the Queen in Right of Canada, 1996), 57.

24. Thomas J. Courchene, *Redistributing Money and Power: A Guide to the Canada Health and Social Transfer* (Toronto: C. D. Howe Institute, 1995), 76–77.

25. Allan M. Maslove, "Reconstructing Fiscal Federalism," in Frances Abele, ed., *How Ottawa Spends 1992–93: The Politics of Competitiveness* (Ottawa: Carleton University Press, 1992), 67.

26. Ronald Manzer, *Public Schools and Political Ideas: Canadian Educational Policy in Historical Perspective* (Toronto: University of Toronto Press, 1994), 251.

27. Thomas J. Courchene, "Canada's Social Policy Deficit: Implications for Fiscal Federalism," in Keith G. Banting, Douglas M. Brown, and Thomas J. Courchene, eds., *The Future of Fiscal Federalism* (Kingston: School of Policy Studies, 1994), 114.

28. G. C. Ruggeri, D. Van Wert, and R. Howard, "Reassignment of Tax Fields and the Changing Federal Role," *Canadian Journal of Regional Science* 18, no. 2 (Summer 1995): 221–234.

THE COMPLEXITY AND COMPETITIVENESS OF FISCAL FEDERALISM: Blending the GST with Provincial Sales Taxes

Hugh Mellon

"The distribution of financial powers between the Dominion and the provinces has been one of the most troublesome of the many problems raised by Confederation and certainly has the longest history."[1] This declaration from R. MacGregor Dawson's landmark *The Government of Canada* stands as one of the great understatements of political analysis. The matching of fiscal resources with governmental responsibilities is one of the most vexing policy challenges for a federation. In the Canadian case, provinces have many costly areas of jurisdiction (health, roads, education, etc.) and substantial policy discretion. However, there are persistent regional disparities in wealth and resources. The federal government has traditionally channelled moneys to the provinces via grants and shared-cost programs, yet debt pressures are restricting this source of funds. Differing governmental agendas at each level add complications. Taken together these pressures produce formidable obstacles to public policy and/or budgetary co-ordination.

The resulting federal-provincial fiscal relationship is a complicated environment marked by competition, distrust, and carefully forged agreements that are little understood by the public. Forging intergovernmental consensus involves specially constructed provisions designed to win pragmatic compromise. Examples of federal-provincial agreement can be seen in such financial matters as tax collection, pensions, regional development incentives, shared (federal-provincial) cost programs and sales taxes. It is with reference to the last of these, sales taxes, particularly the Goods and Services Tax (GST), that our discussion of the fiscal dimension of Canadian federalism will proceed. As a generator of significant government revenues and the subject of active federal efforts aimed at federal-provincial harmonization, this case illustrates many of the critical dynamics involved with issues of public finance in a decentralized federation.

The GST remains one of the most condemned public policy measures in national history. Two successive national governments have been attacked for its implementation. Federal officials are currently engaged in the quest for harmonization of the GST and provincial sales taxes. Harmonization as conceived by Ottawa would involve the integration of federal and provincial taxes, and the encouragement of retailers to have the tax already included in the prices displayed on store shelves, the so-called sticker price. This would eliminate the shock of selecting an item based upon a sale price and then being jolted by the size of the resulting sales tax bill. It might, of course, help mask the size of the GST levy. The federal government persists in the search begun during the Mulroney era for a vehicle to achieve nation-wide sales tax integration. Federal promotion of harmonization comes as the culmination of an unsuccessful Liberal government effort to find a politically palatable alternative to, or adjustment of, the GST, which would allow them to deliver on rash partisan promises to do away with the hated tax. Interestingly, Quebec was the first province to move towards sales tax harmonization. At present there is an effort to bring three Atlantic provinces on side. The 1996 deal with New Brunswick, Newfoundland, and Nova Scotia is a current manifestation of the controversy generated by fiscal matters in the Canadian federation. The issue of harmonization and the associated federal endeavours illustrate the predicaments involved when federalism encounters questions of federal-provincial fiscal resources, governmental discretion, and federal efforts for national solutions. Complexity, competing governmental agendas, debates over supposed special arrangements for various provinces, interest group lobbying, and political unrest, are all present and accounted for in the resulting turbulence.

Meanwhile, the GST also raises issues involving global commerce and debt reduction. Commercial matters surface in diverse ways ranging from the basic tax collection process all the way to the level of international lenders and credit evaluators who monitor public finances and achievement of debt reduction targets. The impact of globalization is seen in the policy goal of not prejudicing exports whatever the tax arrangements and in the desire to prove to international bond raters and credit agencies that Canada is endeavouring to control its governmental indebtedness. All GST revenues, save for credits and rebates built into the design of the program,[2] go towards the federal government's debt-servicing and reduction fund. In 1993–94 the GST produced $15,696 million for this debt fund.[3]

Particular attention will be paid in a later section to the federal-provincial agreement to implement harmonization in three of the Atlantic provinces. Prince Edward Island continues to resist federal blandishments, but the other three provinces are working with the federal government. The negotiations leading up to this agreement and the political fallout resulting from its signing offer food for thought on the underlying political and economic dynamics of Canadian federalism. Political, commercial, and financial pressures intermingle and induce provincial governments to jockey for advantages of various sorts in terms of federal co-operation and in terms of generating appeal for prospective business investors. Over and above its instrumental importance as a revenue source, sales tax policy becomes a source of ammunition in the competitive dynamic among governments.

Before plunging into the deep waters of the GST and discussions of tax co-ordination, several background preliminaries require attention. First is the distribution of taxation authority emanating from the interpretations of the British judiciary and their understandings relating to the application of taxes. Their analytical framework for assessing sales taxes application and government jurisdiction ended up rewarding provincial inventiveness (deviousness?) and influenced subsequent tax collection mechanisms. Second on the agenda is historical information on the GST's introduction and the associated federal-provincial upset. After this, there will be a few words about the GST and the Liberal commitments associated with the

1993 federal election. Together, these sections set the stage for the contemporary debates over the federal-provincial aspects of the GST and the arrangements worked out with New Brunswick, Nova Scotia, and Newfoundland. This case study will exhibit the already identified intricacy of Canadian fiscal federalism and offer insight into the impact of fiscal matters on governmental strategies and aspirations.

TAXATION AND THE CONSTITUTION ACT, 1867

The Confederation settlement of the 1860s contained provisions regarding the division of taxation authority. Federal taxation powers were clearly designed to exceed those granted to the provinces. However, as in various other areas of public policy, a combination of provincial determination and judicial interpretation altered the original consensus. Many of the government services that citizens came to expect in the twentieth century (health care, public education, and extensive road networks) fell within provincial jurisdiction and revenue needs blossomed. Imaginative tactics allowed provincial intrusion into the sales tax field and the overcoming of constitutional roadblocks. The provincial presence in the sales tax field has since become so much a part of the landscape that discussion of both federal and provincial priorities is central to sales tax reform.

The 1867 Constitution Act (henceforth referred to as the B.N.A. Act) awarded the provincial governments authority over "Direct Taxation within the Province in order to [sic] the raising of a Revenue for Provincial Purposes" in section 92(2). On the other hand, section 91(3) recognized federal jurisdiction over "The raising of Money by any Mode or System of Taxation." Customs and excise duties were also assigned to the federal government's authority by section 122. Thus even a cursory reading of the BNA Act makes clear the federal predominance in matters of taxation. Federal authorities had more sources of fund-raising at their disposal and the reference to direct taxation would seem to significantly constrain subjects of provincial taxation. Provinces were assigned taxation powers over only those situations where the burden of the tax could not be passed on to a third party. A property tax levied directly against the owner of land is an example of the type of taxing situation envisioned by the architects of Confederation for provincial jurisdiction.

Over time the growth of government and the increasing responsibilities assumed by the provinces resulted in exploration for new revenue sources. Sales taxes appeared to be a possibility despite the existing division of power. Attempts at sales tax usage led to intergovernmental conflict and constitutional litigation. The Judicial Committee of the Privy Council (JCPC) faced a dispute over taxation in *Bank of Toronto v. Lambe*.[4] The most important ramification of this ruling for purposes of understanding the constitutionality of provincial sales taxes was the decision of the British law lords to frame the direct-indirect taxation distinction according to the writings of John Stuart Mill in his *Principles of Political Economy*. Mill's distinction, as rendered by Peter Russell, Rainer Knopff, and Ted Morton, was that "a direct tax is one which is demanded from the very person who it is intended should pay it; whereas an indirect tax is one which is imposed on one person in the expectation that he will reimburse himself at the expense of another."[5]

Provinces were temporarily stymied. Yet, a way around this direct-indirect hurdle was found by the government of New Brunswick in its Tobacco Act of 1940. Instead of a retailer paying a tax and then indirectly passing it on to consumers through higher prices, the New Brunswick legislation made the retailer the tax collector. Hence the tax would be imposed directly on consumers by the tax-collecting retailer. Retailers were made agents of the provincial government in the interests of tax collection and provincial entry into the sales tax field. This assignment of duties satisfied the letter of the law in the eyes of the British jurists rooted in their literal application of Mill's dichotomy. In the words of the JCPC's Viscount Simon, "It is a tax which is to be paid by the last purchaser of the article, and, since there is no question of further re-sale, the tax cannot be passed on to any other person by subsequent dealing."[6] New Brunswick had found a way over the hurdle through altering tax collection arrangements. Legal manipulation, or what Russell, Knopff, and Morton referred to as "shrewd draughtsmanship"[7] had persuaded the JCPC.

Henceforth, provinces could and did expand their reliance upon retail sales tax opportunities. This is now a significant source of provincial fund-raising. For 1994–95, taking the provinces as a whole, sales taxes raised over $20 billion and contributed about 13.4 percent of total gross general provincial revenue.[8] In terms simply of taxation sources and the revenue they generate (this would exclude transfer payments, for example, which are another type of revenue flowing to the provinces) sales taxes ranked second after income taxes. Nine provinces now apply one. Alberta stands alone in not levying a provincial retail sales tax. Rates for their sales taxes vary among provinces, and in 1995 they ranged from seven percent assessed by British Columbia and Manitoba to 12 percent levied by Newfoundland.[9] In addition to the diversity of taxation rates, provinces also differ with regard to the goods covered and the exemption provisions. Certain goods may be exempted in light of such public policy goals as energy conservation or literacy promotion. Sales tax application or adjustment is a well-guarded instrument of provincial governments.

FROM THE MANUFACTURERS' SALES TAX TO THE GOODS AND SERVICES TAX

Few issues have so galvanized public outrage as the GST. Yet, in light of the partisan rhetoric and heated debate that accompanied the arrival of the GST, it is easy to lose sight of the inefficiencies of its predecessor, the Manufacturers' Sales Tax (MST). Reform of the MST, however, had proven difficult. Introduced in 1924, the MST affected many business and economic interests and tax reform had often proven to be a political quagmire. Incremental rather than radical change had often proved easier to navigate through the treacherous waters of interest group lobbying. Despite this heritage, in June of 1987 when the Mulroney government unveiled its white paper[10] on tax reform, few, if any, could have imagined the cauldron of GST-related strife that would erupt. That the MST had assorted and serious limitations has never been widely contested but its reform was a challenge.

Levied at the manufacturers' level, the MST came early in the production chain. It was assessed on a narrow range of goods and had different rates for different types of products. Its application at the level of the manufacturer meant that it became built into subsequent prices through goods being used as inputs for assembly of more involved goods. This led to what is known as tax cascading,[11] in which the effect of the tax is intensified as taxed products are used as components of other products and resultant prices reflect the impact of taxes paid through the production process.

Openness and citizen awareness were also issues. For most consumers the MST remained invisible as it was already built into prices and production. The existence of different tax rates applicable only against a narrow range of goods complicated matters for nonexperts, who were, of course, the vast bulk of the population. The evils did not end there, though. Imports were favoured over exports as "distortions stimulated imports at the expense of domestic production and reduced Canada's exports."[12]

Few were unhappy with the prospect of terminating the MST. Despite this, the search for an alternative was arduous. Gillespie[13] observes that major calls for reform surfaced in 1956, 1967, and 1975 with momentum for change building through the late 1970s and into the 1980s. Successive federal ministers of finance struggled to find an acceptable option.

Beginning with the 1987 White Paper on Tax Reform, the Mulroney government embarked upon a broad-based effort at tax revision. The initiative reflected a wish for greater efficiency. Allan Maslove depicts Tory motivations in these terms, "the goal has been to reduce the influence of tax considerations on market behaviour, including spending, taxing and investment decisions."[14] The vagaries of the MST would no longer distort prices and comparisons of exports and imports. Government policy was shaped as well by an intention to deal actively with the national debt. Restraint and tighter budgetary management would be governing watchwords.

The subsequent years were filled with interest group pressure, federal-provincial negotiation, partisan antagonism, parliamentary theatre, and public frustration. Members of the general public expressed deep and abiding frustration with what many regarded as a new and unnecessary tax. Finance Minister Michael Wilson laboured long and hard to win support for the reform cause. He promised that the new tax would be visible, revenue neutral when compared to its predecessor, and would benefit the tax system as a whole. He first called for a nine percent tax only to retreat in April of 1989 to a fallback position of seven percent. Wilson searched for provincial support and for possible tax co-ordination. Provinces, meanwhile, were concerned about losing taxation autonomy and about being identified with an unpopular federal initiative.

The GST was far from being the only major issue of the Mulroney government. Free trade pacts, constitutional accords, budgetary restraint, aboriginal unrest, high interest rates, and promotion of privatization were among the other major government concerns. Debates and divisions about the GST always reflected both the issues central to consideration of sales taxes as well as general political tensions. The federal-provincial environment was marked by tensions involving the above-noted issues, particularly the Constitution. Given the national preoccupation with constitutional reform, the more pragmatic issue of tax reform was occasionally overlooked. Wilson's selling task was overshadowed by the unsuccessful struggles to achieve passage of the Meech Lake Accord (1987–90) and the follow-up Charlottetown Accord of 1992.

The diversity of provincial tax rates and the sensitivities of the provincial governments worked against ready harmonization of federal and provincial sales taxes. Some provinces showed early interest, but agreement was elusive. Tax levels, the range of affected goods, and provincial discretion over the sales tax as a policy tool were all major issues. Federal involvement in formal negotiations to win provinces over was terminated by the federal government in the first few months of 1989. Provincial governments generally were not anxious to serve as collectors of one of Canada's most unpopular tax measures. In April of 1989, Hugh Winsor, the *Globe and Mail*'s experienced observer of the national political scene, bluntly asserted that "[Wilson] could not sell the tax to the provincial governments, which refused to combine it with their own sales taxes."[15]

Prince Edward Island and Saskatchewan appeared at different points to be candidates, but in 1991 both opted not to reach final agreement with Ottawa.[16] Only Quebec ultimately indicated that it would pursue an agreement with the federal government for tax integration.

Selling the GST was never an easy task. Extensive federal efforts in the period from 1989 into the early 1990s to persuade Canadians to accept the GST were costly and of very limited success. Jonathan Rose and Alasdair Roberts[17] have documented the tens of millions spent on promotional campaigns, communications efforts, and information services. The GST struggle was played out against a broader debate over the fairness of sales taxes and the federal government's market agenda. Conservative tax policy was seen as reflective of the government's pro-business orientation and debt-fighting determination. Ideological opponents argued for greater progressivity in taxation (taking proportionately more from the better off) and for greater zeal in levying taxes against corporations and the wealthy elite. The Michael Wilson proposals contained provisions for tax credits for low income families, but these measures were limited.

Tax design and the interrelationship of revenue collection, social equity, and efficiency involve important issues whose full exploration is beyond the scope of this paper. General judgments on the effect of the GST's introduction on the existing tax system and its fairness are difficult to arrive at due to the many variables at work. Examples of these variables include the existing combination of taxes and exemptions, the perceived revenue-raising alternatives, and the differing types of criteria one might assign to the tax system—revenue-raising, fairness across income groups, intergenerational fairness, promotion of certain economic outcomes through tax incentives, etc. Thus, even an apparently straightforward characteristic such as fairness generates debate over fundamental divisions relating to ideology, to the purpose of governments and markets, to differing senses of how to rank the currently disadvantaged groups warranting assistance, and to the time period within which one feels results should be felt. Scholarly judgments on the pros and cons of particular tax structures are often, of necessity, highly nuanced.

Specialist commentators have offered useful assessments of the GST. W. Irwin Gillespie has written that the GST made the tax system "fairer and more efficient."[18] Doing away with many of the evils of the MST represented marked improvement. Maslove[19] also prefers the GST over the MST, but points out that greater reliance on the income tax system would have been more progressive. In addition he reminds readers that one can assess the alterations of the sales tax arrangements without considering the tax credits for the disadvantaged that accompanied the GST. Adopting this distinction allows one to acknowledge the effects of the tax credits while questioning the continued reliance upon sales taxes.

Aside from Quebec most provinces were leery of co-operating with Ottawa over the GST. Public discontent about the tax and the Mulroney government generally was not abating. The GST was denounced as contributing to increases in price levels and hardship among provincial citizens. Provincial premiers were sensitive to this and, furthermore, wished to maintain their fiscal autonomy. Provincial freedom to set the level of their own sales taxes and to design the lists of affected goods and services was not to be bargained away lightly.

Acceptance of the federal entreaties would extend taxation to an expanded list of goods and services. Provincial political control might be eroded if the federal government constrained provincial tax discretion. Use of sales tax adjustments for provincial reasons could be jeopardized. Harmonizing down to some sort of average tax level (working from pre-existing federal and provincial tax levels) would run into opposition from both the provinces at the high sales tax end as well as from Alberta, which lacked any provincial sales tax. High sales-tax provinces argued that harmonizing to an average level would cost them funds, while Alberta stood opposed to sales taxes generally.

Federal government motivations obviously differed. Given their center-right political outlook, Wilson and his colleagues felt responsible to make the tax system more compatible with efficient markets. Distortions caused by tax cascading or by the favouritism built in towards imported goods would be removed. When businesses used taxed goods to create other products they would now be able to claim tax credits thereby avoiding the building of taxes paid into the final price of assembled goods. Making a broader range of goods and services eligible for taxation would address the narrowness of the MST's application. Provincial collaboration with the federal government would make it is easier to achieve uniformity. Aside from its policy benefits, uniformity might allow Ottawa to share GST credit (blame?) with the provinces.

As of January 1, 1991, a seven percent GST applicable on a broad range of goods and services finally was implemented by the federal government. Parliamentary resolution was made possible only after the unusual procedure of appointing additional senators to allow the Progressive Conservative–led House of Commons to overcome Senate opposition. Section 26 of the British North America Act had provided for the possibility of appointing added senators to assist the House in the face of determined Senate opposition; however, it had never before been implemented.

THE GST AND PROVINCIAL FINANCES

Provincial reaction to the GST's introduction illustrated the interaction of federalism and political economy. Provincial reactions were conditioned by revenue needs and provincial circumstances. An example of this came in the provincial decisions about whether to apply their provincial retail sales taxes simply to the price of taxable items or to levy their taxes on the combined price of retail items *plus* the amount of GST paid.[20] Opting for the latter choice would result in higher provincial taxes paid, because the sales tax would be applied against a higher amount (the sum of an item's price plus the amount of GST paid). Ontario and the four western provinces decided to pass up the possibility and levied their taxes simply against pre-GST prices. Not everyone could overlook the opportunity. Difficult financial situations intensify the need for revenues, and so Quebec and the four Atlantic provinces opted for the added tax revenues.

The financial weakness of Canada's eastern provinces showed up in other ways. Atlantic officials were hesitant about discussing some sort of integrated federal-provincial sales tax arrangement, for they feared having to lower their relatively high provincial sales taxes. Having the country's highest sales taxes meant that they would lose revenue if a federal-provincial deal harmonized rates at some sort of average provincial tax rate. High rate provinces wanted compensation for any commitment to lower their sales taxes. Tax integration, or harmonization, would cost them in terms of foregone dollars at a time of federal government retrenchment.

Quebec was the first to harmonize federal and provincial sales taxes. This involved the province tailoring its base of taxable items in response to the federal provisions. According to a Montreal *Gazette* commentary "in 1990, the Quebec government jumped at the chance to harmonize ... because it meant that it would be able to tax a broader range of goods and services, albeit at a lower rate than the nine per cent it was charging at the time."[21] Quebec could use the added revenues to deal with provincial deficits and slow economic conditions. The associated trade-off offered additional benefits, including simplified tax administration and paperwork. The federal-provincial arrangement also reflected the close bilateral relationship between Prime Minister Mulroney and Premier Bourassa.

1993—THE GST AND THE HEAT OF PARTISAN BATTLE

Amid the heat of the federal campaign trail in 1993, the GST had vibrant incendiary capabilities. Liberal platform orators indicated that a victory by their party would produce major change. The precise nature of this promised change was unclear, though. Many voters assumed change could mean cancellation. After all, no less a figure than Jean Chrétien himself had declared in October 1990, before an audience of fellow Liberals, "I am opposed to the GST. I have always been opposed to it. And I will be opposed to it always."[22] Deputy Prime Minister Sheila Copps repeatedly urged the scrapping of the GST. While most citizens heard these pronouncements, more restrained comments resided within the Liberal Red Book, the party's campaign bible of commitments and policies. It indicated that a search for an alternative would commence. The substitute would produce "a system that generates equivalent revenues, is fairer to consumers and to small business, minimizes disruption to small business, and promotes federal-provincial fiscal cooperation and harmonization."[23] These words suggested a quest for an alternative taxing arrangement, not outright abolition. Bridging this divide has persisted as a perplexing problem for Liberal strategists.

In keeping with the Red Book provisions, the House of Commons Standing Committee on Finance was assigned responsibility for a detailed GST review over the first half of 1994. Their report featured assessment of assorted policy choices and recommended harmonization of federal and provincial sales taxes. Unfortunately, the committee members had few concrete ideas about how to win the provinces over. Public pressure for GST reform, if not abolition, persisted nonetheless. Liberal MPs feared voter backlash over the GST's retention, while party officials wished to campaign on having delivered upon Red Book commitments. Finance Minister Paul Martin opened negotiations with the provinces, but two and one half years after the election there seemed little to show for these efforts aside from the established trend of tax co-ordination with Quebec. In April 1996, he acknowledged that sales tax reform was more complicated than anticipated in 1993.

AGREEMENT WITH ATLANTIC CANADA

Pro-active measures were required if the logjam was to be broken. Compensation for provinces losing tax revenues through harmonization could be such a measure. Provincial acceptance of the federal harmonization agenda in return for federal compensation became the basis for intensified talks with Atlantic Canadian premiers. The understandings reached between the federal government and the governments of New Brunswick, Nova Scotia, and Newfoundland are an enlightening case study of the fiscal dimension of federalism. It illustrates the labours involved in reaching workable policy compromises, the tensions inherent in deliberations over governmental revenue needs, the competition between provinces, and the interrelationship of federal-provincial and intraprovincial politics.

Rumours of harmonization initiatives involving the Atlantic provinces surfaced in late March 1996. On March 30 the four premiers of Atlantic Canada met at the Halifax International Airport to discuss strategy for dealings with Ottawa. According to the communications directors for New Brunswick Premier Frank McKenna, the Halifax gathering was "an opportunity for them [the premiers and their officials] to get together and discuss the various offers and options that have been presented by the federal government on this issue."[24] The deliberations soon encountered a roadblock. Prince Edward Island premier Catherine Callbeck expressed concern over the scale of lost provincial revenues due to harmonization: "We have great difficulties with the plan; we're not leading the charge on this."[25]

Intergovernmental discussions between officials and politicians ensued through April. Enthusiastic premiers stressed the benefits of lowering tax rates through harmonization. Nova Scotia's John Savage grandly declared that "This could be the biggest boost to business and the biggest boost to individual taxpayers in the history of this province."[26] Such exuberance was not shared by Prince Edward Island's representatives and they remained aloof from the emerging intergovernmental agreement.

By mid-April a memorandum of understanding (MOU) concerning sales tax harmonization had been reached between the federal government and the governments of New Brunswick, Nova Scotia, and Newfoundland. The MOU bound the federal finance minister and his provincial counterparts to work towards harmonization at a 15 percent tax level by April 1, 1997. As part of the agreement, participating provinces had to give up the freedom to alter tax rates unilaterally. The signatories also accepted the application of sales taxes against a range of goods larger than that used for their pre-existing provincial sales taxes. This meant that the new harmonized tax would be applied against goods not previously taxed. Federal authorities agreed in turn to a compensation arrangement for foregone provincial revenues. Compensation would be paid for a four-year period on a declining basis (100 percent of revenue shortfalls greater than five percent of current retail sales tax returns in years one and two, 50 percent in year three, and 25 percent in year four).

Signatory provinces (N.B., N.S. and Nfld.) declared that harmonization would have considerable net benefits. Among these were that it would simplify tax collection and make shopping easier. Prices now would include the amount of tax to be paid and consumer surprise at the cash register would thereby be avoided. There would be no taxes paid on business inputs, thus addressing the tax-cascading problem. Exports would be enhanced. New Brunswick, for example, advertised growth in employment, exports, and GNP. "Our exports will be more competitively priced, free of the hidden retail sales tax on business inputs that currently pushes prices up. The result will be higher sales of our products in the global economy, and more jobs for New Brunswick workers."[27]

Federal finance minister Paul Martin was also vocal in his praise of the harmonization plan. He asserted that this would help commence fulfillment of the Red Brook promise. The money found to fund compensation was justified as simply the latest example of Ottawa's willingness to help those parts of Canada enduring wrenching structural change. Comparison was made with moneys provided to western and eastern Canada to cope with the elimination of certain transport subsidies.[28]

Prince Edward Island premier Catherine Callbeck opted not to join in the agreement. Instead, a special committee was struck by the province to review the sales tax issue and solicit public opinion. Some pundits have suggested that the premier feared acting given her government's low standings in the polls. As for herself, Callbeck stressed the magnitude

of lost provincial revenue and the limited opportunities available within the Island economy to make it up.[29] Whatever the case, it perhaps bears noting that Callbeck shortly thereafter stepped down as premier and her successor lost the subsequent provincial election.

Arriving at the MOU was far from being the end of negotiations. Instead it simply
kicked off months of laborious deliberations on the detailed mechanics of tax harmonization.
This phase in the process lasted until the latter half of October. Administrative details such
as how tax-inclusive pricing would be implemented had to be hammered down so that retailers
and consumers would know what they were dealing with. Simultaneously, lobbying and
public relations efforts began as groups jockeyed for advantage in the newly emerging tax
regime. The most striking example of this came from those in the book trade, who attacked
the GST as a tax on reading and a burden to literacy promotion.

The lobbying campaign related to books offers insight into the interrelationship of intraprovincial and federal-provincial politics. Nationally, Paul Martin had been steadfast in
his opposition to the selective treatment of particular goods. Consistent application of the GST
across a broad range of goods was defended as making the overall tax rate lower, easing public comprehension, and serving as a barrier to selective lobbying tactics. The premiers,
meanwhile, were less resolute as educational material had often been exempted from sales
tax payment and public support for the book lobbyists was pronounced. Furthermore, the
provinces have jurisdiction over education as well as responsibilities related to library systems and literacy efforts, all of which involve books and the literary communities within their
provinces. Support for exempting books was strong within the provinces. As New Brunswick
finance minister Edmond Blanchard acknowledged when asked about the possibility of an
exempted commodity, "New Brunswickers have made it very clear to us that item should be
the tax on books."[30]

Intense intergovernmental negotiation ensued and a compromise was found in the agreement reached in October. Schools, universities, and libraries will get a 100 percent rebate of
tax paid on book purchases. A rebate allows the tax to be assessed, but stipulates that it
then be automatically cancelled out. The provinces also opted to include a rebate of the
provincial portion of the harmonized tax (8 percent of the 15 percent harmonized tax) for all
other book buyers. This was not the only departure from full-scale harmonization as illustrated by Nova Scotia's intent to include a 1.5 percent rebate on tax paid for new home purchases. These amendments to harmonization raise concerns about future growth of tax
exemptions. The *Globe and Mail*'s Barrie McKenna summed it up this way, "Federal officials argue that rebates are compatible with a common base and don't unduly inflate administration costs. But critics worry that the precedent established in Atlantic Canada may
open the door for further customization if or when other provinces come on board."[31]

The deal reached in October included a joint technical paper to explain the administrative details. Save for the already noted rebates, the basic outline of the deal reflected the
understandings contained in the MOU. Harmonization with the three provinces would be implemented on April 1, 1997. The term *blended sales tax,* or *BST,* also came into use, however subsequent opposition attacks on the so-called BS Tax may lead to a short shelf-life for
this label. Tax inclusive pricing was to be implemented by businesses to combat "sticker
shock" at the cash register. Administration of both provincial and federal sales taxes would
be unified.

Interprovincial differences and competition also marked the political debates over the tax
harmonization agreement. Among the Atlantic partners there was jockeying for the head-

quarters of the centralized collection centre for the new tax administration.[32] Among the rest of the country, reaction critical of regional favouritism emerged. Protests that commenced back at the time of the MOU's signing continued to simmer. They served as a backdrop to the widespread public and media condemnation of the Chrétien government's retention of the GST, which they had once so bitterly attacked.

In the spring Alberta's premier, Ralph Klein, issued a public letter to the prime minister condemning the harmonization agreement as an unacceptable federal accommodation towards the Atlantic provinces.[33] Klein was the most outspoken voice, but his western and territorial counterparts shared his opposition. Meeting in the Yukon in early June, they called for a review of federal tax collection policies. Interesting enough this theme of resentment articulated in the West was shared by separatist-leaning Quebec MPs and Ontario's Conservative provincial government. Michel Gauthier, Bloc Québécois leader, spoke out against the compensation payments to the Atlantic governments. He challenged Prime Minister Chrétien to justify the deal to the people of Quebec "when, despite their good faith and their being the first to harmonize their sales tax with the federal tax, they did not get the compensation the Maritimers got."[34] Ontario's premier Mike Harris argued that harmonization at 15 percent would mean tax increases for his citizens at an inopportune time. Ontario has a relatively low provincial sales tax rate, excluding, of course, Alberta's complete absence of a sales tax. The Harris position was consistent with his government's right-wing agenda of tax cuts and smaller government. Despite the outcry, Paul Martin continued the federal push toward harmonization and endeavoured to counter his opponents. Unlike Chrétien, Martin sought to offer an apology of sorts for his party's inability to find an alternative plan for the GST. Negotiations were available for any province wishing to discuss the matter. There was no undue intent to benefit Atlantic Canadians at the expense of others beyond the traditional and constitutional (*Constitution Act of 1982*, sec. 36) recognition that disadvantaged provinces receive assistance.

Premiers McKenna (New Brunswick), Tobin (Newfoundland), and Savage (Nova Scotia) journeyed to Toronto in mid-November to present the case for harmonization to the business community. Noting that harmonization would improve treatment for taxes paid on inputs to the production process and would simplify tax administration, the premiers went looking for prospective investors. Newfoundland's Tobin contended that harmonization meant that these provinces would have "the most efficient sales tax regime" in Canada.[35] Regional rivalry reached even into the Toronto visit, though. Each of the three Atlantic leaders went independently with prepared sales pitches for possible investors.

As of spring, 1997, the harmonization deal seems to be remaining generally on target. Yet, difficulties have arisen. Industries with products that had previously been exempt from sales tax application have articulated fears over negative repercussions. This kind of reaction generally develops whenever tax coverage is adjusted. National retailers have complained about having to adjust sales campaigns and catalogues for the special tax-inclusive pricing system. Presentation of differing pricing schemes for different regions (depending upon whether they were covered by a tax harmonization agreement) would become necessary. This group of critics has found a receptive audience among opposition politicians and senators.[36] In light of the growing outcry, compromises have been reached delaying tax inclusive pricing until more provinces are covered by harmonization deals. Arriving at this consensus has allowed the harmonization package to move more rapidly in the Senate. Despite these irritants, the basic federal-provincial deal of harmonization offset by federal financial compensation seems to be holding.

In light of business opinion, the New Brunswick government began agitating to remove the tax-inclusive pricing feature from the federal-provincial agreement and the corresponding enabling legislation. Alarmed over business unrest, they began lobbying the other parties to the deal. When a Senate committee reviewing harmonization toured Atlantic Canada late in the winter of 1997, New Brunswick finance minister Edmond Blanchard declared, "Can we do harmonization without tax-inclusive pricing? The answer is yes."[37] Faced with this reaction, supplemented by growing concerns on the part of the Newfoundland government, the federal Finance Department accepted the delay of tax-inclusive pricing.

CONCLUSION

Issues involving the fiscal dimension of Canadian federalism are complex, controversial, and often conflictual. Compromise is difficult to arrive at and usually involves compromise on everyone's part. Sales tax application and reform is one example of this set of tendencies at work.

As a specific case study, sales tax reform offers food for further evaluation. Preparations for the harmonization of federal and provincial sales taxes are well under way in the case of four provinces (Quebec and three of the Atlantic provinces). Simultaneously, observers from across the country are keenly watching the experiences with co-ordinated tax administration. Federal officials persist meanwhile in efforts to win over further converts. The odds against their success are high, but the administrative and political advantages would be significant. At the same time, consumers and commercial concerns strive to keep up with developments and defend their interests. How all these forces interact continues to make for a fascinating study.

The detailed look at the harmonization negotiations and ultimate federal agreement with the three Atlantic provinces provides a microcosm of the broader forces of competition and political rivalry that mark intergovernmental negotiations over matters of public finance. Economic circumstances in the different parts of the country dictate differing sets of objectives and strategies for dealing with the federal government. Ottawa cannot dictate that the provinces agree to its every proposal. Understanding how these pressures interact on a selected issue like sales tax reform will facilitate exploration of other major topics in the field of fiscal federalism—the future of equalization, declining federal transfers, etc. Fiscal federalism remains a field with much to explore.

NOTES

I would like to acknowledge the assistance of Norman Campbell and Allan Maher. They are not responsible, of course, for any errors of interpretation. Their advice was very beneficial and their co-operation was appreciated.

1. R. MacGregor Dawson, *The Government of Canada*, 5th ed., revised by Norman Ward (Toronto: University of Toronto, 1973); 99.

2. Perhaps the best simple description of the structure and working of the GST is offered by the Canadian Tax Foundation's annual publication, *Finances of the Nation*. See, for example, Karin Treff and Ted Cook, *1995 Finances of the Nation* (Toronto: Canadian Tax Foundation, 1995), pp. 5:1–3.

3. Treff and Cook, *1995 Finances of the Nation*, p. 5:1.

4. 12 App. Cas. 575. The British Judicial Committee of the Privy Council ruled in favour of a tax on corporations levied by Quebec.

5. Peter H. Russell, Rainer Knopff, and Ted Morton, *Federalism and the Charter: Leading Constitutional Decisions* (Ottawa: Carleton University Press, 1989), 111.

6. Quoted in Russell, Knopff, and Morton, *Federalism and the Charter*, 115.

7. Ibid., 113.

8. This is drawn from the calculations and estimates reported in Treff and Cook, *1995 Finances of the Nation*, p. 5:5.

9. Ibid., 5:4

10. White papers are an example of governmental policy devices known as "coloured papers," which are efforts by government to indicate its thinking on issues and to promote public as well as federal-provincial debate in advance of detailed legislative proposals. See, for example, pp. 146–8 in Kenneth Kernaghan and David Siegel, *Public Administration in Canada*, 3rd ed. (Scarborough: Nelson, 1995).

11. Allan M. Maslove, "The Goods and Services Tax: Lessons from Tax Reform," in Katherine A. Graham, ed., *How Ottawa Spends 1990–91: Tracking the Second Agenda* (Ottawa: Carleton University Press, 1990), 29.

12. W. Irwin Gillespie, *Tax, Borrow and Spend: Financing Federal Spending in Canada 1867–1990* (Ottawa: Carleton University Press, 1991), 217.

13. Gillespie, *Tax, Borrow and Spend*, 219–20.

14. Maslove, "The Goods and Services Tax," 28.

15. Hugh Winsor, "Wilson's Work Cut Out Selling Tax to Public," the *Globe and Mail,* April 21, 1989, A15.

16. Treff and Cook, *1995 Finances of the Nation,* p. 5:5.

17. Alasdair Roberts and Jonathan Rose, "Selling the Goods and Services Tax: Government Advertising and Public Discourse in Canada," *Canadian Journal of Political Science* 28, no. 2 (June 1995), 311–30.

18. Gillespie, *Tax, Borrow and Spend*, 224.

19. Maslove, "The Goods and Services Tax," 34.

20. Material for this paragraph is drawn from Treff and Cook, *1995 Finances of the Nation*, p. 5:4.

21. Reprinted in the Saint John *Telegraph Journal,* May 24, 1996, A13.

22. Quoted in Edward Greenspon and Anthony Wilson-Smith, *Double Vision: The Inside Story of the Liberals in Power* (Toronto: Doubleday, 1996), 373.

23. Quoted in Ninth Report of the Standing Committee on Finance, *Replacing the GST: Options for Canada* (Ottawa: Canada Communication Group, 1994), 1.

24. Quoted in Don Richardson, "Atlantic Premiers' Snap Summit Puts Single Sales Tax on the Table," the *Telegraph Journal,* March 30, 1996, A1.

25. "Atlantic Provinces to Study Tax Merger," the *Globe and Mail*, April 1, 1996, A4.

26. Alan Jeffers, "Agreement Coming Soon on Tax Harmonization," the *Evening Telegram*, April 15, 1996, 1.

27. New Brunswick Government Information Package Insert—"Harmonization: What's in It for New Brunswick?" (Spring 1996), 1.

28. Finance Canada, *News Release 96-035* (April 23, 1996), 8.

29. Stephen McKinley, "Callbeck Isn't Ready to Harmonize Taxes," the *Telegraph Journal*, May 13, 1996, A4.

30. Don Richardson, "Province Joins Battle to Have Tax Removed from Books," the *Telegraph Journal,* September 4, 1996, A5.

31. Barrie McKenna, "Tax Harmony on Long Road," the *Globe and Mail*, October 28, 1996, B1.

32. Note, for example, the appearance of the following press report at the time of the October harmonization agreement, Dale Madill, "N.B. Siphons Off BST Centre Jobs," the *Chronicle-Herald*, October 23, 1996, A1.

33. Barrie McKenna, "Klein Demands Lower GST Rate for Alberta," the *Globe and Mail*, May 3, 1996, B1.

34. *House of Commons Debates,* April 24, 1996, 1888.

35. Bruce Little, "Atlantic Premiers Tout Their Advantage," the *Globe and Mail*, November 20, 1996, B7.

36. Note, for example, Laura Eggerston, "Blended-Tax Bill Hits Snag as McKenna, Senate Balk," the *Globe and Mail*, March 11, 1997, B1, B4.

37. Quoted in Don Richardson, "N.B. Wants Out of Tax-In Pricing," the *Telegraph Journal,* March 10, 1997, A1.

P a r t

VI

CHALLENGES AND FUTURE DIRECTIONS

Federal systems of government are vulnerable to diverse challenges and pressures. The task of maintaining national unity amid decentralizing pressures (regionalism, interprovincial conflict, etc.) is a demanding assignment. So, too, is the effort to preserve regional prerogatives and distinctive local communities amid the centralizing forces of modern life (the widespread influence of American culture, corporate concentration, consolidation of national media chains, etc.) In the existence of these two sets of political tensions and the interplay between them, we find the source of many of the fundamental difficulties that surround Canadian political life. Sorting through and analyzing these tensions is a critical task.

Canada is undergoing major social, economic, and political changes. Dynamism and controversy are exhilarating, but there are threats lurking. Events in Quebec suggest that the very future of the country is in doubt. Heated debate ensues about economic direction and the role of government. National unity is an appealing slogan for many, but there often seem to be few shared national objectives or projects. Nation-building is frequently regarded as being at odds with province-building.

The following essays grapple with the assignment of exploring the key controversies and challenges at the core of the contemporary federal scene. They raise the disturbing problems which often perplex us as a country.

Some of the underlying difficulty is played out in the constitutional arena. Canadians have endured several gruelling rounds involving efforts to reform our governing arrangements. These leave a complex legacy not only for future participants, but also for the national psyche. Debate involves the interplay of French-English linguistic and cultural duality as well as disputes over the place of Quebec. This duality is widely sensed in Quebec, while elsewhere many people point to Canada's multicultural characteristics and aboriginal peoples, as well as emphasizing individual rights over the collective claims of cultural distinctiveness. Yet another depiction of the challenge facing the Canadian federation is offered through reference to central Canadian political and economic dominance and the hegemony of Ontario influences over economic policy-making. Reference is made to a string of issues (freight rates, tariff policy, energy pricing, etc.) wherein the concerns of outlying regions seem to have taken a back seat to the wishes of central Canadian elites.

The essays that follow represent three thoughtful and exciting presentations. It is not suggested, though, that they or any other three essays could encompass all ways of assessing the current federal malaise. The national political diet is replete with quarrels and historic antagonisms. These three essays mark insightful efforts to give meaning to the diverse winds blowing across the land. Students are encouraged to reflect upon the arguments presented and upon the possibilities for improvement.

Andrew Cohen offers his views on the legacy of the Meech Lake Accord effort at constitutional reform. During the period 1987–1990 the country was absorbed in the labour of assessing, and responding to, this initiative worked out in mid 1987 by Prime Minister Mulroney and the ten premiers of the time. Once agreed to by the first ministers, the Accord needed to be approved by all their respective governments and legislative bodies within three years, the constitutionally prescribed time limit. Early agreement gave way to discord as governments (those of New Brunswick, Manitoba, and Newfoundland) seemed to waver or edge into the opposition camp. Even a last-ditch week long bargaining session involving the first ministers in Ottawa on the eve of the 1990 deadline failed to generate sufficient momentum to have the Accord pass.

Central to the Accord was a list of basic demands put forth by the Liberal government of Quebec under Premier Robert Bourassa. Achievement of these would produce Quebec's formal approval of the constitutional agreements reached in 1981–82 by Prime Minister Trudeau and the other nine provincial governments. Quebec's demands were constructively received by the other provinces, who added a few touches of their own. The Meech Lake Accord's main provisions included recognition of Quebec as a distinct society, reaffirmation of Quebec's powers in the field of immigration, provision of lists from the provinces of names for Senate and Supreme Court appointments, guarantees of future federal-provincial first ministers' conferences, an increased range of items for which unanimous consent (federal and provincial governments) would be needed for constitutional amendment, and financial protection for provincial governments opting out of new federal cost-shared programs in areas of provincial jurisdiction. Critics of the package, including former prime minister Pierre Trudeau and former Newfoundland premier Clyde Wells, argued for an alternative vision emphasizing individual rights, provincial equality, and a nationalizing leadership role for the federal government.

Pierre Coulombe focusses upon the place of Quebec and its uneasy connections to national political life. Successive provincial governments have formulated strategies for preserving the province's culture, language, and governing authority. This quest has often led to confrontations with other elements within the country. When premiers René Lévesque (1976) and Jacques Parizeau (1995) conducted referendums on Quebec's place within Canada, the fires of political passions burned brightly. Liberal governments have also fought to guarantee provincial distinctiveness. Former premier Robert Bourassa rejected the constitutional reform project of the early 1970s associated with the Victoria Charter. More than a decade later he returned to the constitutional bargaining table with the Meech Lake round. In addition, he utilized the notwithstanding provisions of the Constitution Act, 1982, to protect use of the French language. Section 33 of the Constitution Act, 1982, is the notwithstanding clause which allows either the federal or a provincial government to pass a law notwithstanding the charter provisions of section 2 "Fundamental Freedoms," sections 7-14 "Legal Rights," or section 15 "Equality Rights," through the passage of a bill declaring the government's intention. (This can have effect for up to five years and may be renewed.)

John Conway offers a political-economy viewpoint that questions the elitist patterns of Canadian political life. This elite consensus has, he would argue, been dominated by a right-wing, pro-business orientation, a central Canadian bias, and a fear of popular democracy and referendums. His arguments are rooted in a portrait of Canada's Confederation and its emphasis upon establishing governments and institutions, not a truly open, participatory political community.

On the contemporary landscape, Conway fears a rising neoconservative tide. Neoconservatism is one of a number of labels given to the recent policy trend among governments that emphasizes limits upon government's role in the economy, deficit reduction, privatization of government corporations, freer international trade, and a general preference for marketplace solutions rather than government intervention. Sceptics fear a lack of government initiative will leave the disadvantaged without protection and will undermine the possibility of citizen involvement and community action.

Students attempting to grasp the social and economic arguments in the country at large should work to assess Conway's depiction of Canada's evolution. It stands as a position contrary to much of our traditional nation-building mythology.

DISCUSSION QUESTIONS

1. How do you feel about the provisions of the Meech Lake Accord that were designed to reconcile divisions between Canada and Quebec? What is your assessment of Cohen's arguments about the legacy of the Meech Lake Accord effort?

2. Is there necessarily a contradiction between the efforts of a provincial community to collectively protect their values or language and the modern emphasis on individualism and rights? Why or why not? How might we evaluate arguments made from these differing perspectives?

3. What might constitute a "distinct society"? Could we set out criteria of political distinctiveness?

4. How does the history or character of Quebec's culture compare with your sense of your own province? What has struck you about Quebec from your travels or reading?

5. How much do you think provincial governments *can do* to preserve a province's particular culture or language? How much *should* they do?

6. Assess the impact of the Quebec Referendums of 1980 and 1995. What influence have they had on Quebec society and on the Canadian political community?

7. Assess and explain John Conway's portrait of Canada's development. How does it compare with other accounts you may have heard or read?

8. Do you have any feelings about the appropriate role and range of activities for Canada's national government? Should it be involved in economic planning or should most decisions be left to the market?

9. Is Canada led by a central Canadian elite? What evidence or example(s) would you offer of elite influence?

10. Is Canada in a state of crisis? Why or why not? If you believe it is, what is your perception of (a) the nature of the crisis and (b) its fundamental character?

REVISITING THE MEECH LAKE ACCORD, TEN YEARS LATER

Andrew Cohen

On April 30, 1987, the premiers and the prime minister gathered in an Edwardian retreat on the shores of Meech Lake, a footprint of water in the Gatineau Hills of Quebec. Officially, the purpose of the meeting was to discuss changes to the Constitution that had emerged during months of unpublicized intergovernmental negotiations among senior civil servants. The expectation was that the meeting would be informal in tone, exploratory in content, inconclusive in outcome. Few observers, including most of the journalists waiting outside, thought it would produce much of substance. As Roland Penner, the attorney general of Manitoba, described the invitation from the prime minister, "Brian Mulroney just wrote us and said, 'Come down to Meech Lake for a little chat,' said the spider to the fly." And so Penner and his colleagues did.

The first ministers gathered at noon and met all afternoon. By late evening they had reached agreement on the five proposals put forward by the government of Quebec, and added two more. After five years of self-imposed isolation, Quebec had agreed to endorse the Constitution Act of 1982. When Brian Mulroney emerged that night to proclaim a new Age of Unity, he and his fellow nation-builders were jubilant. One by one, they stepped forward to applaud their vision and their patriotism.

To listen to the first ministers, the two solitudes had been reconciled. After years of threats and promises, the provinces and federal government had, in the space of an afternoon, re-organized the powers and responsibilities of Confederation. To its proud architects, the Meech Lake Accord was an epochal achievement, and epochal it would be.

Good or ill, something strange and wondrous had happened at Meech Lake. Although the Accord never became part of the Constitution, it became a statute of consciousness no less binding than a statute of law. Today it remains an emotional splinter in the national psyche, a lost opportunity to some and a residual fear to others. In death it remains divisive. Years later Pierre Trudeau and Lucien Bouchard were still blaming each other for the failure of Meech Lake with an antipathy that suggested both had supported it, though neither had.

A decade later, the waves from Meech Lake still break across the country's soul. The expectations it raised and the hopes it dashed endure. Historians may well see it as the division between the old and new Canadas, marking the last time that the first ministers were ready to make a deal, quickly and quietly, confident that they could deliver their electors. Today the discourse is so poisoned that even raising the Constitution—and the promise of reconciliation it once held—is incendiary.

Indeed, Meech Lake has become True North on the country's constitutional compass. Since the collapse of the Accord in June 1990, any subsequent proposal for constitutional change—from the omnibus Charlottetown Agreement of 1992 to the modest platform of the Quebec Liberal Party of 1996—has been measured in terms of the Meech Lake Accord. Does it offer more? Does it offer less? If it is less, it is certain to go nowhere in Quebec; and today, Meech Lake itself would not seem sufficient to Quebec nationalists.

For the champions of the Accord, which includes most of the political class, its failure was the failure of Canada. They said it then and they say it now. Had it passed, they argue, Canada would be bounding happily into the next century, addressing the social and economic challenges of the globalized world. For critics of the Accord, which polls suggest included most Canadians, the failure of the Accord was the salvation of Canada. Had it passed, they argue, Canada would be even more fragmented and unwieldy. Decentralization would be irreversible. There would still be a constitutional debate, and there would still be a separatist government in Quebec, presenting an endless set of demands. So would the rest of the provinces. Canada would still be in question, as it has been for most of its history.

Far from ending the unhappy conversation over the country's future, Meech Lake renewed it. It revisited the hoary struggle of rights and powers and stirred the ugly passions of separatism. The trouble with Meech Lake is that it wasn't just another constitutional failure, like the Victoria Conference of 1971 and others, which were forgotten. Meech Lake was an *aggressive* failure, which continues to resound as a high-pitched echo and a throbbing ache.

No other single event has so influenced the politics of Canada over the last decade. Following Meech Lake, the Liberals were defeated in Ontario in 1990. The Spicer Commission was created in 1991. The Charlottetown Accord was approved by the first ministers and rejected by the people in a national referendum in 1992. Brian Mulroney resigned and his Conservatives were obliterated in 1993. The Bloc Québécois was born, led by Lucien Bouchard. The Parti Québécois was elected in Quebec in 1994. The separatists won 49.4 percent of the vote in the provincial referendum in 1995. Subsequently, Parliament recognized Quebec as a distinct society and extended to it a constitutional veto.

In revisiting the Meech Lake Accord, contemplating the consequences of its adoption is as difficult as re-arguing the debate. Much as both sides like to cite the events of the last ten years to support their case, there is no definitive answer; examining the past here is as frustrating as divining the future anywhere else. As long as the country remains whole (and arguably, even if it were to splinter), the question remains speculative, which isn't to say that a self-absorbed people will not continue to ask it.

So, the questions. Had Meech Lake passed, would Canada be united and happy today, gazing into a cloudless sky and sunlit uplands? Would it have been spared the constitutional contortions, the referendums of 1992 and 1995, the dark warnings of the imminent apocalypse? Would the separatists in Quebec be in retreat, their referendum defeated, if it had even been held? Would Lucien Bouchard be prime minister in Ottawa, or practising law in Chicoutimi?

If is the longest word in the English language, longer still in contemplating Canada's constitutional angst.

During the three years of debate over the Accord, both sides argued their cases with steely confidence. Reviewing those arguments in light of the events of the last decade reveals the mythology that has grown up like a rain forest around the shores of Meech Lake. To illustrate what might have happened in Canada had Meech Lake passed, let us consider two of the more prominent arguments in favour of the Accord.

The first argument was that Meech Lake identified Quebec's traditional demands and finally addressed them. Ottawa had thought that it knew what Quebec wanted when it proposed the Fulton-Favreau Formula and the Victoria Charter, both of which Quebec rejected. Ottawa thought it knew when Quebec agreed to join seven other provinces in April 1981 and give up its constitutional veto. Ottawa thought it knew when successive governments of Quebec, of different political stripes, embraced *égalité* or independence, *deux nations*, profitable federalism, or the distinct society.

What made Meech Lake so different, the Fathers of Re-Confederation argued in 1987, was that this time Quebec had asked and Canada had answered. As Brian Mulroney and the premiers claimed, "Canada said yes to Quebec. Quebec said yes to Canada." The message was that Meech Lake would satisfy Quebec. It would end an enervating discourse, if not forever, at least for now.

Having won concessions at Meech Lake, Quebec would go home satisfied. Its historic demands would be met. Its desire for respect and recognition would be answered. Quebec would become a full, functioning member of Confederation. No more humiliations, no more empty chairs at conferences. Quebec would no longer be *demandeur* and petitioner. For Canada, post–Meech Lake, this would be the end of asking, as seminal to the United States, post–Cold War, as the end of history.

While few would say that Meech Lake would stop the constitutional carousel, that was the popular expectation. Of the many arguments marshalled by supporters, this was the most appealing. "Meech would've solved the problem, and it was a modest little accommodation, symbolic," said David Peterson, the former premier of Ontario, years later.[1] The prospect of resolving this tiresome question, finally and completely, was attractive to a country that had been absorbed by wasting constitutional discussion for a quarter century. After nine years of a separatist government in Quebec between 1976 and 1985, after a referendum on sovereignty-association in 1980, after "the exclusion" of Quebec in 1982, after four unsuccessful rounds in 1968, 1971, 1978, 1979, who wouldn't have embraced the promise of constitutional peace?

The message of Meech Lake, though, was far different in Quebec. It was portrayed there as a beginning, only a prelude, to something bigger. During the debate over Meech Lake in the National Assembly on June 23, 1987, Premier Robert Bourassa said to Jacques Parizeau, "May I remind the Leader of the Opposition that there will be a second round?" He added: "I say to the leader when he begins to cite a number of areas not yet settled, there will be another round of negotiations."[2]

Bourassa had always re-affirmed the right of Quebecers "to put an end to the federal union with Canada" if it did not satisfy them. In other words, Meech Lake would not bring constitutional peace. As Pierre Trudeau put it, here was a man who had just signed a marriage contract re-affirming his right to file for divorce. No, this wasn't the end of it; indeed, it wasn't even a moratorium on constitutional discussion, which would have been a reasonable expectation. Always one to keep his options open, Bourassa was preparing to ask for more.

This position, however subtle its expression, never really changed in the life of Meech Lake. A month before the Accord collapsed in 1990, Quebec Justice Minister Gil Rémillard told an audience in Paris that "the Quebec government wanted to establish on a solid basis the foundations of a comprehensive constitutional reform to come in a second stage of negotiations."[3] As William Johnson points out, this was not stated clearly at the time. How could it be? To do so would be to make liars of the premiers and the prime minister, who wanted their publics to believe something else. If Meech Lake had become a junk bond in English Canada, it was still a promissory note in Quebec.

The key to a stronger Quebec was the distinct society clause. What was seen as symbolic to the premiers (Don Getty of Alberta dismissed it as "window dressing") was seen as fundamental by Quebec. Robert Bourassa billed it as the key to more powers even without that anticipated second round. "It cannot be stressed too strongly that the entire Constitution, including the Charter, will be interpreted and applied in the light of the section proclaiming our distinctiveness as a society," he told the National Assembly on June 18, 1987. "As a result, in the exercise of our legislative jurisdictions we will be able to consolidate what has already been achieved, and gain new ground."[4]

But even if Quebec had not demanded another round of talks, the other premiers would have. From the beginning, when they met at their annual conference in Edmonton in 1986, the premiers had declared that the next round was to be the Quebec Round, addressing Quebec's agenda. (As it turned out, that wasn't quite so; worried about charges of granting Quebec special status, all provinces got what Quebec got, other than the distinct society). Now, having satisfied themselves that they had satisfied Quebec, the other provinces wanted to address their concerns. To that end, they entrenched in the Constitution an annual federal-provincial conference on the Constitution. The first two items were to be Senate reform and "the roles and responsibilities of the fisheries." In addition, they entrenched an annual conference on the economy and "other matters."

Thus, the premiers committed themselves to talking about the Constitution *ad infinitum*. This provision virtually ensured that the provinces and the federal government would meet twice a year to discuss the same two items; the meetings would be called whether or not they were necessary. The provision mandated debate and enshrined discord. As constitutional scholar Peter Hogg warned, "changing the Constitution is a stressful and time-consuming exercise which should be attempted only occasionally, and only when there is reason to believe in the likelihood of success."[5] The premiers disregarded that advice. Section 148 would have obliged them to return to the agenda year after year, regardless of political conditions or public interest.

Any suggestion, then, that Meech Lake would bring an end to the discussion was belied by the declarations of the government of Quebec, which promised a second round, and by the wording of the Accord, which required one. Here was the new muscle of executive federalism. Had Meech Lake passed, it isn't hard to imagine how things would have unfolded. Each year the first ministers, acting as a *directoire*, would have been summoned to their two conferences, the ten premiers ranged against the prime minister. Each meeting would have provided an opportunity for the provinces to advance their regional agendas, whether it was the Senate or the fishery or property rights or job training. And each time Quebec would have used its newly acquired veto over changes to federal institutions (such as reforming the

Senate and introducing proportional representation in the Commons) to block those changes outright or to seek concessions elsewhere in exchange for its support.

Perhaps the two levels of government might have decided to cancel these meetings. If so, they would have had to issue the same disclaimer every year, akin to invoking the notwithstanding clause (which allows government to pass legislation that contravenes the Charter by opting out of some of its sections.) Even without Meech Lake, it is important to remember that the first ministers would have had to review the Constitution in 1997 under the terms of the Constitution Act of 1982. That was only one meeting, and it could have been dispensed with by a conference call. (Some suggested that it had when the prime minister and the premiers met in 1996 and discussed constitutional change for five minutes.) In contrast, the meetings mandated by Meech Lake would have been unrelenting, offering a bi-annual forum for the provinces to confront the federal government. Given the psychology of these meetings, this would, over time, have enhanced the stature of the provinces in Confederation and weakened the central authority.

If there is any doubt about Quebec's appetite for more powers, recall how that appetite grew after Meech Lake. The commission established in 1991 by the Quebec Liberal Party and chaired by Jean Allaire demanded the federal government transfer virtually every remaining power to the province, including exclusive control over unemployment insurance, agriculture, the environment, and health. It would have left Ottawa with defence, customs, currency and debt, and equalization. Some of these powers demanded by Allaire would certainly have appeared on Bourassa's wish list in the next round.

Sharon Carstairs, the leader of the Manitoba Liberal Party, who had strongly opposed the Accord but had relented under intense pressure during the negotiation in June 1990, eventually saw the Allaire Report as proof of the Quebec Liberal Party's hidden agenda: "There was a naiveté among first ministers. They seemed to believe that if Quebec obtained what it wanted through the Meech Lake Accord it would then go away satisfied, and Canada would go happily into the twenty-first century without further constitutional wrangling. My opinion was that if Quebec obtained all they wanted in the Meech Lake Accord this would simply whet their appetite, and demands for more power would quickly follow. Allaire substantiated my thinking in spades."[6]

As for the Charlottetown Agreement, Bourassa said repeatedly that he could never have accepted it if it hadn't offered more than the Accord. But if polls were correct, Quebecers rejected it in 1992 because it didn't offer enough. In fact, every government in Quebec in recent memory had asked for more than Bourassa did at Meech Lake. Given Quebec's historic demands and the rise of provincialism elsewhere, it is hard to believe that the provisions of Meech Lake, modest as they were said to be, would ever have been enough.

Indeed, it is also unclear that Meech Lake was ever what Quebec truly wanted, whatever Bourassa's claims. As political scientist Max Nemni argues, more than 80 percent of the briefs submitted to the National Assembly during its hearings on the Accord opposed it.[7] And while Quebecers initially supported the Accord, their support declined sharply in the months before its collapse on June 23, 1990. On balance, the Accord was probably the maximum that Robert Bourassa thought he could get from Canada and the minimum he could sell to Quebec. But let there be no misunderstanding: for Bourassa, Meech Lake was always a floor, not a ceiling.

The second argument for the Accord flowed from the first. Pass Meech Lake, Canadians were told, and it would stem the tide of separatism. Reject it and renew separatism, and break up Canada. The chorus of Cassandras was led by Brian Mulroney, echoed by the premiers, and the political and business establishment. As former prime minister Kim Campbell recalls in her memoirs, Mulroney predicted another referendum in Quebec after Jacques Parizeau came to power. "If that referendum succeeded, as the PM knew very well it was likely to do, what would we say to our children when they asked, 'You mean all this could have been avoided if Meech Lake had been ratified?'"[8]

This was the refrain that so antagonized Clyde Wells as premier of Newfoundland. In the talks in Ottawa in June 1990, he was warned that if he didn't go along he would destroy Canada. As one premier put it, when Wells said he'd resign if he were wrong, "I said, "Clyde, you are immaterial to this whole thing. We all are. If the deal fails, the country's gone, so who cares if you resign?'"[9]

Joe Ghiz, the premier of Prince Edward Island, put it this way: "I really believe in my heart that unless Quebec is reconciled, it will go. It's not scaremongering. Any reasonable interpretation of our history cannot lead to any other conclusion."[10]

Of course, many said that was scaremongering. The dark warnings about the consequences of reconciling Quebec on these terms or losing the country started with Meech Lake. They were repeated in the referendum campaign over the Charlottetown Agreement in 1992, and reverberate today, sotto voce, among those who insist that re-opening the Constitution is the only way to satisfy Quebec and save Canada.

That Meech Lake failed and that Canada survives is a matter of fact, not conjecture, one of the few demonstrable truths in this debate. That Canada did come within a hair's breath of rupture—assuming that Quebec would have declared independence had the secessionists won the referendum on October 30, 1995—is also fact rather than conjecture. Would passing Meech Lake have disarmed or deflected the separatist movement, as some maintain? Or, did the failure of Meech Lake actually renew separatism in Quebec, bringing Canada closer to collapse than ever?

To argue that Meech Lake would have doused the fires of separatism is optimistic at best. It implies that Quebec, having won that much-coveted recognition as a distinct society, would have lived happily ever after in Canada, even if the courts were to rule subsequently that the distinct society clause didn't make Quebec that distinct after all. It implies as well that the Parti Québécois never would have been returned to power, and if it had, that it would have abandoned its long-standing commitment to sovereignty. Lastly, it implies that the Quebec Liberals—or any other avowedly federalist provincial government in the future— would have stopped asking for more powers from Ottawa, and if they did not, that at least they would have given up using the threat of separation as leverage to gain more.

To accept all that is to live in a fool's paradise. Only a Pollyanna could believe that Meech Lake would have silenced the separatists for very long. In the absence of a credible alternative to the Liberals, the Parti Québécois would have come to power sooner or later in Quebec's two-party system. Had Robert Bourassa not been diagnosed with cancer, it is conceivable that he might have run and won re-election in 1994. But he would have run against the odds, knowing that no government of Quebec had won a third consecutive term since 1951.

Assuming the Meech Lake Accord had passed, the Péquistes presumably would have campaigned differently. True, the success of Meech Lake would have robbed them of another "humiliation" at the hands of English Canada and denied them another helpful example of the failure of federalism. Given a quiescent public in 1994, they might have recast themselves as moderates, purporting to honour the wishes of Québécois and promising change within the system, playing down sovereignty as René Lévesque did in the election of 1981, months after he lost his referendum on sovereignty-association.

But that mask of moderation would have fallen eventually. Once in power the PQ was certain to search for offence. Having found or fabricated it, the secessionists would have picked up their soiled banner and returned to their agenda. With apologies to Joe Ghiz: any interpretation of our history could not lead to any other conclusion. The *raison d'être* of the Parti Québécois is sovereignty, and Jacques Parizeau was an unreconstructed sovereigntist. He quit the party in 1984 after it refused to take a tougher line on independence, and he resigned as premier the day after he lost the referendum in 1995. Meech Lake or not, he did not come to office to collect a salary and cut ribbons; his sole purpose, his *idée fixe*, was to take Quebec out of Canada.

Had the Péquistes come to power in the Canada of Meech Lake, not only would they have pursued that second round of constitutional negotiations Bourassa had promised, they would have used it to frustrate and challenge federalism at every turn. To this mischievous end, the provisions of the Accord—such as the right of the province to nominate judges and senators, to opt out of federal spending programs with compensation, and to claim a quarter share of Canada's annual immigration—would have strengthened their hand. But their greatest weapon would have been the distinct society, a chisel Parizeau and his confederates would have used to chip away at Confederation.

Like Bourassa's Liberals, the Péquistes would have invoked Quebec's distinctiveness to justify seeking more power from the federal government over banking, communications, culture, language, job training, and foreign policy, to name just a few areas. They would have launched a series of court challenges, forcing the courts to define, in each instance, what the distinct society meant and what power it conferred. The Parti Québécois never hid its intentions here. In an interview on October 25, 1989, Parizeau said: "If we come to power, there is no doubt that I'm going to use [the distinct society clause] ... for everything that it's worth. It's remarkable how much one could get through that clause if the courts say, Well, yes, in some circumstances, it can override certain dispositions of the Charter of Rights. If the courts ever say that, my God, what a weapon it could be for people who have the sort of—shall we say, political project that I have."[11]

It would have been disturbing enough for federalists if the Supreme Court began ruling in favour of Quebec, a prospect enhanced by the presence of three sympathetic judges on the bench from Quebec, which a separatist government in Quebec would have insisted on nominating. (True, the federal government could have refused to appoint Quebec's nominees. But for how long? Worried about giving the separatists a pretext for another humiliation, Ottawa would probably have relented.) Over time—albeit a long time—power would have shifted to the province, undermining the Charter of Rights.

But what if the courts had said no to Quebec, ruling in case after case that the distinct society offered no new legislative authority to the National Assembly? What of the backlash then? Rest assured the day the high court issued such a judgment, an enraged Jacques Parizeau would have leapt to his feet in the National Assembly, claiming that the distinct society was the empty promise that all the premiers had said it was—all, that is, but Robert Bourassa—and that Quebecers had been misled in the worst sort of deceit and treachery.

Pierre Trudeau had warned of just that when he testified against the Accord in 1987. "We have made peace with Quebec by letting it believe that 'distinct society' means Two

Nations. If the courts hold that it does have that meaning, Canada is doomed. If they hold otherwise, Quebec will have been tricked, and the howls of protest will strengthen separatism."[12]

There is another interpretation here. Supporters of the Accord argued that the courts would not have interpreted the clause broadly. As critics of Meech Lake cited constitutional scholars who argued that it would confer power on Quebec, supporters produced their own scholars denying it conferred any at all. It is possible that the Supreme Court would have interpreted the clause narrowly, which would have given Quebec no substantial new powers. And it is also possible that Quebecers, uninterested in arcane judicial questions, would never have cared, content with the symbolic recognition implied by the "distinct society." Perhaps.

Looked at this way, the critics of the Accord were alarmist; Trudeau overstated the dangers of Meech Lake as he overstated the dangers of the notwithstanding clause, which did not substantially weaken the Charter over its first fifteen years. While Meech Lake had flaws—the process was secretive, the salesmanship was poor, the wording was unchangeable, the period of ratification by the provinces was too long—it was unfairly maligned. Moreover, given the price of accommodating Quebec at Charlottetown, let alone today, the minimalist Accord was a bargain.

The case for adopting Meech Lake, then, is not that it was good law-making, but that it was fundamental nation-building. It takes time and space to accommodate two peoples, and Meech Lake would have created a little of both. Indeed, the Accord would have bought peace.

The argument is that Meech Lake would have neutralized the anger and silenced the debate long enough to allow Quebecers to feel more comfortable about their place in Canada. Kim Campbell argues that the social transformation in Quebec that began with the Quiet Revolution is not over. Despite the secularization of society, there is still an ethnocentric view of history and a demonization of anglophone society that is at the core of separatist ideology. Her hope was that as Quebecers began to see Canada more favourably, they would become less defensive. "I supported Meech because I thought that if we could buy another 20 years to complete the opening up of Quebec, the result would be a strong, united, vibrant Canada," she writes.[13]

That argument has been made often over the last decade, most effectively when the country was in crisis, as it was during the Quebec referendum. There is a wistful, hopeful quality to it, suggesting that if Meech Lake had passed, we would have erected a bridge of understanding across the gulf separating the solitudes. In the narrowest of votes, who can say that adopting Meech Lake might not have fostered enough goodwill among Quebecers to have given the federalists a modest margin of victory? Who is to say that margin might not have dealt the separatists enough of a body blow to deflate the issue, as the first referendum seemed to do in 1980? Given polls showing a strong affection for Canada among Quebecers, even as they resolved to leave, it is a strong argument. Still, only politicians and dreamers believe the referendum would have put separatism to rest for very long. After all, the one in 1980 didn't.

Ten years later, we can argue that passing Meech Lake would have bought time to accommodate Quebec. Or we can argue that it would have ended the constitutional debate or eliminated the threat of separatism. Beyond those central questions, what of the ebb and flow of events and the rise and fall of parties and politicians whose fortunes were linked to the success or failure of Meech Lake? Like George Bailey in the Hollywood film, *It's a*

Wonderful Life, we wonder how Canada would have been different if the Meech Lake Accord had never been written, or, if it had been written and adopted.

Contrary to what Brian Mulroney and others maintained, Meech Lake did not have to happen when it did. There was no pressing need to re-open the Constitution in 1987. It was scarcely five years after patriation, and separatism was at its nadir. Robert Bourassa allowed later that there was no need for him to act at all. "We could have waited until next year. We could have waited until after the next federal election," he said in 1990. "We were under no pressure."[14]

In the end, re-opening the Constitution without completing it proved to be worse than letting it lie dormant. The failure of Meech Lake gave the separatists new hope and new life. By the time Meech Lake failed in 1990, support for sovereignty in Quebec surpassed 50 percent.

But to argue that the failure of Meech Lake single-handedly resuscitated separatism isn't to say that separatism was ever truly dead. As we have noted, the Parti Québécois would have returned to power eventually and embraced independence, even it were to be called something else. The key difference is that the PQ wouldn't have had a cause to exploit (the failure of Meech Lake) or a new power to wield (the legislative authority conferred by the distinct society clause). Separatism would have been denied both of the conditions necessary for its revival. In the meantime, in a world without Meech Lake, we would have hoped that the forces of globalization would have encouraged an increasingly confident Quebec to recognize the value of aligning itself with Canada in the modern world, understanding the increasing limitations of sovereignty at the end of the century. Looked at in this light, if Canada had wanted to buy time to maintain the peace, surely the best way would have been to ignore the Constitution entirely.

Raising the issue opened Pandora's Box and unleashed the demons. The debate over Meech Lake—from the process to the substance—ignited what Keith Spicer called "a fury in the land." Of course, it wasn't the Meech Lake Accord alone that angered Canadians. A cocktail of explosive issues—the recession, free trade, deregulation, deficits, the Goods and Services Tax—all conspired to produce this reign of discontent in the peaceable kingdom.

But Meech Lake became a lightning rod for all that Canadians disliked about their government, and it helped realign power in Canada in 1993. Provincially, the first casualty of Meech Lake was the Liberals in Ontario, who had enjoyed staggering popularity in their five years in power. David Peterson was seen as having been too generous at Meech Lake and that helped defeat his government in September 1990. As it happened, almost all the premiers who signed the Accord were gone within five years. Richard Hatfield of New Brunswick was defeated in 1987, Howard Pawley of Manitoba in 1988 and Grant Devine of Saskatchewan in 1991. Brian Peckford resigned in 1989, John Buchanan and William Vander Zalm in 1990, and Robert Bourassa in 1994. All their governments were subsequently defeated. Joe Ghiz, John Buchanan, and Don Getty retired in 1993, and their successors were re-elected.

The reasons for the change in leadership varied by province. But it is safe to say that Meech Lake soured the public mood and discredited the political class. For most of the politicians associated with the Accord, Meech Lake dealt a blow from which they never recovered.

Of all the casualties, the most dramatic was Brian Mulroney and his party. Mulroney had twice tried to orchestrate constitutional change and he had twice failed. He resigned in 1993, and when asked about his greatest disappointment, he cited the failure of Clyde Wells to pass the Accord. The Conservatives were reduced to two seats in the federal election that year, the greatest loss ever suffered by a political party in Canada.

As some political parties melted away in the fires of Meech Lake, others rose from their ashes. The Reform party drank from the well of anger; its opposition to concessions to Quebec and its call for a new Canada of equal provinces helped it win 52 seats, all but one of them in western Canada. But the real child of Meech Lake was the Bloc Québécois. Founded by disaffected Liberals and Conservatives, it won 54 seats in a five-party Parliament and became the official Opposition.

It is easier to argue that without Meech Lake there would have been no Bloc Québécois than that there would have been no referendum in Quebec. The party's raison d'être is the defence of Quebec's interests in Ottawa and its roots are clearly set in the frustration over the collapse of the Accord (though Bouchard had left the government before the Accord died). Had Meech Lake passed, Lucien Bouchard might well have stayed in Ottawa, conceivably succeeding Brian Mulroney. Given his opportunism and ability, he might have been prime minister of Canada today rather than le *premier ministre de Québec.*

Bouchard was not the only beneficiary of Meech Lake. Other critics of the Accord also gained stature and popularity. The three premiers who opposed the Accord at different stages—Frank McKenna in New Brunswick, Gary Filmon in Manitoba, and Clyde Wells in Newfoundland—were all returned to power. Wells retired in 1995. Filmon and McKenna remained in office in 1997. Elijah Harper, who stopped the Accord in Manitoba, entered federal politics in 1993. Lastly, there was Pierre Trudeau. Unique among prime ministers, Trudeau continued to wield enormous influence as a private citizen. Through his best-selling books and telling public statements, he articulated his unwavering vision of Canada and rejected the revisionism of the nationalists, much to the applause of English Canadians.

But even if the Reform party and the Bloc Québécois sprang whole or in part from Meech Lake, what has been their lasting impact on Canadian politics? In 1997, it is still uncertain. The Reform party probably has shaped the political agenda adopted piecemeal by the Liberals, who have moved right on the deficit, taxation, immigration, and crime. But its popular support hasn't grown and it remains a Western party, even as official Opposition. The Bloc Québécois, for its part, is a single-issue party. It had little impact as official Opposition. And its attack was so ineffectual in Parliament during the referendum campaign—what was to be its defining moment—that Bouchard abandoned Ottawa to campaign in Quebec. While he is said to have reversed the direction of the campaign, it was the force of his personality, not the appeal of the party, which was decisive. After the referendum, the party lost not only its leader, but its *raison d'être.* In the 1997 federal election, its share of the vote dropped, it lost seats in Parliament, and it was dislodged as official Opposition.

What's vexing about revisiting Meech Lake ten years later is that rather than clarifying the issue, time has clouded it. A definitive referendum in 1995 would have emboldened those on either side of the divide to put their case more strongly. Had the separatists lost decisively, for example, critics would have taken that as proof that Quebecers, if not happily reconciled to Canada, had at least resolved to live within it. Had the separatists won decisively, supporters would have taken that as proof that Meech Lake—and Charlottetown—were the last, best hope for an honourable compromise. And so it goes.

What is undeniable is that Canada remains whole in 1997—despite the failure of two constitutional rounds in the last decade, despite a separatist official Opposition in Ottawa, despite a separatist government in Quebec, despite a near-loss in the referendum in 1995. What's more Canada remains secure, prosperous, tolerant, and democratic. Whatever the country's constitutional bugbear, it has managed since Meech Lake to lower its deficit, create jobs, absorb immigrants, restructure its economy, expand its foreign markets, create more wealth, and assert its voice in international councils. In other words, it remains a successful nation of imperishable promise, which, reluctant as Canadians are to celebrate it, is saluted by the United Nations and the international community.

That Meech Lake would have made any of this success more likely is improbable. That it would have fostered a stronger sense of nation and accommodated Quebec is even less probable. Rather than a shield of unity, the distinct society might well have become a sword of division. Quebec would have continued to retreat behind its walls, its people looking to Quebec City to protect its interests while the rest of the country gave up trying to accommodate them. Only to those who believe that Canada is inevitably two nations and can only survive with distance between them, is the passing of Meech Lake mourned.

More ominously, devolution would be further advanced and more deeply entrenched than it already is. It would be *de jure*, not *de facto*. In concert with Quebec, it is easy to imagine the other provinces arriving in Ottawa twice a year, eager to press their claims for more powers. The federal government would still be beholden to the provinces on the Senate and the Supreme Court and forced to compensate them for opting out of federal spending programs. (Having balanced its budget, the federal government would now be able to consider establishing new national social programs again, something thought unlikely in the deficit-ridden days of Meech Lake. The Accord would have frustrated them). If Ottawa is weak today, it would have been weaker still under Meech Lake.

The longer Canada endures, though, the more likely it is that Meech Lake will be seen as one struggle of many in Canada's Constitutional Wars. It is a struggle which could last indefinitely, having no discernible end and no discernible winner. Meanwhile, the country will survive and succeed. It goes to show that the fundamental lesson of the decade since the Meech Lake Accord is that Canada works better in practice than in theory.

NOTES

1. Patricia Best, "Citizen Peterson," *Toronto Life*, October 1995, 63.

2. Cited in Donald Johnston, ed., *With a Bang, Not a Whimper: Pierre Trudeau Speaks Out* (Toronto: Stoddart, 1988), 99.

3. Cited in William Johnson, *A Canadian Myth: Quebec, Between Canada and the Illusion of Utopia* (Montreal: Robert Davies Publishing, 1994), 210.

4. Cited in Johnston, ed., *With a Bang, Not a Whimper*, 85.

5. Peter Hogg, *Meech Lake Constitutional Accord Annotated* (Toronto: Carswell, 1988), 52.

6. Sharon Carstairs, *Not One of the Boys* (Toronto: MacMillan, 1993), 190.

7. Cited in Johnson, *A Canadian Myth*, 213.

8. Kim Campbell, *Time and Chance: The Political Memoirs of Canada's First Woman Prime Minister* (Toronto: Doubleday, 1996), 146.

9. Claire Joy, *Clyde Wells: A Political Biography* (Toronto: Stoddart, 1992), 201.

10. Andrew Cohen, *A Deal Undone: The Making and Breaking of the Meech Lake Accord* (Vancouver: Douglas and MacIntyre, 1990).

11. Cited in Johnson, *A Canadian Myth*, 211.

12. Pierre Trudeau before the parliamentary committee, May 27, 1987, cited in *With a Bang, Not a Whimper*, Johnston, ed., 35.

13. Campbell, *Time and Chance*, 127.

14. Cited in Cohen, *A Deal Undone*, 80.

QUEBEC IN THE FEDERATION

Pierre A. Coulombe

Students of Canadian federalism, however weary they may sometimes feel about timeworn conflicts involving Québec, cannot avoid looking into the intricacies of its place in the federation. To say this is not to endorse a vision of Canadian history that revolves around these conflicts, and to lay aside as peripheral issues those that relate to other aspects of the federal dynamic. The aboriginal issue—to name the one that evokes a special moral urgency—has certainly found its rightful place on the national agenda and in the minds of scholars old and new. That the Québec issue would be so enduring, aside from the sheer captivation it often resuscitates, has more to do with a sense that when we consider the future of the federation, the Québécois can make it or break it. Alongside former prime minister Pierre E. Trudeau's doctrine on federalism, this kind of realpolitik was certainly central to his conduct towards Québec. No doubt this also underlies the actions of today's political leaders in their attempts to preserve national unity, though at times, it can be surmised, without any profound accompanying vision of why federalism should matter.

It has become customary to ask, What does Québec want? But it should come as no surprise that there has never been any clear-cut answer. Québec has wanted different things, depending on when the question was asked and to whom it was addressed. To expect a single answer is to assume a monolithic view about Québec's ideal political status and to overlook the evolution of nationalist discourse over the last two centuries. It is an approach that also neglects the interactive dimension of Québec's aspirations, that is, how these have been partly shaped by what the rest of Canada also wants. Still, as shorthand for inquiring about what Québec's grievances (and praises) of federalism are all about, the question remains as relevant as its answers are multiple. We may try to sort out amongst these various answers those that have continuity over and above passing fads, and hope they can illuminate our understanding of the Québec-Canada relationship on the eve of the new millennium.

THE SEARCH FOR IDENTITY

When the Second World War ended, Québec society still was infused with a conservative ideology that elevated to the rank of mission the survival of the French-Canadian culture and Roman Catholic faith in North America. The control exercised by the church, not only in spiritual but in temporal matters as well, had allowed the ideology of survival to pervade various institutions. The educational system, a major agent of political socialization, was the prerogative of the clergy. Private schools, including the *écoles normales* (teachers' colleges), the elitist *collèges classiques*, and the universities were administered by the clergy, while Catholic public schools were governed by Catholic committees made up of a majority of clergy members. French Canadians learned they were the carriers of a language, culture, and faith that had to be transmitted to future generations. They found in an idealized view of rural life the conditions for survival, away from the evils of urbanization and industrialization, and looked upon clergy men and women for guidance. The influence of the church extended to labour unions as well. Following Pope Leo XIII's *Rerum Novarum* (1891), which encouraged greater solidarity of the church with workers, the Québec clergy had created Catholic unions—which incidentally also served to keep at bay international unions. The church thus provided French Canadians with a moral outlook by which they could lead their lives, as it were, insulated from the modern world.

How could it have been any different when we consider that the clergy was the only remaining elite the *Canadiens* could rely on after the British conquest of New France in 1760 left them with little or no political leadership of their own. Moreover, the great liberal revolutions in the United States and France did not take root in French Canada, despite calls from Americans to join them in their fight against the British. And any hope of building a liberal, secular society in Québec died along with the Patriotes' failure to overthrow the British in 1837 and to declare the independence of Lower Canada (present-day Québec). The church and its teachings from then on penetrated Québec's social, cultural, and political spheres and became an inescapable component of everyday life. Perhaps this was worth the price if it meant ensuring the survival of French Canada's social fabric. But it can also be said that the church stifled French-Canadian society and hindered its modernization.

By the time the 1950s came along, that was certainly the feeling among a growing number of critics of the dominant ideology, notably the *Cité libristes*. The dogmatism and authoritarianism of the church had indeed ensured the integrity of the nation, and its more conservative leaders intended to continue to do so with the blessings of the Union Nationale government of Maurice Duplessis. But it had also suppressed critical thinking under the weight of a rigid moral order that permeated cultural and intellectual life as well as political institutions. Besides, growing industrialization and urbanization were bringing about new challenges, and many felt the church was ill-equipped to meet the new demands. The Québécois increasingly felt alienated from an official ideology that no longer resonated in their daily lives. Within the church itself were progressive individuals who challenged the status quo. Among them was Montreal bishop Monsignor Charbonneau, who, during the Asbestos Strike of 1949, brutally repressed by the Duplessis government, called upon the church to support the working class against the regime, thus breaching the church-state alliance.

When Maurice Duplessis died in 1959, the forces of change could no longer be contained. Duplessis's popular successor, Paul Sauvé, had planned numerous reforms, but his premature death a few months later left the Union Nationale vulnerable to a more critical electorate.

The Liberals of Jean Lesage formed the new government in 1960, and some of the reforms they implemented would profoundly change the face of Québec society—a period aptly dubbed the Quiet Revolution. First on the agenda was an overhaul of the educational system, a task that was given to the commission of inquiry on education, led by Monsignor Parent, and to a star minister, Paul Gérin-Lajoie. It was decided that the new educational system would be accessible and secular. But also significant were the dramatic changes brought about by Vatican II between 1962 and 1965. Pope John XXIII wished to rejuvenate and modernize the church: recognizing the autonomy of the temporal realm, rediscovering the church's original vocation, democratizing the institution, insisting on Christian values rather than dogmas and rituals. These would have a profound impact on the secularization of Québec society, as freedom of conscience replaced the prefabricated answers to the questions of life, large and small. French Canadians would lose their moral leadership—not unlike the way they had lost their political leadership at the time of the conquest—and religiosity would be relegated to the private sphere. Religious practice dropped off, a number of men and women of the cloth left the priesthood, monastery, or convent, and recruiting novices became increasingly difficult.

The Quiet Revolution thus accelerated Québec's passage to modernity. The foundations of the public discourse would no longer be steeped in tradition, but in the domain of self-determined individuals, authors of their own lives. The pursuit of common ends would be the product of democratic public deliberation rather than being predetermined by history. Community would take second place to personal will. "Who I am" would be determined by "what I choose to be." The free development of individuality, not blind adherence to tradition, would now be considered the main ingredient of happiness and well-being. The breakdown of the French-Canadian cosmology therefore transformed the Québécois' sense of identity.

To say this, to some degree, is to say that Québec has become a province not unlike the others. At a deeper level at least, the Québécois want what other Canadians want, that is, material comfort, the freedom to choose life plans, and equality in the public sphere. But this is not to say that they have no claim to exist as a nation or to carry on their lives in their own political community—inside or outside Canada. Such a claim is not based on deep differences between the Québécois and other Canadians (as it was before the Quiet Revolution), nor is it based on a supposedly superior way of life (as was conveyed by the traditional clerical nationalism), but rather on a sense that their collective existence is simply their own. The claim is to distinctness, not difference or superiority.[1] It may very well be true that the youth of Montreal are just like the youth of Toronto, or that the truly different province in Canada is, say, Newfoundland, not Québec. But this remains a weak answer to modern claims to distinctness.

The new nationalism is also in sharp contrast to the old. Today's main nationalist current embraces a civic and pluralistic definition of the nation, where membership in the nation is not based on ethnic or historical criteria, but on the will to live in Québec. The contours of the Québec nation no longer overlap with those of the French-Canadian ethnolinguistic community. The French language today, to take the most salient feature of that identity, is detached from the Roman-Catholic faith and even from the French-Canadian culture. The promotion of French is unrelated to the realization of a special destiny, it is said, and officially has its source in the desire to integrate immigrants around a common public language. Now it may not be persuasive to state that modern nationalism has completely discarded the French-Canadian identity from its discourse. We could well argue, for instance, that such a justification for language laws is but a liberal rationalization rendered necessary by modern discourse, and that the wish to see the French language flourish is still rooted in *survivance*. Nonetheless the new moral vocabulary reflects profound changes in the ideological mind-set of the Québécois, not mere double-talk. Any analysis of contemporary Québec politics must take into account this modern identity.

THE SEARCH FOR POWER

Observers of the Québec-Canada relationship will doubtless see that the growth of modern nationalism in Québec has weighed heavily on the federal system. Province-building is one thing, nation-building quite another. But the strain is, after all, built into the system itself. When state sovereignty is divided between two orders of government, and when that is done in large measure to reassure a historical community of its right to continue to exist, even prosper, we should expect some friction as to how to go about sharing sovereignty. To be sure, there is an old quarrel about how to interpret the British North America Act of 1867. For some, the federation was to be a façade for a unitary system where the central government would be the locus of sovereignty and provinces mere administrative units. The sweeping powers given to the federal government in 1867 is evidence that this was not far indeed from the intentions of one of the architects of Confederation, namely, John A. Macdonald. For others, the federation was to reflect a genuine philosophy of federalism where each order of government would be sovereign within its own jurisdiction along with the corresponding financial resources. Ontario premier Oliver Mowat certainly subscribed to this vision when he led the provincial autonomy movement against the central power, claiming that the BNA Act was foremost a contract between colonies and hence the federal government a creation of provinces. That French Canadians would come to construe (rightly or wrongly) the founding document as reflecting a pact between French and English communities, needless to say, would contribute to the federal imbroglio.

The pact has deep historical roots in the collective memory. Already in 1774, the British had recognized the right to the distinct existence of the French and Roman Catholic people within its North American empire. In the face of growing uneasiness in the Thirteen Colonies, it was felt that ensuring the loyalty of the *Canadiens* required that the policy of the 1763 Royal Proclamation be reversed. Thus the Québec Act re-established civil law, the seigniorial system, and the right of the church to collect tithes, while the oath of allegiance to the Church of England as a prerequisite for holding office was abolished. This was in itself in continuity with previous forms of accommodations. Under military rule (1759–63), the articles of capitulation had provided for the free exercise of the Roman Catholic religion and for most of the laws of the French regime to continue to be in effect. Even the terms of the Royal Proclamation were not applied to the letter, owing to Governor James Murray's admiration for the *Canadiens* and his desire to disrupt as little as possible their way of life. When hard-liner Guy Carleton was called to replace the governor judged too lax, he eventually developed the same respect for the French. The next step was to grant the colony its own elected assembly. The immigration of Loyalists to western Québec (present-day Ontario) prompted the authorities in 1791 to separate the colony in two, Upper Canada and Lower Canada, each with its own Parliament. The drawback was the lack of responsible government, which led to political unrest in 1837–38. Following the famous investigation of the rebellions by Lord Durham, who felt that the source of the problem was the lack of responsible government and past attempts to preserve the French nationality, the British abandoned the policy of accommodation and adopted one of assimilation under the 1840 Act of Union. The act implemented responsible government, but also provided for a single assembly that underrepresented the French. The British had not foreseen, however, that the policy would be undermined by the desire of English and French Canadians to co-exist: a tacit system of double majority vote became the norm in the Assembly, a dual structure of government departments gave each region some administrative autonomy, and French was tolerated in the Assembly after member of Parliament Louis-Hippolyte Lafontaine defied the law by making his first speech in French.

So during the first century of British constitutional rule over its new possessions, the presence of the French community was dealt with at times by recognizing its right to exist, at other times by favouring its absorption into British society, depending on the dominant ideology and strategic imperatives of the day. But always there were some who preferred the politics of diversity over the politics of uniformity. That this spirit of accommodation, which had underlain much of our history by 1867, would have guided those who believed in a pact between two communities is consistent indeed. It was this attitude that ensured that Québec would have provincial rights in matters considered crucial to its cultural integrity. The choice of federalism, in this context, seemed like the best one.

Those who felt that Québec's particular aspirations and challenges justify a revamping of the Constitution were few before the 1960s. The question was not of vital importance to Maurice Duplessis. After all, why demand additional powers for Québec when his government did not even exploit to the fullest the powers it already had at its disposal? His economic conservatism and aversion to the Keynesian practices of the day, for one thing, dictated a laissez-faire approach that could only please Anglo-American investors. Moreover, the idea of the welfare-state was incompatible with the role the regime encouraged the church to play in social institutions. What was of vital importance, however, was preventing an increasingly ambitious federal government from encroaching on Québec's jurisdiction, and indeed the centralizing tendencies that the federal government had acquired during wartime hit a wall of resistance in the province, most notably with federal subsidies to universities. Although Duplessis would not demand additional constitutional powers, he saw how Québec's sovereignty over its areas of jurisdiction were undermined by a lack of fiscal revenues and insisted that the power to tax is the power to govern. What room Québec should occupy in the taxation field became a contentious point between the federal government of Louis Saint-Laurent and the Duplessis regime, which marked the beginning of a new era of Québec-Canada relations.

Again the Quiet Revolution has an important bearing upon an understanding of these relations. The initiatives of the Lesage government in various sectors of society were in sharp contrast with the laissez-faire approach of Duplessis. Like his predecessor, Lesage also resisted Ottawa's attempts to intervene in Québec's jurisdiction. But the new interventionist government now saw itself as the motor of socio-economic development in the province, and on that basis required substantial financial resources that only the federal purse could make available. The challenge of reconciling provincial autonomy with federal transfers was met by allowing provinces to opt out of shared-cost programs and still receive financial compensation—a practice Québec would take advantage of more than any other province and would later wish to see entrenched in the Constitution. Moreover, the Lesage government multiplied its efforts to help Québec develop an international personality of its own, despite

Ottawa's disapprobation. Co-operative agreements were signed with France and other countries of the *Francophonie* and foreign missions were opened world-wide. The Québec government's faith in federalism did not flag for that reason. In fact, Lesage often expressed the belief that with mutual goodwill Québec could grow and prosper within the federation with few formal amendments to the Constitution.

But the Québec state was changing rapidly. The first years of the Quiet Revolution had seen the nationalization of hydro-electric companies, government support of Québec-owned businesses, the creation of crown corporations in the mining and steel industry, the highly successful Caisse de dépôt et de placement to invest the pension fund,[2] and a number of new provincial social programs. All of these, and more, translated into the professionalization and growth of a public service that would absorb the rising educated middle class. And significantly, nationalist discourse served to legitimate the growth of the Québec state, for it was now viewed as the primary instrument of French-Canadian emancipation. It is no wonder that the central government began to fear that this new purpose would put an obstacle to pan-Canadianism and undermine national unity. The rise of the French Power in Ottawa, as it was called during the first years of Trudeau's government, and the push for official bilingualism as a nation-building policy, can be understood as a reaction to the modernization of the Québec state. The rivalry became more acute upon the return of the Union Nationale in 1966 with Daniel Johnson as its leader. Federalism, he argued, needed more than minor alterations. Québec had to have full control over human matters (education, social security, health care), economic matters (economic and financial instruments), cultural matters (arts, language), as well as an international presence. Equality or Independence was the new slogan.

Some actors of the Quiet Revolution were bound, sooner or later, to consider that the federal system hindered Québec's progress. The 1966 elections had seen two separatist parties in the running, but none had succeeded in gaining much popular support, let alone winning seats. René Lévesque's departure from the Liberal party in 1967 brought a new impetus to the movement. The chief architect of Hydro-Québec had tabled a proposal for sovereignty at the annual congress of the Liberal Party, but upon its defeat left the party to form the Mouvement souveraineté-association (MSA), and soon after the Parti Québécois (PQ). His credibility, charisma, and popularity brought to the sovereigntist project the respectability it needed to be propelled into power just a few years later. Many did not join Lévesque, however—amongst them Paul-Gérin Lajoie, who called for special status for Québec within the federation. Different though the shape of debates may be today, they are derived from these two fundamental propositions: sovereignty or recognition within the federation.

THE SEARCH FOR RECOGNITION

Public debate over the Meech Lake Accord (1987) revealed deep disagreements over the issue of entrenching a clause in the Constitution which states that Québec constitutes a distinct society within Canada. Those who opposed it invoked various reasons. For some, the clause was unwarranted since all regions and all peoples of Canada, not exclusively Québec, can be considered distinct in their own way. For others, entrenching differences between Canadians, especially the Québec difference, does not bode well for the building of a common nationality. The Charlottetown Agreement (1992) tried to alleviate these concerns, first by proposing a Canada clause, which gave constitutional status to other communities as well, and then by ensuring that the sense of nationhood would not be lost in this myriad of historical acknowledgements. What began, in bold simplicity, as the entrenchment of the distinct society clause turned into one of the thorniest, still unresolved, constitutional issues.

Isaiah Berlin once wrote that human beings seek not only freedom and security, but also recognition, so much so that they are sometimes ready to barter the former for the latter. As individuals and as peoples, we want more than freedom from coercion, we want our uniqueness to be properly recognized. Since how we feel about ourselves partly depends on how others feel about us, we are not indifferent as to whether or not they sufficiently value our distinct existence.[3] Berlin rightly pointed out the importance of grasping this phenomenon if the ideals and actions of peoples and nations are to be intelligible to us. That is how Canadian philosopher Charles Taylor interprets our constitutional predicament. For Taylor, it is not the perceived lack of powers that could justify the independence of the Québec nation, nor is it the idea that the federal system is supposedly a threat to its cultural survival; rather, it is foremost the lack of official recognition, the sense that the Québécois identity is still unrecognized in the Constitution.[4] In fact, nationalist discourse sustains the viewpoint that the patriation of the Constitution in 1982 without Québec's consent constitutes on the part of Canadian governments the antithesis, the official negation of a recognition sought since the late 1960s. The half-hearted statements that no one denies Québec's distinctness, only they don't want to see it entrenched in the Constitution, are of little avail in the campaign to persuade the Québécois to stay.

The desire for recognition is a by-product of a profound need for collective self-esteem and authenticity.[5] Be it the domination of whites over blacks, Europeans over aboriginals, men over women, or British over French Canadians, what is involved is the well-known phenomenon by which the dominated groups internalize the degrading images that the dominant group has of them. The consequence is low self-esteem, a sense of being morally, culturally, or otherwise deficient. Liberation begins with a rejection of that negative self-image, and three possibilities present themselves. The first is assimilation into the dominant group, that is, a kind of self-destruction of identity through the search for similitude. That some women reject patriarchal feminine stereotypes only to adopt male gender values and behaviours is an example of partaking in such a self-destruction of identity. Cultural and linguistic assimilation is also a common strategy to join the prestigious group and assure all that there remains no vestige of the former identity that might question one's belonging. It is this kind of liberation Lord Durham had in mind for the *Canadiens*, and this is the choice of a non-negligible number of francophones even today. The second option is separation, understood here as a resignation to the fact that the dominant group's attitude will not improve and that a life apart (to various degrees) is consequently the only solution. It is the preferred solution for some minority groups, who, having failed to adequately reform mainstream (cultural, social, educational) institutions, decide to develop their own, and for some women whose rejection of the patriarchal system altogether translates into the building of a parallel community. Of course this is the option of a good number of Québec separatists, notably those disgruntled federalists who have lost all hope in amending the Canadian Constitution[6]. But it is also what underlies, though perhaps unconsciously, the growing disinterest and indifference of the Québécois vis-à-vis their Canadian compatriots. The third option is recognition, where a group's authentic identity is celebrated by the dominant society, where its voice is not only heard but listened to.

It is safe to say that in the aftermath of the Quiet Revolution, the Québécois shed the degrading image of themselves they had long internalized as a colonized people, and began to rebuild their collective self-esteem. Recognition became a cardinal issue, especially when many began to think that it was the only alternative to René Lévesque's new sovereigntist project. But the Québécois were not alone in seeking status. Aboriginal peoples' claims as the first inhabitants gained visibility and eventually occupied a fair share of the constitutional agenda. So did the claims of ethnic minorities other than those with French or British origins, as immigration from non-European countries increased. These, and others, too, found in the Constitution of 1982 and its Charter of Rights and Freedoms some form of rights-based recognition, while the two-nations thesis quickly floundered. Québec nationalists felt it all the more important to call for a recognition of Québec as a distinct political community and thus avoid a folklorization of its identity into the multicultural whole, while Charter groups were adamant in their opposition to demands that might challenge their newfound official status. The dynamics of recognition brought about a constitutional overload and a zero-sum game that makes mutual recognition an even greater challenge.

Most Québec sovereigntists no longer wish to meet this challenge. The distinct society clause, if it ever comes, will be too little too late, they say. To be sure, the evolution of Québec society in the last forty years, coupled with the new nationalist discourse, has led to a territorialization of the Québécois identity and the consolidation of the Québec state as their only national state. Berlin has argued that "the only persons who can so recognize me, and thereby give me the sense of being someone, are the members of the society to which, historically, morally, economically, and perhaps ethnically, I feel that I belong."[7] When much of the Québec intelligentsia claims to be indifferent to the entrenchment of the distinct society clause, are they not saying that they no longer belong in Canada, and that recognition from Canadians has lost its appeal and is no longer relevant to them? And are they not calling for the majority of the Québécois to express their disaffection by voting for what really matters, sovereignty? Taylor believes that this seeming indifference is a reaction to recognition denied, that while the sense of rejection following the Meech Lake Accord may very well be irreversible among some Québécois, recognition by their Canadian compatriots still matters to a majority of them.[8] Should his impression turn out to be overly optimistic, and the manufacturing of indifference succeed, Canadians will face an impasse as any future formal recognition of Québec will meet with indifference.

CONCLUSION: THE VALUE OF FEDERALISM

Federalism springs from, and thrives on, disagreement. That is why Canadians chose it back in the 1860s, for they knew they could not agree on all matters. We are missing the point if we believe that our inability to share common ends is a symptom of the inadequacy of the federal system. On the eve of Confederation, British and French Canadians had already experienced a century of relative peace and prosperity together (considering the circumstances under which their destinies were joined), and the spirit of federalism had periodically resurfaced despite setbacks. So federalism appeared to be the best institution to manage our differences and carry us forward into the twentieth century. Of course if a federal system can allow for the cohabitation of distinct nations within a single state, it also has to be nourished by some idea of why union was desirable in the first place, a kind of founding principle. No doubt geography had something to do with it in our case, so did the business opportunity it represented for some intercolonial negotiators, and perhaps even sheer habit. But there was more to it than that, it will be said, something akin to a common nationality. How French Canadians went about contributing to the building of this common nationality is not unrelated to the relative success of the enterprise so far. It could seem paradoxical indeed that some of the most eloquent advocates of Canadianism were Québécois, leaders like George-Etienne Cartier and Henri Bourassa, and more recently Jean Lesage and Pierre E. Trudeau. But while all of them understood that Canadian citizenship requires us to transcend our differences, they were also acutely aware that the French-English duality has to be carefully managed. That is why federalism mattered to them.

This delicate balance between unity and diversity is not easily achieved. Different motives can run counter to federalism, of which one of the more important is the desire to strengthen one's preferred community of allegiance. While federalism divides loyalties insofar as citizens belong to two communities simultaneously, in the minds and hearts of many, one community of belonging tends to supersede the other. It is but a small step from this to wanting undivided sovereignty for the community with which we identify most, to perceiving the sharing of power as inevitably implying a loss of power, in short, to moving away from the federal principle. Since the Quiet Revolution, the identity of the Québécois has become firmly embedded in the Québec community, while the identity of other Canadians has increasingly defined itself in relation to the pan-Canadian community. We cannot exaggerate this point, since the Québécois continue to be sentimentally attached to Canada, and since regional feelings are quite strong across the country. But the territorialization of the Québécois identity is enough to impact significantly on the workings of the federal system. Canadians outside Québec, for instance, are less likely to accept a decentralization of powers to provinces, since this is perceived as a weakening of "their" national government. Conversely in Québec, transferring powers to the central government would be construed as depriving the National Assembly of the legislative instruments it needs to ensure the well-being of the Québec nation. Moreover, many Canadians outside Québec would like to reform national central institutions, notably the Senate, in order to make them more responsive to regional concerns. The Québécois, however, worry about reinforcing such institutions, however sensitive these might be to regional needs, and thus prefer an increase of legislative powers for the Québec National Assembly. A way to bypass these conflicts is to favour more asymmetry in the federation, that is, to allow the government of Québec to hold more powers while other provinces can turn to Ottawa if they wish to do so. But while some measure of asymmetry has been institutionalized since the 1960s, a number of Canadians fear that a further push in that direction will undermine the principle of the equality of provinces and create a two-tiered system of federal-provincial relations. These problems, incidently not insurmountable, illustrate how redesigning federalism is not an innocent process, for it often reflects normative choices that favour one's preferred community of belonging. A healthy federal system cannot allow for one community to supersede the other, whether it be that of the entire country or that of a particular region.

In the ongoing public debate about the future of Canada, it might be worthwhile to critically re-examine the value of federalism in plurinational states. Of course there are Canadians outside Québec who will always deplore the absence of a single, unhyphenated, Canadian identity, a notion that is foreign to the philosophy of federalism. And in Québec there will always be some who simply cherish the thought of having their own country, regardless of how well federalism might work. They have something in common in that they are both calling for undivided sovereignty and for a single community made in their image. These views are not without merit. But the others for whom unity and diversity are equally desirable will continue to find virtue in federalism.

FURTHER READING

Beaudoin, Gérald-A. *Le partage des pouvoirs*. Ottawa: Les Éditions de l'Université d'Ottawa, 1983.

Behiels, Michael D. *Prelude to Quebec's Quiet Revolution: Liberalism Versus Neo-Nationalism, 1945-1960*. Montreal and Kingston: McGill-Queen's University Press, 1985.

Berlin, Isaiah. *Four Essays on Liberty*. Oxford: Oxford University Press, 1969.

Brun, Henri and Guy Tremblay. *Droit constitutionnel*. Cowansville: Les Éditions Yvons Blais, 1982.

LaSelva, Samuel V. *The Moral Foundations of Canadian Federalism: Paradoxes, Achievements, and Tragedies of Nationhood*. Montreal and Kingston: McGill-Queen's University Press, 1996.

Linteau, Paul-André et al. *Histoire du Québec contemporain: Le Québec depuis 1930*. Montréal: Boréal, 1989.

McRoberts, Kenneth and Dale Posgate. *Développement et modernisation du Québec*. Montréal: Boréal Express, 1983.

Mill, John Stuart. *On Liberty*. Harmondsworth: Penguin, 1974.

Quinn, Herbert F. *The Union Nationale: A Study in Quebec Nationalism*. Toronto: University of Toronto Press, 1963.

Taylor, Charles. *Reconciling the Solitudes: Essays on Canadian Federalism and Nationalism*. Montreal and Kingston: McGill-Queen's University Press, 1994.

Trudeau, Pierre Elliott. *Federalism and the French Canadians*. Toronto: Macmillan, 1968.

Tully, James. *Strange Multiplicity: Constitutionalism in an Age of Diversity*. Cambridge: Cambridge University Press, 1995.

NOTES

I would like to thank Diane Roussel and the editors for their helpful comments.

1. John Stuart Mill (*On Liberty*, 1859) made a similar distinction in his discussion of individuality and, more recently, the distinction was examined by Richard Vernon, "Moral Pluralism and the Liberal Mind," in *Unity, Plurality and Politics* (London: Croom Helm, 1986). They might not agree, however, with how it is used here.

2. When the federal government set up the Canada Pension Plan, the government of Québec decided to opt out and set up its own Régie des rentes du Québec. This large pool of capital would be managed by the Caisse de dépôt et de placement, a highly successful financial institution.

3. Isaiah Berlin, "Two Concepts of Liberty," in his *Four Essays on Liberty* (Oxford: Oxford University Press, 1969).

4. Charles Taylor, "Impediments to a Canadian Future," in his *Reconciling the Solitudes: Essays on Canadian Federalism and Nationalism* (Montreal and Kingston: McGill-Queen's University Press, 1994).

5. See Taylor, "Impediments to a Canadian Future," and also "Why do Nations Have to Become States?" in his *Reconciling the Solitudes*.

6. On the issue of Québec secession, see Robert Young's essay in this book.

7. Berlin, "Two Concepts of Liberty," 156.

8. Taylor, "Impediments to a Canadian Future," 196–97.

THE POLITICAL ECONOMY OF CANADIAN FEDERALISM: A World Without Canada? Approaching the Next Millennium

J. F. Conway

Canadians continue to embrace a whole series of myths about Confederation. We talk of the "Fathers of Confederation," politely overlooking the self-seeking motives of the businessmen-politicians who conceived the plan. We speak of the "national dream," focussing on patriotism and other fine sentiments in an effort to elevate the bargaining and trade-offs that resulted in Canada to some higher, moral plane. Our history is "prettified," revised, often completely reconstructed. Even the London *Times* of 1865 revealed a clearer insight into Confederation than most Canadians today have, when an editorial said, referring to Confederation, "Half the useful things that are done in the world are done from selfish motives under the cover of larger designs."[1]

Three great events shaped the essence of Canada long before Confederation was even contemplated. These events ensured that Canada would remain a nation bedevilled by the English-French conflict, characterized by unremitting conservatism, and beset by a deep suspicion of popular movements and aspirations. The conquest of Quebec by Wolfe, the immigration of the fleeing counterrevolutionary United Empire Loyalists, and the defeat and repression of the 1837–38 Rebellions all had a great deal to do with determining the essential character of the Dominion which emerged in 1867. As they approached Confederation, Canada's rulers, encumbered by this legacy, were determined to contain and humble Quebec, to resist extreme democracy, and to view popular assertions as seditious. Confederation was never conceived as a plan to address the long-festering grievances of the Québécois; nor was it viewed as an orderly progression to popular democracy; nor, indeed, as a way to fulfill the yearnings of the people for nationhood. The plan was conceived by the business and political elites of the various British North American colonies, inspired by the elite of the colony of Canada, for no other reason than to assure their futures.

A somewhat reconstituted ruling class, more open to this "political dream of wonderful audacity,"[2] in the words of George Brown, had emerged from the ashes of the 1837–38 Rebellions. Forced reluctantly to grant responsible government, cast adrift by Britain as free trade was embraced in the 1840s, the new ruling class became dominated by the "progressive Conservative" (in Sir John A. Macdonald's words)[3] elements of the hard Tory merchant bloc that had ruled before, a rising group of industrial capitalists, landowners, railway and steamship entrepreneurs, and financial adventurers in the growing Canadian banking and insurance system[4]. This group, and their backers in the British Colonial Office, recognized that some form of federation was the only road to the survival of an independent British fact on the continent, as well as the only road to the establishment of an expanded national economy within which they could realize their aspirations. In the absence of such a British federation, American hegemony over a growing portion of the continent was inevitable. And in the absence of an enforced east-west national home market, the rising Canadian capitalist class would see its hopes dashed, confined by localism, undercut by American economic competition.[5]

The new federation would not go too far down the treacherous road of democracy. As Macdonald had so candidly put it at the 1864 Quebec Conference, what was being established was "constitutional liberty as opposed to democracy."[6] The House of Commons would not be elected by universal male suffrage, but tied to British qualifications for electors. Indeed, the principle of adult suffrage was not won until women were granted the vote in the context of World War I, and registered Indians were finally allowed to vote in 1960. Furthermore, there was to be a Senate, just in case the Commons got out of hand, which would be "the representative of property."[7] As Macdonald said, "A large qualification should be necessary for membership of the Upper House, in order to represent the principle of property. The rights of the minority must be protected, and the rich are always fewer in number than the poor."[8]

When Queen Victoria signed the British North America Act on May 19, 1867, the Canadas, now to be Quebec, Ontario, Nova Scotia, and New Brunswick, became the federal Dominion of Canada. It was a new variation on the old theme. The new federal government would borrow capital, or guarantee investments, in order to unite British North America from coast to coast through an expansion of the transportation system westward by rail. Ultimately, in the West, vast quantities of wheat and other natural resources would be extracted to join the similar flow from central and Atlantic Canada to feed Europe's industrial markets, especially that of Great Britain. Central Canada, especially Ontario, would additionally prosper in a variety of other ways: railway promoters and forwarding interests would move grain and other resources to market and manufactures back; the protective tariff would lead to a growing industrialization to supply the national home market expanded by a vast immigration of settlers to build the West; retailers and wholesalers would benefit through the general commercial boom; financial empires would rise on the growing demand for credit. Atlantic Canada would benefit from a growing demand for coal, fish, and the products of its long-established industries. The strong central government would play the crucial role: it would finance railway development, promote immigration, construct a wall of protective tariffs, and acquire the Prairie West as a colonial possession, while continuing to put pressure on British Columbia to join the federation. The job of the federal state was to "clear and prepare the way for the beneficent operation of the capitalist."[9]

For the first three decades, the grand Confederation scheme failed, largely due to the greater attractiveness to immigrants of the U.S. By 1896 the Dominion government was heavily in debt, with over one-half of the government's current outlay committed to debt charges and new development programs. The same held true for all provincial governments, except Ontario. This had occurred due to the prevailing, if dubious, political wisdom of the proper role of government—"the traditional role of government in British North America as an agency for creating conditions in which private enterprise might thrive" was assumed by all but a few politicians, according to the Rowell-Sirois Commission report of 1940.[10] The fly in the ointment was that vast sums had been expended on creating conditions, yet private enterprise had refused to thrive. The mood abroad was anything but hopeful and, according to the Rowell-Sirois Commission, there were "forebodings about the success of Confederation."[11]

In 1896 prosperity began to dawn as the "wheat boom" of 1896–1913 began.[12] The key to the boom lay in declining transportation costs and rising prices for wheat, which overnight made the production of Prairie wheat profitable. Free and cheap land further stimulated the process, providing a strong magnet for the land-hungry from around the world. Add to this the fact that the American frontier was for all practical purposes settled, and the conditions for a massive jump in population and wheat production on the Prairies were amply fulfilled. The subsequent speed of settlement and agricultural development was unprecedented in Canadian history. From 1896 to 1913, over one million people moved into the three Prairie provinces, occupied lands increased by seven times, and wheat production leapt by more than ten times. The industrial component of the original design was also working beautifully, as the net value of manufacturing production almost tripled between 1890 and 1910. It would not be an overstatement to say, as the Rowell-Sirois Commission did, that, in the 1896–1913 period "the settlement of the Prairies dominated the Canadian economic scene."[13]

During the period 1896 to 1984, the central contradictions embodied in the political and economic strategy behind Confederation—a state-guided industrialization and modernization in the context of a federation characterized by a strong central government and weak provincial governments—dominated Canadian politics, as confrontations and crises resulted in compromises, concessions, and minor reforms. These central contradictions, though inseparably interlocked, can be analytically subsumed in four areas: class conflicts and struggles; problems of political legitimacy; regional discontent; and the Quebec question.

The class contradictions involved demands by the labouring popular classes—farmers and workers—for a greater share of the wealth produced (for workers, collective-bargaining rights and higher real wages; for farmers, lower costs of production and marketing reforms; for both, the establishment of a social wage through universal, state-sponsored and -financed social, health, and educational programs). The class conflicts among capitalists at the national level reflected deep divisions in interests among finance, commercial, and industrial capitalists, as well as demands from local and regional capitalists for a development strategy more amenable to their interests and opportunities.

The problems of political legitimacy arose from Canada's imperfect and corrupt democracy and these were addressed with concessions and reforms in the context of successive waves of popular discontent, the strongest of which was the populist uprising led by the Progressive party in the post–World War I era, followed by smaller eruptions throughout the Great Depression and the post–World War II period. Movements to address regional grievances—typically conflating regional and class conflicts with crises of political legitimacy—demanded changes in the political and economic terms of Confederation, and frequently advocated profound modifications in Canada's political economy, as in the case of the western-based Social Credit and CCF movements. The successes of such efforts were significant but still at the margins of the Confederation strategy, and always stopped short of a basic restructuring and re-orientation of the national strategy.

The Quebec question, from the Conquest onwards, haunted the Confederation strategy, based as it was on the oppression of the Québécois nation as a source of cheap labour and as a captive market; on open, cheap access to Quebec's rich resources, and on excluding the Québécois nation from a prominent role in westward settlement and expansion. The successful containment of the Québécois nation in a constitutionally weak province under the hegemony of a strong federal government, involving as it did the risk of defying Lord Durham's post-1837–38 advice never again to allow that nation political control of an elected assembly, was premised on a coalition among the privileged and protected English minority in Quebec, a conservative Québécois political and economic elite, and the Catholic church, in order to forestall popular agitations and uprisings. Though there were episodes of troublesome popular outbursts in response to the hanging of Riel, the suppression of French outside Quebec, and conscription during the two world wars, this strategy of isolation and containment of the Québécois nation was largely successful until the Quiet Revolution and the subsequent growth in support for sovereignty.

As a result of the various concessions, compromises, and reforms over the years, and particularly after the combined world crises of the Great Depression and the rise and defeat of fascism, as well as the awakening of the Québécois nation from its imposed slumber, a consensus emerged, just as it had emerged in most advanced industrial capitalist nations in response to the dual threat of internal conflicts and demands for justice, and of external pressure from the Soviet Union's competitive state-socialist model for modernization and development. The reconstructed and modified Canada was a society based on a mixed economy, generally committed to incremental increases in a universal social security net, a humane regulation of the worst features of unregulated, free enterprise capitalism, and slowly advancing standards of living for wage- and salary-earners. In this way, Canadians were assured by all political parties, Canada could enjoy the best of socialism, with its concern for distributive justice and security for all, and of capitalism, with its evident economic efficiency, without sacrificing individual choice and freedom. Further, problems of regional discontent and Québécois aspirations could be addressed through an assertive federal government sponsoring programs of regional redistribution, regional development, and redress of justified Québécois grievances. The superior powers of the federal government would be voluntarily restrained in the context of a consultative executive federalism involving multilateral negotiations among first ministers. Just as in the case of the original Confederation strategy, this mixed economy/welfare state consensus was significantly based on activist and interventionist governments—at both the federal and provincial/regional levels—guiding the federation, economically and politically, in order to ensure stability and prosperity.

The mixed economy/welfare state consensus came under increasing attack throughout the then-called Free World during the late 1970s and early 1980s. As international capitalism endured a serious cost of production crisis due to OPEC's oil embargo, forever robbing the western industrial system of cheap energy, as well as a need for massive capital investment to renew the industrial infrastructure and to invest in the new information-based, computer/robotics industrial technology, there was a dramatic if temporary decline in the rate of return on capital investment. The collapse of the Soviet threat and the concomitant decline in the ideological power of the socialist/communist option in world and domestic politics presented an historic window of opportunity for an attack on all the popular gains made in the last century, and there commenced throughout the advanced capitalist world a neoconservative counterrevolution.

Although Canada's neoconservative era will be forever inseparably linked with Brian Mulroney, Canada's Tory prime minister from 1984 to 1993, the origins of Canadian neo-conservatism in fact lay in the West, the federal Liberal party, and the newly aggressive business lobby. In the West, Manitoba's Tory premier Sterling Lyon, after defeating Premier Ed Schreyer in 1977, initiated a hard program of public spending cuts and program re-straints, leading to defeat by the NDP's Howard Pawley in 1981. British Columbia's Socred premier William Bennett, called by the free enterprise coalition to fill his father's shoes to defeat NDP Premier Barrett in 1975, won a third term on May 5, 1983, and embarked on a surprise neoconservative revolution in July 1983. The resulting political storm marked the beginning of the end for Bennett, who left office in 1986 rather than face certain defeat. Key lessons were learned from these early neoconservative failures. As Oliver Letwin, in the past a privatization adviser to British prime minister Margaret Thatcher and to Saskatchewan Premier Grant Devine, and head of Rothchild's International Privatization Unit, said, "What is important is to develop—slowly and effectively—momentum. It's the momentum and gradualness that makes things happen." Most importantly, the "right psychology" among the public must first be cultivated.[14]

The contributions of the federal Liberal party and government to the neoconservative agenda have been lost in the mists of political myth, particularly as a result of John Turner's unsuccessful anti–free trade battle in the 1988 election and Jean Chrétien's successful Red Book, anti-neoconservative assault on Kim Campbell in 1993. Responding to the reces-sion, in 1982 the Trudeau government established the Royal Commission on the Economic Union and Development Prospects for Canada, chaired by former Liberal finance minister Donald Macdonald, a well-known friend of corporate Canada. The Macdonald Commission reported in September 1985, after thirty-four months of hearings and research involving the expenditure of almost $21 million.[15] A great deal of what was to become Ottawa's neo-conservative agenda can be found in the report's major recommendations[16]. While much of the Macdonald Report might have collected dust on government shelves had the Liberals re-mained in office, the dramatic victory of Brian Mulroney the year before ensured that Macdonald's "glorification" of the free market, as the *Financial Post* put it later,[17] would fall on fertile soil.

The final key element in the neoconservative counterrevolution was the newly aroused and surprisingly aggressive business lobby in Canada. Finding inspiration in the successes of Thatcher and Reagan, supplied with intellectual weapons by the corporate-funded Fraser Institute and C. D. Howe think-tanks, angry over the intrusiveness of government in man-aging the economy, and determined to re-assert capital's power to restructure Canadian so-ciety, the business lobby flexed its muscles. The traditionally restrained Canadian Manufacturers' Association (CMA) and Chambers of Commerce were joined by the more politically aggressive Business Council on National Issues, the Canadian Federation of Independent Business, the Canadian Citizens' Coalition, and a whole host of antitax busi-ness front groups. Previously the business lobby had been split. On the one hand, there was the small-business lobby, forever reactionary and backward looking, demanding a return to the nineteenth century, tirelessly repeating demands for cuts in welfare and unemployment benefits, for a lower minimum wage or none at all, for deregulation, for an end to the so-cialistic public economic sector. On the other hand, there were the citadels of big capital, tak-ing pride in their progressivism, proud of their decisive role in the Canadian national project from the National Policy onwards, purveying a sense of paternalistic *noblesse oblige* and social responsibility, even often conceding the importance of the welfare state and a carefully curtailed public sector in a managed, stable, and humane capitalist economy. Suddenly the big- and small-business lobbies, increasingly on the political ascendancy, found unity and abandoned all constraints. In October 1984, the CMA presented a wide-ranging brief to the federal cabinet and to the Macdonald Commission[18]. Among the things lamented in the brief were laws regulating child labour, minimum wages, health and safety in the workplace, lay-off procedures, and statutory holidays. Not only were such interventions too expensive, but they undermined business competitiveness. During the same month, the Royal Bank released a similar submission at a press conference. The good bank wanted to reduce if not eliminate labour-market "rigidities" and investment "distortions" afflicting the free market: trade unions, minimum-wage laws, unemployment insurance, social assistance. The bank proposed "flexible wages" in a free labour market. Furthermore, the bank wanted an end to investment "distortions" caused by public interventions in the marketplace through extensive public ownership or intrusive national policies. In fact, the united business lobby in Canada was toying with a return to nothing less than social barbarism in the context of dismantling effective government on behalf of the public or national interest.

When Brian Mulroney swept aside Turner's Liberals on September 4, 1984, few Canadians realized what had been set in motion. Mulroney was a man of profoundly conservative views, with few scruples and intimate links to the corporate sector which paid handsome political dividends in furthering Mulroney's insatiable political ambitions.[19] By the time Mulroney finally won the Tory leadership in 1983, on the heels of a well-financed campaign to destroy Clark, he was on the boards of directors of ten leading companies, including Provigo and the Canadian Imperial Bank of Commerce, and counted as personal friends people like Conrad Black as well as Paul Desmarais. His corporate credentials were, therefore, impeccable, yet remained those of a loyal servant to capital, a reliable lieutenant on whom the captains of industry and finance could rely. Upon election the new prime minister openly embraced the neoconservative agenda from the outset and, despite artful zigs and zags required to manipulate and reassure the public, proceeded with its loyal implementation. Armed with the Macdonald Report, which Mulroney enthusiastically characterized as "some excellent ideas" with an analysis "essentially the same as my own,"[20] and the new government's shorter, more succinct *A New Direction for Canada: An Agenda for Economic Renewal,*[21] issued two months after the election and which clearly laid out the government's intentions, the Mulroney government went to work. The business lobby was delighted, and the alliance between the Mulroney government and corporate Canada was cemented. As Laurent Thibault, president of the CMA said, "They [the Mulroney government] began with a basic agenda, and they stuck to it."[22] Thomas d'Aquino of the Business Council on National Issues was equally pleased, endorsing the government for successfully achieving "a very strong public acceptance of what I call some of the very fundamental values important to business."[23]

The key ingredients of the agenda have been well documented.[24] The agenda included: (1) cutbacks in social spending, including the significant erosion of Canada's social, educational and health security net; (2) an assault on the incomes and living standards of wage- and salary-earners, while increasing the total share of wealth generated flowing to capital and its privileged servants;[25] (3) a weakening of federal power *vis à vis* the provinces; (4) a program of deregulation and privatization, and a move to free-market forces as the engine of social and economic development; (5) a free trade deal with the U.S. as a prelude to the establishment of a continental free market encompassing Canada, the U. S., and Mexico; and (6) a deliberate process of discrediting and disabling government as a popular democratic tool available to the people to shape the economy and society, largely by deliberately burdening governments with huge annual deficits and a crippling debt at high interest rates, and by shifting the increasing tax burden from the rich and the corporate sector to those in the middle and lower income categories.[26] This was an ambitious agenda, involving nothing less than a major restructuring of Canadian society and the economy by overturning the mixed economy/welfare state consensus and turning the clock back fifty years and more to the era of the unregulated free market, private greed, and unrestrained individualism, and a modified social Darwinism as the basic creed governing interventions to assist the weak, the afflicted, and the vulnerable.

What we are in fact witnessing is ascendant world capital's abandonment of the national project as a key tool in realizing its ambitions and interests. The Canadian business lobby, representing the giants of corporate Canada, deeply committed to neoconservatism, free trade, and globalization, has accordingly virtually abandoned Canada as a national project. Indeed, the new globalization/neoconservative cant insists the truly successful corporation must now compete on the world stage and aspire to transnational status. For a corporation even to have a vision of "nation" or a "national stage" on which to act, is considered backward, old-fashioned, and an impediment to success. At its most basic economic level this simply confirms a central law of capital—grow and expand, or die—and should not therefore be surprising. But at the political level the implications are profound. What corporate capitalism is telling the people of Canada is that having used Canada in the initial stages of development, the success stories of corporate Canada now want to abandon nation-building. Indeed, given the central and successful role of the business lobby in our neoconservative politics of the last decade, Canadian business has done everything it could to dismantle what has been constructed since 1867. Let us recall that these corporate success stories have roots in the nineteenth- and early twentieth-centuries and unashamedly fashioned and then used Canadian national policies— the tariff, protection of Canada's banks and financial institutions, subsidies, grants of public lands and mineral rights, tax breaks, etc.—to build their successful enterprises. Now, having achieved success, they are ready to meet world competition and understandably wish to move onto the world stage. But these enterprises want to do so unencumbered by any commitment to Canada as a national project. The very country they established and exploited to achieve success, the business lobby now wishes to renounce, to put behind them.

The corporate reasoning is clear. The old National Policy, the core economic strategy of Canada as a nation, is finished. But Canada has developed no new National Policy, no new core economic strategy, but free trade, free markets, and globalization—the very circumstances imposed upon Canada's political and economic elite when Britain moved to free trade in the 1840s. It goes without saying—as our elites of 150 years ago realized—that an economic strategy singularly characterized by free trade and free markets amounts to no economic strategy at all. The old National Policy really amounted to an industrialization/modernization strategy in order to build the east-west economic foundation of the nation, rooted in tariff protection to keep the home market for local industries, protection for financial institutions, and the extraction of resources for world markets. This strategy depended heavily on exploiting the Canadian people as a captive market, and exploiting the natural environment in the rapid extraction of resources for export. Above all, the strategy required strong and interventionist federal and provincial governments.

That strategy had clear regional dimensions. The peripheral regions—the West, the North and Atlantic Canada—provided captive markets and resources. Southern central Canada—a narrow, heavily populated region along the Great Lakes and the St. Lawrence—was the focus of industrialization. Quebec played a mixed role: there, industrial development was more heavily based on the exploitation of cheap and plentiful labour, Quebec's vast natural resources were opened up, and the Québécois provided a lucrative captive market. Ontario shared these characteristics with Quebec, but tended to enjoy the advantage of being the focus of more modern, technologically innovative industrial development. Ontario also enjoyed the advantage of being the dominant province in the nation, politically and economically; the location of head offices for transportation, financial institutions, and the great houses of wholesale and retail commerce; and the centre of political power where national goals were defined. Confederation was really the project of the political and economic elite of Ontario, and that elite jealously guarded its domination and prerogatives in setting the national agenda.

That era is now over. The end has been coming for some time, politically and economically. The north-south economic pull, especially for Quebec and the West, and political alienation, challenged east-west economic ties. Increasingly, trade with the U.S. became more and more free—by the mid-1980s 80 percent of trade between Canada and the U.S. was free of tariff barriers, and protection was less and less important to Canada's economy. The FTA and NAFTA put a decisive and final end to the old National Policy, and further undermined the east-west national economy. From 1991 to 1995 Statistics Canada reported that interprovincial trade grew by under seven percent, as a result of a dramatic shift to foreign markets, especially the American market.[27] This shift to foreign markets was biggest in Alberta and Quebec. In fact, Quebec's 1995 interprovincial exports were lower than those of 1990, and Quebec suffered a $1 billion trade deficit with the provinces in that year, while enjoying a $3.8 billion surplus in foreign trade. Meanwhile Alberta's deficit in interprovincial trade grew from $2 billion in 1991 to $3 billion in 1995 at the same time as its foreign trade surplus grew to almost $11 billion. In fact, Ontario was the only province to report an interprovincial trade surplus in 1995 of almost $26 billion, and a foreign trade deficit of just over $5 billion. In terms of trade between Ontario and Quebec, Ontario's trade surplus with Quebec more than doubled to almost $6 billion in 1995. But, of course, the essence of both free trade agreements was that no new national policy would be put in place by Ottawa or the provinces as the remnants of the old are phased out—and the Canadian economy was expected to go naked into continental and world markets. One therefore searches in vain for the new national policies on the fisheries, the grain trade, agriculture in general, forestry, water, natural resource extraction and exportation in general. There is no new national industrial strategy, nor is there an overarching national economic strategy to tie the regions together in a viable and symbiotic way. With neoconservatism, free trade, free markets, and the withdrawal of government from the economy, the Canadian economy, as such, is on the verge of ceasing to exist. Meanwhile economic growth and vitality is increasingly linked, especially for Quebec and the West, to continental economic integration, and the tattered remnants of the east-west national economy are increasingly seen as impositions and impediments.

Consequently, the long-existing centrifugal forces that have repeatedly threatened the federation—from the West and from Quebec—have been strengthened and given renewed confidence, straining national unity to its limits. The existence and success of the Canadian federation very much rested on the dual pillars of a coherent and integrated national economy that delivered reasonable levels of economic security and prosperity, and of an assertive federal government prepared to use its superior fiscal and constitutional powers to address failures, crises, and grievances springing from the inequities of capitalism and regional disparities. The most persistent and troublesome problems for the federation were repeatedly posed by Quebec and the West, and national unity depended on a reasonably effective response to the grievances of the West and the Québécois nation. Canada, as a result of the ascendant neoconservative consensus, has largely abandoned both the tools essential to the success of the federation—a coherent national economic strategy and the aggressive use of the state. Without both elements, the Canadian federation would never have come into existence, and in their absence today and into the future, the viability of the federation is increasingly uncertain.

The grievances of the West and of Quebec are not trivial and have deep and persisting historical roots. It is no accident that in order to incorporate the West and Quebec into, and retain them in, Confederation, Canada's political and economic elite repeatedly drank from the poisoned chalice of legal force and political and economic oppression, particularly in the case of Quebec. These two regions—together with the aboriginal nations—stand alone in the history of the Canadian federation as the objects of federal military conquest, occupation, and suppression, and endured a period of subsequent colonial status. In a sense, the successful establishment and initial survival of the federation are firmly founded on this legacy of force and oppression, and this legacy continues to sit, like an unwelcome ghost, at every federal-provincial negotiating table.

Efforts to redress these grievances have often had, and continue to have, contradictory results. Gestures to the Québécois nation—linguistic concessions, economic development programs, the removal of discriminatory barriers to francophones in business and government, maternal language education rights—have frequently provoked resentment in the West, where politicians have opportunistically sustained an abiding popular hostility to the Québécois nation. Gestures to the West, though usually met with more generosity in Quebec, can still provoke deep fears in Quebec, especially constitutional gestures like the equality of provinces doctrine and multiculturalism. Incumbent politicians in government in Ottawa and the provinces have often manipulated such divisions effectively. The most recent example was the betrayal of Lévesque by the western premiers in 1981 in exchange for higher oil prices, a regional constitutional veto, a notwithstanding clause to override the Charter, and more complete provincial constitutional control of natural resources, an event that has helped propel Quebec to the threshold of sovereignty.

Rather than rising to the challenge by granting more effective and structural remedies to Quebec and the West, Canada's political and economic elite papered together a federal system based on historical misconceptions, minor crisis-management adjustments, a rejection of the reality of Canada's two nations, a trivialization of Quebec's fears as merely questions of language, and a dismissal of the West's agitations as quaint and regionally-specific curiosities. Furthermore, the federalist elite commenced first to construct and then to embrace a series of political and constitutional myths. These myths concealed the reality of Quebec as the political and constitutional home of the Québécois nation, granted the appearance of concessions to the aggrieved people of the West, while providing a false but reassuring sense of Canadianism. Canadians will have to free themselves from these myths that make a settlement impossible. One myth is the assertion that the Québécois are only one small piece of the Canadian mosaic, no more or less distinct than other groups in other provinces.

This belief is absurd. The constitutional recognition of Quebec as a distinct society is a minimum demand of the Québécois, who see it as merely a recognition and affirmation of historical and sociological reality. To continue to refuse it is to invite Quebec independence.

The second myth Canadians will have to abandon is constitutional multiculturalism. Before we can reach a successful resolution of our differences, Canadians will have to stop embracing multiculturalism as an alternative constitutional reality to Canada's three nations, English Canadian, Québécois, and aboriginal. While ethnocultural diversity is a key feature of Canada, it is a malicious fiction to insist it is *the* key feature of Canada, when three out of four Canadians have British or French roots, and when all Canadians have integrated with either the English or French language groups. The most convenient aspect of multiculturalism, which was used quite cynically by Trudeau and other first ministers, is that while masking the reality of anglophone domination, it diminishes the significance of the French fact in Canada. The doctrine has proven a potent weapon against Quebec (and, later, against the aboriginal nations). English Canadians, especially in the West, and the many ethnic minorities that justifiably felt excluded, grasped the concept to offset demands both from francophone minorities across English Canada and from the Québécois nation, and later from the aboriginal nations.

Finally, before Canada can achieve a resolution of its constitutional differences, the myth of the equality of provinces must be abandoned. Confederation was not premised on the doctrine of the constitutional equality of provinces as a federal principle. Indeed, such a principle was explicitly rejected in favour of enumerating a specific and limited list of provincial powers, while granting the federal government a list of specific powers, a series of key dominant powers, and all residual powers. All provinces were constitutionally equal in the exercise of the powers assigned to them within their borders, but that notion of equality did not extend to an equal say in the federation, to an equal share of power in the central government. On the contrary, the basic doctrine underlying the federal power was a slightly modified version of *representation by population*. That is, each province would enjoy and exercise a share of power in the central government commensurate with the size of its population. This principle was modified to the extent that when readjustments were made in representation in the House of Commons after each census, the number of MPs for any province was not to be allowed to fall below the number of senators designated for that province. This provides the safeguard that, despite the principle of "rep by pop," each province will continue to enjoy reasonable levels of representation in the House of Commons. Not all provinces were equal at the time of their entrance into Confederation. Each of the four original provinces—Ontario, Quebec, New Brunswick, Nova Scotia—entered Confederation under somewhat different arrangements in 1867, including a very special and distinct status for Quebec, and different deals were struck as each additional colony opted to join. The three Prairie provinces were in an entirely different constitutional category. Ottawa acquired the region as a colonial possession, and the Prairie provinces were simply the constitutional creations of the central government. Upon their creation, Ottawa denied them control of their lands and natural resources, a clear provincial power enumerated in the BNA Act, yet successfully withheld by Ottawa until 1930, "for the purposes of the Dominion."[28] Nothing makes clearer the historical supremacy of Ottawa than this power to create provinces by federal statute and, furthermore, to create a different constitutional class of province; that is, those whose attainment of full constitutional provincial status could be delayed at the pleasure of Ottawa.

A further confirmation of federal supremacy lies in the fact that Ottawa retains key powers that can be exercised in the national interest and at the peril of provincial powers.[29] These include the power to disallow or reserve any provincial statute; all residual powers; the general power "to make laws for the peace, order and good government of Canada"; and the power to declare that any local work in a province is "to be for the general advantage of Canada or for the advantage of two or more of the provinces." The federal powers of disallowance and reservation have not been exercised since the 1930s during the heady days of Social Credit under William Aberhart in Alberta. But these powers have not atrophied from a lack of use. Indeed, they are designed not to have to be used. Their mere existence imposes a certain self-discipline on the provinces, particularly in the face of an assertive federal government. The federal declaratory power has been used more frequently to establish central authority over things like railways, the grain trade, telecommunications, and nuclear energy. Its possible use was debated during the energy crisis of the 1970s when Premier Lougheed of Alberta cut the flow of oil eastward in retaliation to Ottawa's efforts to establish a national energy policy. Any federal system that abandons such powers will slowly bleed to death as a result of a self-inflicted wound.

The recent emergence of the doctrine of the constitutional equality of the provinces was another device in the arsenal developed by Trudeau to deal with Quebec and to appease the West. By insisting that all provinces were constitutionally equal, Trudeau was able to insist that Quebec was a province just like the others. Quebec's demands should therefore simply be put on the list along with the demands of all other provinces. In this way, Trudeau was able to sidestep Quebec's demand for a bilateral negotiating process between Ottawa, representing English Canada, and the Quebec government, representing the Québécois nation, while at the same time including the annoyed western premiers in the process as equals. Ironically, Trudeau's opportunistic use of the doctrine gave it a degree of respectability, turning it into a Canadian constitutional convention and achieving a degree of realization in the amending formula adopted in 1982 (changes in the constitution require the consent of Ottawa and seven of 10 provinces representing more than 50 percent of the population). Provincial rights premiers, and Mulroney and his neoconservative allies, were able to use the doctrine in nearly successful efforts to transform Confederation into a loose amalgamation of powerful provinces presided over by an increasingly impotent central government, as envisioned in the Meech Lake Accord and the Charlottetown Agreement. Furthermore, the doctrine allows provincial rights premiers to insist that Quebec can obtain nothing not granted to all other provinces. This doctrine makes our current Quebec–English Canada impasse insoluble. To give all provinces exactly what Quebec needs to advance and protect its uniqueness will destroy the federation. Yet the reality is that not to give Quebec at least some of what it needs also risks the breakup of Canada.

CONCLUSION

The Canadian federation is at risk economically and politically, and is on what could be an irreversible trajectory to breakup. To survive, the federation urgently requires a new national economic strategy, free of the neoconservative business agenda, to bind the interests and futures of Canadians of all regions together into an effective national economy characterized by universal social wage programs and higher levels of distributive justice. The federation cannot continue in political and constitutional crisis indefinitely, and some mutually acceptable constitutional resolution of the grievances of the Québécois, the West, and aboriginal Canadians is essential.

There are no easy blueprints, no magic solutions. But the last 50 or 60 years contain clear lessons of what has not worked. The use of draconian federal constitutional and military powers has typically failed and frequently has had the opposite effect to that intended, as the use of disallowance and reservation powers proved in the case of Aberhart of Alberta, and the imposition of the War Measures Act during the 1970 October Crisis in Quebec demonstrated. The federal actions against Aberhart increased the popular support both for his regime and for his Social Credit and debt protection programs. The use of the WMA, in retrospect, in the long run provided a boost to the Quebec sovereignty movement, just as the 1981 constitutional betrayal of Lévesque did. Furthermore, the Conquest of 1759, the repression after the 1837–38 civil war, and the illegal suppression of French outside Quebec, for the Québécois nation; and the two Riel Rebellions, the subsequent military occupations, and the hanging of Riel, for westerners, have become defining moments in the history of western and Québécois alienation from the federation. Efforts among the political and economic elite to concoct private deals in secret and then to try to browbeat, threaten, and cajole the people into acceptance have failed (though such methods were effective in the beginning in bringing off the Confederation project). The Meech Lake Accord and the Charlottetown Agreement experiences have made this crystal clear. The neoconservative consensus, successfully imposed by the business lobby, has proven to be an economic and political disaster for Canada, despite high profit levels for corporations and financial institutions, provoking a growth in injustice, anger, and despair, and leading to mounting civil disorder. The abandonment, or defeat, of this consensus is essential if Canada, by again becoming a humane society worthy of an individual's loyalty and love, is to survive into the next millennium—and about that there is a clear popular consensus to which elected politicians have closed their ears.

Further, the last fifty or sixty years, and especially the recent past, tell us, again in broad strokes, what is needed. The problem of regional alienation, especially in the West, must be successfully addressed economically and constitutionally. The aboriginal question urgently requires a constitutional, political, and economic settlement. The yearnings of the Québécois nation for special constitutional status must somehow be reconciled with the majority sentiment in English Canada for a strong central government. The crisis of political legitimacy that now afflicts our political system needs to be addressed and Canada's deeply flawed and imperfect democracy badly needs reform in order to regain the confidence and trust of the people.

Certain measures are self-evidently necessary if Canadian democracy is to be deepened and made more responsive to the regions and to popular aspirations. First, the Senate must be abolished as an undemocratic impediment in our political system—as we learned again during the GST fiasco and the Newfoundland schools debate. The Senate has no credibility and its continued existence is an affront to democracy. Next, establish a constitutional minimum number of House of Commons seats below which a province or territory cannot fall should its population decline below a threshold for representation by population. Then, amend the Constitution to require that the Commons seats granted to each province be assigned on a proportional basis to each political party according to levels of popular support. The results of the 1988 and 1993 elections, if proportional representation were in place, would have been quite different under such a system, resulting in both cases in minority governments, strong representation from the other two national parties, and much less of a regional sweep in 1993 for Reform and the Bloc.

Under proportional representation, the House of Commons would have been a very different place after 1988 and 1993, and our recent political history would probably have been less divisive and crisis-ridden.[30] The basic principles of fair and democratic representation of the popular will would have been more perfectly realized. There would have been the clash of debate including class, region, nation, and party. Each party would have had to deal with regional issues—language and self-determination for Quebec, energy resource policy for the West, the fisheries in British Columbia and Atlantic Canada—in the context of the party's ideological line. On occasion, cross-party regional alliances might have occurred. The chance of the kind of regional polarization by which Trudeau could write off the West, or the pre-Mulroney Tories could write off Quebec, or the current Chrétien Liberals could write off Quebec, would be greatly lessened; indeed, would be highly unlikely.

A House of Commons based on proportional representation would be difficult to effect in Canada. The major parties would resist it, and it would be a disaster, critics allege. There would rarely be a majority government, the "Italian disease" would afflict us, and Canada would become ungovernable. Prime ministers would be constantly jockeying for majorities, governments would fall, and we would have annual elections. One easy remedy is to have fixed elections—elections shall occur on the second Monday of June every fourth year, for example. In between, the parties would have to work harder at putting together ministries with the confidence of the House, which, after all, is the basic principle of parliamentary democracy and responsible government. Furthermore, Canada's experience with minority governments—Diefenbaker in 1957–58, the Pearson years of 1963–68, Trudeau in 1972–74 (let's forget Joe Clark in 1979, who pretended he had a majority)—has not been particularly bad. Some argue such governments are the most sensitive and productive, and this was most particularly true of the Pearson years. They have to work harder at governing and refrain from arrogant assertions of undiluted power, not necessarily bad things. Indeed, one could argue that the governments of Mulroney in 1988 and that of Chrétien in 1993 may prove to have been the worst in our history—both governments won strong parliamentary majorities with minority popular support and proceeded to brutally impose controversial, divisive, and damaging policies contrary to the popular will, and contrary to much of what was promised in order to secure election.

Supposing the results of 1988 and 1993 been expressed in a proportional system, we should contemplate the answers to a series of questions about our recent political history. With only majority support in Alberta and Quebec, would the free trade agreements have been put in place and retained? Indeed, would they have even been proposed in their present form? Would the Meech Lake disaster have occurred? Would the GST have passed? Would our pro-corporate and prowealthy tax system have remained unreformed? Would the social, educational, and health program cuts and the downloading have occurred? Would we have been subjected to the divisive Charlottetown referendum? Would Brian Mulroney have remained prime minister after the 1988 election, particularly given his betrayals of the electorate on the "sacred trust" of social programs and his 1984 opposition to free trade? Would Chrétien have remained prime minister after his flagrant reversal on his Red Book promises?[31] Would the undiluted corporate, neoconservative agenda remain in place, despite explicit and repeated rejections of that agenda by the electorate in provincial and federal elections? Would Chrétien be able to continue his bullying and scare tactics against Quebec? The answer to all these questions is arguably no. And had Canada's democratic institutions faithfully reflected the popular will on such matters, today the Canadian federation would be in a much less parlous state.

These are big reforms. None of the political parties, nor none among our current crop of party leaders, would be willing or able to provide the leadership to achieve them. Levels of public mistrust, rancour, and hostility between English Canada and Quebec, and popular disaffection from Canadian politics and institutions, make it impossible to imagine any scenario that might work. Perhaps only a popular and democratic solution would win public confidence. One approach worth considering as a possible road out of our present impasse is that of a constituent assembly, elected popularly, and assigned the task of formulating constitutional solutions for presentation to the people in a referendum and then to the House of Commons and the provincial legislatures for ratification. Given the urgency of Canada's situation, and the current crisis of political leadership and legitimacy, such a solution may be the only one available if we wish to salvage the Canadian federation.

FURTHER READING

Many of the arguments in this article are developed more fully in the following books, articles, and papers by the author.

Debts to Pay: A Fresh Approach to the Quebec Question. 2nd ed. Toronto: Lorimer, 1997.

The West: The History of a Region in Confederation. 2nd ed. Toronto: Lorimer, 1994.

"Reflections on Canada in the Year 1994." In James de Finney et al., eds. *Canadian Studies at Home and Abroad.* Montreal: Association for Canadian Studies, 1995, 145–7 (also published in *Journal of Canadian Studies* 29, no. 3 [Fall 1994]).

"Quebec and English Canada: The Politics of Territory." *Constitutional Review Constitutionnel* 6, no. 1 (Fall 1994): 19–23.

"The Mulroney Counter-Revolution, 1984–1993," Learned Societies—CSAA, Calgary, 1994.

"Canada and the U.S.: What Makes Us Different?" *Labour/Le Travail* 28 (Fall 1991): 311–21.

"Fractions Among Prairie Farmers" (with R. Stirling). In G. S. Basran and D. A. Hay, eds. *The Political Economy of Agriculture in Western Canada.* Toronto: Garamond Press, 1988, 73–86.

"The Rising of the New West." In Paul W. Fox and Graham White, eds. *Politics: Canada.* Toronto: McGraw-Hill-Ryerson, 1987, 223–36.

"The Crisis of Social Democracy in Canada," *Labour/Le Travail* 17 (Spring 1986): 257–65.

NOTES

1. London Times, April 13, 1865, quoted in P B. Waite, *The Life and Times of Confederation, 1864–1867* (Toronto: University of Toronto, 1962), 323.

2. Quoted in Waite, ibid, 329.

3. The phrase appears in a letter from Macdonald to Captain Strachan, February 9, 1854, see J. K. Johnson and Carole B. Stewart, eds. *The Letters of Sir John A. Macdonald, 1836–1857* (Ottawa: Public Archives, 1968), 202.

4. Stanley B. Ryerson. *Unequal Union: Confederation and the Roots of Conflict in the Canadas, 1815–1873* (Toronto: Progress Books, 1968), 276–77.

5. From an 1865 speech by Macdonald in the Assembly of Canada, reproduced in P B. Waite, ed.. *The Confederation Debates in the Province of Canada* (Toronto: McClelland and Stewart, 1963), 39.

6. G P. Browne, ed. *Documents on the Confederation of British North America* (Toronto: McClelland and Stewart, 1969), 95.

7. Ibid, 133.

8. Ibid, 98.

9. D G. Creighton, "Economic Nationalism and Confederation," in R. Cook, ed. *Confederation* (Toronto: University of Toronto, 1967), 4.

10. *Report of the Royal Commission on Dominion-Provincial Relations, Book I* (Ottawa: King's Printer, 1940), 61. Cited hereafter as *Rowell-Sirois Report, I.*

11. Ibid, 74.

12. All figures used on growth are from the *Rowell-Sirois Report, I*

13. Ibid, 74.

14. Regina *Leader Post*, January 26, 1988, April 8 and July 8, 1989.

15. *Globe and Mail*, September 21, 1985.

16. *Report of the Royal Commission on the Economic Union and Development Prospects for Canada* (Ottawa: Minister of Supply and Services Canada, 1985).

17. *Financial Post*, September 21, 1986.

18. *Globe and Mail*, "Report on Business", October 17 and 18, 1984

19. John Sawatsky, *Mulroney: The Politics of Ambition* (Toronto: Macfarlane Walter and Ross, 1991); N. Auf der Maur, R. Chodos, and R. Murphy, *Brian Mulroney: The Boy from Baie-Comeau* (Halifax: Good Read Biographies, 1985); Claire Hoy, *Friends in High Places: Politics and Patronage in the Mulroney Government* (Toronto: Key Porter, 1987); Jeffrey Simpson, *Spoils of Power: The Politics of Patronage* (Toronto: Collins, 1988); Stevie Cameron, *On the Take: Crime, Corruption and Greed in the Mulroney Years* (Toronto: Macfarlane Walter and Ross, 1994).

20. *Globe and Mail,* September 6, 1985.

21. Department of Finance, *A New Direction for Canada: An Agenda for Economic Renewal* (Ottawa: Minister of Supply and Services Canada, November 8, 1984).

22. *Financial Post*, September 5, 1988.

23. *Globe and Mail,* November 19, 1988.

24. John Calvert, *Government Limited: The Corporate Takeover of the Public Sector in Canada* (Ottawa: Centre for Policy Alternatives, 1984); Duncan Cameron, ed. *The Free Trade Papers* (Toronto: Lorimer, 1986); Stephen Clarkson, *Canada and the Reagan Challenge* (Toronto: Lorimer, 1985); Daniel Drache and Duncan Cameron, eds. *The Other Macdonald Report* (Toronto: Lorimer, 1985); Cy Gonick, *The Great Economic Debate* (Toronto: Lorimer, 1987); Herschel Hardin, *The Privatization Putsch* (Halifax: Institute for Research on Public Policy, 1989); J. Krieger, *Reagan, Thatcher and the Politics of Decline* (New York: Oxford, 1986); James Laxer, *False God: How the Globalization Myth Impoverished Canada* (Toronto: Lester, 1993); James Laxer, *Leap of Faith: Free Trade and the Future of Canada* (Edmonton: Hurtig, 1986); Warren Magnusson et al. *The New Reality: The Politics of Restraint in British Columbia* (Vancouver: New Star, 1984); Patricia M. Marchak, *The Integrated Circus: The New Right and the Restructuring of Global Markets* (Montreal: McGill-Queen's, 1991); Lawrence Martin, *Pledge of Allegiance: The Surrender of Canada in the Mulroney Years* (Toronto: McClelland and Stewart, 1993); Stephen

McBride and John Shields, *Dismantling a Nation: The Canadian Agenda* (Halifax: Fernwood, 1993); Linda McQuaig, *Behind Closed Doors* (Toronto: Penguin, 1987); Linda McQuaig, *The Wealthy Banker's Wife: The Assault on Equality in Canada* (Toronto: Penguin, 1993); John W. Warnock, *Free Trade and the New Right Agenda* (Vancouver: New Star, 1988); Mel Watkins, *Madness and Ruin: Politics and the Economy in the Neo-conservative Age* (Toronto: Between the Lines, 1992); Allan Tupper and Bruce G. Doern, eds. *Privatization, Public Policy and Public Corporations in Canada* (Halifax: Institute for Research on Public Policy, 1989); James J. Rice and Michael J. Prince, "Life of Brian: A Social Policy Legacy," *Perception,* June 1993, 6–8, 30–33; Maude Barlow and Bruce Campbell, *Straight Through the Heart: How the Liberals Abandoned the Just Society* (Toronto: HarperCollins, 1996). The *CCPA Monitor*, published ten times a year by the Canadian Centre for Policy Alternatives in Ottawa, is a good source of information on the neoconservative agenda and its implementation in Canada.

25. Colin Lindsay "The Decline in Real Family Income, 1980–1984," Statistics Canada, *Canadian Social Trends,* Winter 1986, 15–17; Statistics Canada, *Charting Canadian Incomes, 1951–1981,* Ottawa 1984; *Globe and Mail,* February 13, 1988; *Globe and Mail, "Report on Business,"* February 3, 1991; Reference Table 14, "Structural Change in the Sources and Disposition of Personal Income, 1947–1991," in Canada, Department of Finance, *Economic Reference Tables,* August 1993, 25; Statistics Canada, *Income Distribution by Size in Canada, 1991,* Catalogue No. 13-207, December 1993, 151.

26. Lars Osberg and Pierre Fortin, eds., *Unnecessary Debts* (Toronto: Lorimer, 1996); Neil Brooks, *Paying for Civilized Society: The Need for Fair and Responsible Tax Reform* (Ottawa: Canadian Centre for Policy Alternatives, 1990); H. Mimoto and P. Cross, "The Growth of the Federal Debt," *Canadian Economic Observer,* Statistics Canada, Catalogue No. 11-010, June 1991; David Savoie, *The Politics of Public Spending in Canada* (Toronto: University of Toronto, 1990).

27. *Globe and Mail,* "Report on Business", December 26, 1996.

28. This phrase appears in the Manitoba Act, 1870. W. L. Morton, *Manitoba: A History* (Toronto: University of Toronto, 1957); Chester Martin, *"Dominion Lands" Policy* (Toronto: Macmillan, 1938).

29. Federal powers are enumerated in sections 56, 90, 91, and 92 (10) of the British North America Act, 1867.

30. For example, under a straightforward PR model, in 1988 the Tories would have won 129 seats, the Liberals 97, the NDP 62, and Reform 7 (the actual results were 169, 83, 43, and none, respectively) In 1993, the Liberals would have won 124 seats, the Tories 51, the NDP 28, Reform 54, and the Bloc 37 (the actual results were 177, 2, 9, 52 and 54, respectively). The Bloc would be much less dominant in Quebec and would not have achieved the status of official Opposition. Reform seats would have been distributed more evenly across Canada—21 in Ontario, 2 in Atlantic Canada, and 31 in the four western provinces. Under our present system, Reform won 51 of its 52 seats in the West.

31. Liberal Party of Canada *Creating Opportunity: the Liberal Plan for Canada* (Ottawa, 1993) [The Red Book]. On page 9, one reads, "For far too many Canadians, after nine years of Conservative government, [the Canadian] dream has turned into a nightmare. Our economy is in disarray:...Over a million Canadian children live in poverty. Many of our national institutions have been shaken. Our cultural and social fabric has been weakened....Hope for tomorrow has turned into fear of the future....For Canadians, the next election is about one simple question: what kind of country do we want for ourselves and our children?"

List of Contributors

Paul Barker is Associate Professor of Political Science at Brescia College, The University of Western Ontario. He has written on health policy, cabinet decision-making, and Canadian federalism. His current interests include educational policy in Ontario and Canada.

Patrick Boyer has been described by many public commentators as "Canada's resident expert on direct democracy." Three of his books (*Lawmaking by the People* [1981], *The People's Mandate* [1992] and *Direct Democracy in Canada* [1993]) address direct voting by the population through the democratic instrument of referendums and plebiscites. From 1984 to 1993 Boyer represented Etobicoke-Lakeshore constituency in the House of Commons. An active parliamentarian, he chaired committees on election law reform, equality rights, and the status of disabled persons—recommendations from these three committees resulting in major changes in Canadian law in the ensuing years. He holds an Honours B.A. degree (first-class honours) in Economics and Political Science from Carleton University in Ottawa (1968), a Master's degree in History from the University of Toronto (1975), and a Bachelor of Law degree from the University of Toronto (also 1975).

Andrew Cohen is a member of the Editorial Board of the *Globe and Mail*. A native of Montreal, he studied Political Science at McGill University and holds graduate degrees in journalism and international affairs from Carleton University. He has worked at the *Ottawa Citizen*, United Press International and the *Financial Post*. He is the author of *A Deal Undone: The Making and Breaking of the Meech Lake Accord*, a study of Canada's constitutional politics published in 1990. In 1995 and 1996, he won National Newspaper Awards for editorial writing.

J. F. Conway, Professor of Sociology at the University of Regina, is the author of *The West: The History of a Region in Confederation* (first edition, 1984; second edition, 1994), *The Canadian Family in Crisis* (first edition, 1990; second edition, 1993), and *Debts to Pay: English Canada and Quebec from the Conquest to the Referendum* (first edition, 1992; second edition, 1997), translated and published in Quebec as *Des comptes á rendre: Le Canada anglais et le Québec, de la Conquête à l'accord de Charlottetown* (1995); and of monographs on the place of the Prairies in Confederation and on the re-emergence of separatist sentiment in western Canada during the early 1980s. In 1991 he was elected as a Trustee to the Regina Public School Board. He was re-elected in 1994 and appointed Vice-Chair in 1995.

Pierre A. Coulombe currently lectures at the University of Ottawa, McGill University, and previously taught at the University of New Brunswick and The University of Western Ontario. His research focusses on the problem of community in liberal society. He has written on language rights, constitutional reform, and Québec politics.

Nathalie Des Rosiers is an Associate Professor in the Faculty of Law at The University of Western Ontario. She graduated from the University of Montreal in 1981 (LL.L.) and from Harvard University in 1984 (LL.M.). She is a member of the Quebec Bar and the Law Society of Upper Canada. She served as Law Clerk to Justice Chouinard of the Supreme Court of Canada (1982–83) and was a Commissioner of the Ontario Law Reform Commission (1993–96).

Rand Dyck is Professor of Political Science and Vice-Dean of Social Science at Laurentian University. He is the author of two widely used texts in Canadian political science: *Canadian Politics: Critical Approaches* (second edition, 1996) and *Provincial Politics in Canada: Towards the Turn of the Century* (third edition, 1996).

Roger Gibbins is Professor of Political Science at the University of Calgary, where he served as head of the department from 1987 to 1996. He has pursued a variety of research interests spanning western alienation, Canadian constitutional politics, political belief systems, Senate reform, American and Australian politics, and new social movements such as environmentalism and feminism. He has authored (or edited) fourteen books and more than sixty refereed articles and book chapters. Publications include *Prairie Politics and Society* (1980), *Regionalism: Territorial Politics in Canada and the United States* (1982), *Parameters of Power* (with Keith Archer, Rainer Knopff, and Les Pal, 1995), *Western Visions* (with Sonia Arrison, 1995), and *Mindscapes: Political Ideologies Toward the 21st Century* (with Loleen Youngman, 1996). From 1990 to 1993 Dr. Gibbins was the English language co-editor of the *Canadian Journal of Political Science*.

Samuel LaSelva is Associate Professor in the Department of Political Science at the University of British Columbia. His research interests focus on political theory and the Canadian Constitution. His recent publications include *The Moral Foundations of Canadian Federalism: Paradoxes, Achievements, and Tragedies of Nationhood*.

Hugh Mellon is Associate Professor of Political Science at King's College, The University of Western Ontario. His teaching interests include Canadian government and public policy. His work has been published in *Canadian Public Administration* and the *Journal of Canadian Studies*.

Jonathan Rose is Assistant Professor in the Department of Political Studies at Queen's University. His research on mass communications has been published in the *Canadian Journal of Political Science* and *Canadian Journal of Communication*. His current research project is an examination of government advertising.

Richard Vernon is Professor of Political Science at The University of Western Ontario. His publications include *Citizenship and Order* (University of Toronto Press, 1986) and *The Career of Toleration* (McGill-Queen's University Press, 1997). From 1993 to 1996 he served as Editor of the *Canadian Journal of Political Science*.

Robert Vipond is Chair of the Department of Political Science at the University of Toronto. He has written extensively on Canadian and American political thought, federalism, and constitutionalism, most notably *Liberty and Community: Canadian Federalism and the Failure of the Constitution* (SUNY, 1991).

Martin Westmacott is Associate Professor of Political Science, Department of Political Science, and Associate Dean, Faculty of Social Sciences at The University of Western Ontario. His teaching interests include the introductory course in Political Science, Canadian politics, and constitutional reform. He has co-edited two books of readings on Canadian federalism.

Robert Young is a Professor of Political Science at The University of Western Ontario, where he has taught since 1980. He is currently Chair of the Department. He has published many works on federalism, industrial policy, Maritimes politics, and voting behaviour. For the past few years he has been working on Canadian federalism and Quebec secession. He is the author of *The Breakup of Czechoslovakia* and of *The Secession of Quebec and the Future of Canada*.